The trouble with freedom

Manchester University Press

The trouble with freedom

Love, hate and America's future

Melissa Butcher

Manchester University Press

Published by Manchester University Press
Oxford Road, Manchester, M13 9PL

www.manchesteruniversitypress.co.uk

British Library Cataloguing-in-Publication Data
A catalogue record for this book is available from the British Library

ISBN   978 1 5261 8541 9   hardback

First published 2026

The publisher has no responsibility for the persistence or accuracy of URLs for any external or third-party internet websites referred to in this book, and does not guarantee that any content on such websites is, or will remain, accurate, accessible or appropriate.

EU authorised representative for GPSR:
Easy Access System Europe, Mustamäe tee 50, 10621 Tallinn, Estonia
gpsr.requests@easproject.com

Typeset by Newgen Publishing UK

Contents

Preface: Writing freedom

From this moment on, America's decline is over. Our liberties and our nation's glorious destiny will no longer be denied [...]. For American citizens, January 20th, 2025, is liberation day.[1]

Donald J. Trump, 2025

Why did almost 77 million people vote for Donald Trump in November 2024? Since I began writing this book, that is a question I have been asked multiple times by strangers and colleagues, in the USA and elsewhere, often with a sense of bewilderment. Put another way, the question is: why is a country so strongly associated with freedom taking a turn towards authoritarianism? I hope this book will provide some answers.

Documenting the five years from Trump's loss in 2020 to the aftermath of his second presidential victory, this is a story about the trouble created when an idea of freedom, placed at the heart of a nation's sense of identity, begins to shift and buckle under the weight of history, a precarious present and an anxiously imagined future.

As a journalist and researcher for ten years in my homeland of Australia, and an academic in London for the last fifteen, I've specialised in working with people to understand cultural change and conflict. Within this field, my interest in the USA and freedom began to grow in a year when both the UK and USA seemed to have a collective aneurism: 2016 – the Brexit referendum and Trump's first election victory. In the febrile political environment of that time, narratives of freedom in political speech appeared to be travelling along the transAtlantic cultural switchboard. An American-style nationalist populist focus on freedom emerged in the Brexit debate and wider British politics, along with references to global conspiracy theories and the shadowy 'Deep State'.[2]

These connections, and the use of freedom to demarcate this new politics, have only deepened in the interim years.[3] A turn to conservatism and populism in times of change is nothing new. But as society has polarised, and democratic and civil institutions have been weakened both in the USA and UK, my once securely imagined future on the edge of Europe has begun to look much more precarious. I felt an urgent need to understand how a desire for freedom, of all things, had become a driver of resurgent authoritarianism and its mirroring across continents. This led me to relocate to the source, the USA, in 2021 to begin work on *The trouble with freedom*.

I can only ever bring an outsider's eye to this story, but as I have learned as a writer over many years, sometimes the outsider's eye is useful. You are allowed to ask the naïve question, to make no assumptions. You are not seen as being on anyone's 'side'. I also bring to this story several decades' experience as a human geographer. I have always been curious about why we do the things we do in the way we do them, how we live together with all our differences in complicated spaces and how we can miraculously keep going within the messiness of being human. That curiosity allows for conversations that hopefully move beyond soundbites and try to find answers to the question of 'why?'

I started by focusing on prominent debates that centred freedom, including education, incarceration, immigration, medical freedom, reproductive rights, freedom of/from religion. Throughout 2022, I travelled across the country, snowballing personal and professional contacts to meet people from New York to Texas, the Adirondacks to Louisiana, from Gen Z to Boomers, capturing geographical and intergenerational differences. I gathered stories at meetings and rallies – in person and online – in documents and audio-visual content from organisations involved in diverse freedom campaigns. I sat in on study groups and cottage meetings and read hundreds of reports, mission statements, flyers and posters. I recorded conversations with over 130 people, as well as noting hundreds of informal discussions. Since returning to the UK, I have spent the last two years continuing conversations and immersing myself in the social networks of 'conservative' and 'liberal' organisations.

This research builds on a wealth of historical, sociological and journalistic work that has focused on the lived experiences and practices of freedom (see the 'Further reading' section at the end). As historian Eric Foner found, there are expressions of freedom in 'plantations and picket lines, in parlours and bedrooms'.[4] In *The trouble with freedom*, this work is updated to include diners, universities, tech hubs, malls, sports fields, bars and community centres.

The result, I hope, is a cultural map of contemporary America, written in the midst of a raging culture war, the run up to the 2024 presidential election and the first 100 days of Donald Trump's second term. The book documents diverse understandings of freedom and the changes accumulated over decades of social, economic and legal transformations that people feel threaten those freedoms. The subsequent responses to those threats have impacted on politics, society and communities internationally, including driving a turn towards Trump's version of nationalist populism.

However, while addressing concerns that freedom has been re-appropriated by the political and economic interests that fuel authoritarianism, *The trouble with freedom* attempts to move beyond caricatures of 'red neck deplorables' and 'radical leftists'. The book blurs the 'good' and the 'bad', elaborating on the cracks and inconsistencies in America's freedom story. It brings to light the limitations and trade-offs that people recognise as necessary to live in a complex, changing society. The inherent tensions within freedom are captured in its diverse meanings and contested possession; its impact on everyday life; its inclusive and exclusionary dimensions and the processes people use to reconcile these contradictions.

Conversations highlight quiet voices from outside the noise of political punditry and social media troll fests, creating openings into others' lives that illustrate a complicated nation at a difficult time. The USA is a country of immense wealth and opportunity and equally immense inequality: glass and marble global cities and failing rural towns with dollar stores and shuttered shops; a diverse, unsettled nation still reconciling a history of slavery and dispossession, immersed today in bitter, polarised politics.

Conversations were also about getting out of my own echo chamber and caring about what others had to say from very different world views. With a large caveat on the increasingly meaningless nature of political labels, I am vaguely liberal on most issues. I would like an end to environmental destruction, and economic reform that puts communities first. I support abortion rights, I don't like guns and I think free speech comes with responsibilities.

But the conversations were challenging not only because of disagreement. There were times when I agreed with speakers I didn't think I would find common cause with. It was disturbing when I found myself laughing at Tucker Carlson's jokes during a Turning Point USA (MAGA) rally. I agree with Steve Bannon when he says that middle-class incomes for working-class jobs no longer exist because of deindustrialisation and outsourcing, but not when he argues that the 2020 election was 'stolen'.[5] I agree with medical freedom activists that the World Economic Forum and transnational corporations can have too much power, Big Pharma can profit out of ill health and governments have been known to distort facts and lie to their citizens. But I do not agree that the global economy and population is going to be reset in 2030 on the orders of a shadowy transnational cabal. It is possible to see a slippery slope without wanting to go down it.

Where we did agree in nearly all conversations is that there is a democratic deficit in America and other nominally liberal countries. We share moments of being fed up and swap experiences of being politically orphaned when it comes to deciding who to vote for. A possible point of consensus for a future America may then rest on campaigns that link freedom with a system of democratic governance that actually does represent 'we the people'.

A note on the terminology used in this book. All labels are inadequate, as conversations will indicate, yet terms such as 'conservative', 'liberal', 'progressive', 'radical', 'left' and 'right', as well as derogatory terms such as 'fascist' and 'communist', are used in everyday speech. More often than not, they are used to stereotype and demarcate difference.

'America First/MAGA' is used to denote those who support Trump and his policies. America First generally refers to politicians and organisations, and MAGA to the popular movement that underpins it. I also use 'nationalist populism' to frame this political ideology, although there are fracture lines, for example differences over migration, military intervention and economic policy.

I refer to both 'America' and the 'USA'. I recognise that 'America' can refer to the continents, but it is widely used in everyday speech as an abbreviation for the United States of America. Occasionally, the term 'liberty' is used by people interchangeably with freedom. Academics may argue there is a distinction, but this is not always borne out in everyday use. For the most part, it is 'freedom' that is used throughout the book.

Words are capitalised when referencing an organisation or movement, for example National Conservatism.

When using direct quotes from conversations, I have included the narrative as spoken, editing only where necessary for clarity. Pauses and other speech inflections are maintained where possible, denoted by ellipses, while text edited for brevity is denoted by [...]. Pseudonyms are used and details of places changed to maintain anonymity where necessary.

At times, conversations were uncomfortable, and this is a warning that there are occasionally swear words, overt racism, misogyny, trans- and homophobia. This material is included not to condone these views but to try to understand where they come from.

To those who gave up their time to have a conversation, sometimes for just an hour, sometimes an afternoon, or if I was lucky, a day or two ... the anarchists, libertarians, independents, Democrats, Republicans, the undecideds, the hopeful and despairing, the religious, pastors, shamans, agnostics, deists, the secular, fellow diners, the formerly incarcerated, the lawyers, the farmers, moms, dads, young people, elders, First Nations, Asian, Black, Hispanic, white, hyphenated, from the North, the South, the east coast, the Midwest, blue and white collars, hunters, first responders, lobbyists, activists, politicians, entrepreneurs, techies, nurses, teachers, students, gay, straight, non-binary, the gun owners, pro-abortion, pro-life, the differently abled, the veterans, the painters and pool players, those in large houses and those in none ... Thank you.

In tackling freedom, we grappled with immigration, incarceration, who gets to own Jesus, who gets to define history, what it is to be a man and what might happen if we rewrote the Constitution. In the end, as we sat with coffee and cake or some other distraction, this became a story about re-imagining America's future with trust, empathy and the capacity to re-find small spaces of communion with difference.

All change

We all declare for liberty but in using the same word we do not all mean the same thing.

Abraham Lincoln, 1864

In the future days, which we seek to make secure, we look forward to a world founded upon four essential human freedoms. The first is freedom of speech and expression – everywhere in the world. The second is freedom of every person to worship God in his own way – everywhere in the world. The third is freedom from want [...] everywhere in the world. The fourth is freedom from fear [...] anywhere in the world.

Franklin D. Roosevelt, 1941

Let us rise to the call of freedom-loving blood that is in us, and send our answer to the tyranny that clanks to its chains upon the South.

George Wallace, Governor of Alabama, segregationist, 1963

Things will change. We won't be free any more.

Trump supporter, 2020

I'm lost among 10,000 young people who've been told I hate them because I am a childless, unmarried, atheist academic who occasionally teaches critical race theory (CRT) and gender studies. I try not to take it personally. It's December 2021, and I'm at AmericaFest (AmFest), a rally in Phoenix, Arizona, led by the conservative youth organisation Turning Point USA (TPUSA).[1] The word 'hate' is repeated often. Americans are being taught to 'hate their country'. Jeff Bezos and Mark Zuckerberg are 'plutocrats that hate you'. 'The left hates election integrity'. This is a Manichean world of good and evil: a divine, righteous, natural order, with God and the 'truth' on one side defending freedom, and the 'tyrannical', 'godless', 'socialists', 'Marxists', 'communists', 'trans-rights activists', 'liars', 'cheats' and 'ideologues' indoctrinating children and threatening freedom on the other.

'How did we get here?' has become a question asked multiple times over the course of recent years. But there is bound to be this kind of trouble when that much-revered and sought-after human condition, freedom, is placed at the centre of a nation's sense of identity and exceptionalism. Historian Eric Foner has argued that freedom is a 'master narrative', the key organising principle that underpins the USA's identity. 'No idea is more fundamental to Americans' sense of themselves as individuals and as a nation than freedom.'[2] Part of the 'DNA' of the country, it is embedded in culture, in everyday conversations, the media landscape. It is a founding myth enshrined in the Constitution and attached to a foreign policy that defends the 'free' world and 'free' markets. Freedom is part of a cultural map that tells Americans who they are and where they belong, creating a sense of place and coherence while marking out others, the unfree, as different.

Across the conversations that make up this book, it becomes a running joke that on a Likert scale of importance, freedom is closer to '11 out of 10'. Yet, taken for granted, as a 'natural' thing, like breathing, it is difficult at times to articulate what freedom is. People grapple with finding the right words, like Betty, a member of a Free Thinkers group in Evansville, Indiana:

> It's the high note in the song that everyone's trained to sing as a child, 'land of the free'. And then, you know, we all get confused, because it's not [in] reality as much as we might hope it would be. Okay, for some and for different situations. It's very hard to discuss.

It has become even harder to discuss in recent years, as freedom now demarcates 'sides' in a struggle for the 'soul of the nation' within a context of rapid, profound changes to America's cultural infrastructure. I'll be returning to AmFest in the next chapter, but first I want to introduce some of the voices and stories to come, which offer divergent understandings of what freedom means. I'll identify points of change perceived as threats to those freedoms, and the emotional responses that follow as the master narrative and all that it represents shifts and slips out of reach. There is anger, shame and fear, but also care and love that may still rescue us as we re-imagine a future holding different ways of being free.

Defining freedom

Despite its status as a master narrative, there has always been more than one definition of freedom, and therefore of America. It has been continually renegotiated, reshaped and replaced over time and in different contexts.[3] Its meaning has incorporated racialised, classed and gendered definitions that move beyond the simple absence of coercion to include interpretations associated with aspiration and morality, as well as legal, religious, social, economic and political practices. Freedom can be felt as safety, the absence of physical and psychological threat, a state devoid of ambivalence and shame.

Freedom can also be enumerated as a list of things to do, the written rules that delineate a set of practices, like the rights set out in the Constitution: press, speech, religion, assembly, bearing arms, voting. That list can be added to, and meanings debated, interpreted within the law or stated as immutable principles that set the USA apart. Then there are the unwritten rules, the cultural norms we don't know we're breaching until stung by a sense of shame or discomfort, learned from family, school, religion, reinforced by law and political systems, challenged by intergenerational change and social upheaval.

Within this framework of rules, both written and unwritten, come the associated expectations that freedom carries in the USA: choice, opportunity, agency, autonomy and mobility. The freedom to share in 'the American Dream'.[4] Greg, a millennial entrepreneur based in Florida, started his online retail business with a website and an email to his friends. For him, freedom is 'theoretically guaranteed': 'You can just come [to America] and do anything theoretically that you would want to do.'

We'll return to that 'theoretically' later, but Greg expresses the rhetorical freedom embedded in a complex patriotism that supports a sense of exceptionalism and settles the inevitable contradictions embedded in founding myths. The historic sacrifices made to attain independence from religious persecution and European feudalism, gained through dispossessing others of their freedoms, have been rationalised as the price paid for a utopian freedom made real on earth, in the establishment of 'the greatest country ever in the history of the world'.

Collective agreement to a national idea of freedom is signalled through the recitation of rituals and synchronised hands on hearts. In families and institutions across the country, a Pledge of Allegiance is made. In yards and on porches, there are flags and lawn signs as reminders. There are also forms of censure for non-compliance, as Mark, a former Democratic Party candidate in Pennsylvania outlines:

> You have to say the Pledge of Allegiance, you have to stand for the national anthem, or you will be lambasted. [...] [T]he concept of America has been changed to the word freedom and that's been changed to a loyalty. So if you have an issue with something then you hate America.

The conviction that the USA is a model for liberal democracies is as much founded on the myth of freedom as on America's natural resources, technology and military power. This exceptionalism is epitomised by former USA Secretary of State, now Director of the public policy think tank the Hoover Institution, Condoleezza Rice: 'If not for America, who would rally freedom-loving nations to defend liberty and democracy in our world?'[5]

The counter to exceptionalism often comes from those who have lived elsewhere and looked back, seeing the contradictions more clearly, like Alice, a Black entrepreneur and single mother, living in South Carolina, who I met in a Democrat Facebook group:

> Oh, I thought I had freedom in America and then I go to Germany, and you know, they have social programmes where they have support for parents for childcare, for schooling, they can go to school for free! I'm like, for free to college! That's so amazing! Trade schools for free! To be able to have the opportunity to have a free education if you want it.

The baton of overseas intervention in the name of freedom was carried by successive governments, Republican and Democrat, but dropped by Trump and the America First/MAGA movement, who see freedom better preserved by not getting involved in 'forever wars'. Borders to the unfree have been hardened. Freedom has become a limited resource, to be accessed only by those already within the perimeter. While there is a general feeling across the political spectrum in these conversations that 'we have got the most freedom in the world' in the USA, not all feel that it can be shared. There is a desire to 'close the borders' in order to exert control, to restore a feeling of safety, because outsiders 'just want to reap our freedoms'.

For some, the first, paramount freedom that must be protected is 'the right to do whatever I want', unrestricted by government or society. Or as Gary, a libertarian, put it, 'the right or power to think, speak or act in whatever way you want without hindrance'.[6] Centred on personal responsibility, 'individual liberty' is 'essential to the moral and physical strength of the nation', according to the Freedom Conservatism movement.[7] Dan, a 'conservatarian' journalist and gun advocate in Texas, is succinct: 'It's the ability, the unfettered ability to pursue happiness with all of the benefits and costs that go along with it. So if you screw up [or] if you make it, that's on you.'

Yet for others, personal moral codes set limits, including that they should not always persist in 'doing what we like', but instead have 'the right to do what we ought'; a difficult option at times in a culture of free market capitalism that prioritises individual property rights and hyper-consumerism. Individual freedom has become weighed down by choice: from as many soda flavours or toppings on your pancakes as you want, to having an abortion or not, to re-making self-expression, to making choices that will lead to wealth or poverty.[8]

Yet freedom of choice also has to be reconciled with others: family, community, the nation. Freedom can only ever be experienced in relation to someone else, in comparison with the unfree, for example. There is always tension along this fragile border between individual and collective freedoms, or as Helen, a retiree in rural Colorado, described it: '[R]ugged individualism is butting up against behaving as a community.'

Nowhere was this seen more clearly than in conflicts emerging from the COVID-19 pandemic and the rise of a medical freedom movement. Those happy to wear masks, socially distance and get vaccinated took the view they were supporting 'more collective action that limits immediate personal freedom [for] the sake of larger societal gains'.

While for others: 'Yeah, that definitely took some of your freedom away.' The divisions of COVID-19, hardened by the fear of 'tyranny' felt by some following the imposition of mandates, continue to shape American society and politics, including influencing the outcome of the 2024 election campaign.

There are similar tensions in debates centred on gun ownership: that it is wrong to suppress an individual's right to be free from the threat of others' violence versus the collective harms guns generate. Theresa, a delegate for Women for Gun Rights, believes that the government has no place interfering with what she feels is her right to defend herself: '[T]his is my autonomy, this is my being, and as long as I'm not hurting anyone else I believe that I have a right to do that without interference from another person. It is deeply personal.'

However, there is general recognition that there are limits to how much freedom we really have. There are 'rules and laws', but there is above all else, 'theoretically', the principle of 'do no harm': people are free to do what we want up until we bump into someone else's freedoms. References to 'borders', 'boundaries' and 'perimeters' indicate there is little room for complete detachment or indifference. It was repeated in many conversations that 'there is no such thing as absolute freedom'. There must be trade-offs and compromises in order to avoid incursions. Even Texas libertarians have their limits.

However, where the limits lie, and what trade-offs are required in order to feel free, is up for debate. Will, a retiree in Evansville, Indiana, for example, wouldn't want to give up his freedoms entirely but is okay with 'cutting some of them back a little bit'. He and his friends, military veterans, wouldn't give up the Second Amendment for example, and most of them are carrying a gun as they play pool in a seniors' community centre. Linda, a Republican, executive assistant and resident of a mobile home park in Colorado, would make compromises in the name of national security but didn't want to make them in the name of freedom. It was too discomforting to have that word used with a negative connotation such as 'trade-off' or 'limited'. Steph, an evangelical Christian, retiree, living in rural Colorado, also didn't like my title 'The trouble with freedom', so engrained is the idea that freedom is a positive.

Freedom is also embedded in the idea of mobility. Historian Stephen Tomkins hints at the idea that this stems from Protestant dissent.[9] Don't like your local church authorities? Break away and set up your own church down the road. Move west and settle the country. From Alexis de Tocqueville's nineteenth-century observations in *Democracy in America*, to Jessica Bruder's *Nomadland* and Sebastian Junger's contemporary musings along railway tracks, there has been freedom to move for some throughout America's history.[10] Naomi, now retired, lives in a small town on the western slopes of Colorado. For her, there is still 'freedom to move where I choose to move, and freedom to seek out organisations and resources that offer me what I value'.

According to the influential postmodernist Jean Baudrillard, freedom in the USA is 'spatial and mobile' – 'the empty, absolute freedom of the freeways'.[11] Fair to say that postmodernism is despised by some of the ideologues of conservatism, as we'll see in later conversations, but Baudrillard seemed to quite enjoy driving around the country. He was also prescient in noting the conditions that would give rise to twenty-first-century populists like Trump. 'In the future, power will belong to those peoples with no origins and no authenticity who know how to exploit that situation to the full.'[12] Or perhaps more appropriately, we are witnessing 'the debauched excess of middle age'.[13]

The contemporary ability to be mobile is enabled by technology and flexible working. Millennial entrepreneurs like Greg and Lindsey are excited by the digital world and the possibilities of this freedom. Lindsey, who runs an online travel company 'promoting the freedom to explore', lives between the USA and Greece. All she needs is 'a laptop and good internet connection'. For online retailer Greg, innovations like cryptocurrency have the potential for 'even crazier freedom right now':

> You don't even have the constraints of your identity to be kind of free in this country, which is like wild. [...] [T]here's not gonna be things like race and gender to hold anyone back. [...] [T]here's concerns with it always but it's a net positive, it's like now you are just who your true self can be.

We can look forward to the day when race and gender don't hold anyone back, but it's certainly not today or the foreseeable future.

Freedom is never so simple. Negotiating or refusing to negotiate freedoms highlights inequalities in social, economic and political power: who determines where the borders lie and what happens within them? Who gets to feel free within those borders, and therefore safe, and who doesn't? Who gets the freedom to move, to cross a border or not? Who gets to allocate rights and distribute freedoms? 'Freedom to' start your own business, vote, own a gun and so on, the positive freedoms, must be held in balance with 'freedom from'. Freedom 'to be your true self', 'to be authentic', is more likely when there is freedom from debt, from astronomical medical bills or racial violence.

Freedom may be considered an inalienable facet of being human, foundational to the political thinking that established the USA, but it is framed, judged, disciplined, controlled, corralled and constrained. Freedoms are pitted against each other. Privileges, geography, race and ethnicity, gender and class impact on how we experience freedom. The rules can be questioned by some, and it can never be assumed that everyone agrees on them. Asymmetric fracture lines and entanglements drive an unmaking and remaking of freedom, and with it, American identity.

Such limits are acknowledged by everyone in the conversations in this book, even the most patriotic, as a sign that freedom is not equal. Some have always had more freedom than others, including the freedom to take advantage of the opportunities the USA provides. In the reality of structural inequality, debt and health care are two areas that presented acute 'freedom-limiting qualities' for many, particularly those without health insurance. Poverty is marked out as a state of being unfree in that consistent equation that 'money equals freedom', as Clara, an elder member of a migrant association in New York City points out: 'When you got a lot of money you do everything [...]. Everything here is about the money. Remember, everything is about the money [banging on the table to emphasise the point].'

The USA is one of the most unequal countries in the Organisation for Economic Co-operation and Development (OECD) and has the highest level of income inequality in the G7 (2023).[14] Such statistics have fed the rise of populism, according to historian Timothy Snyder, who argues that 'without inequality, without a sense that the future

8

was closed, [Donald Trump] could not have found the supporters he needed'.[15] Nostalgia for a time of economic security is gift wrapped by America First/MAGA as a time when there was also more freedom.

Race also continues to be a key marker of unequal freedoms, referencing the history of enslavement at the heart of the country's founding.[16] As Nikole Hannah-Jones writes in *The 1619 Project*, there have been more years of enslavement and segregation than freedom for Black Americans, and this legacy is ongoing, as seen in experiences of incarceration. Pew Research in 2023 found the median wealth of white families was $250,400 but $27,100 for Black families and $48,700 for Hispanic.[17] There is no escaping America's legacy of slavery, although people try through a teleological, entrepreneurial narrative – 'that was then', but we can fix it for the future. We can do better.

Historian Tyler Stovall describes the idea of freedom in America as a white ideal that has resulted in the continued subjugation of Black and minority communities.[18] At the USA's inception, freedom was limited to property-owning white men; those who sang freedom from the same hymn sheet. The residue of this beginning remains scattered over America's cultural and institutional bones.[19] Those who already have freedom determine the freedom of others. For Jean, a Black activist and educator in Alabama, the whole notion of patriotism in the USA, underpinned by a narrative of freedom, is tied to a history of white supremacy: 'There's no universal understanding or acceptance of the fact that everyone has a right to this notion of freedom.' For the poor, the Black, the brown, the incarcerated, the very existence of freedom comes into question, as articulated by Jorge, a Mexican immigrant living in a mobile home park in suburban Denver, Colorado: 'I really think freedom doesn't exist.'

Inequalities make freedom irrelevant for those who cannot access its benefits. This drives a continued struggle to release the USA from the cultural monopoly that appropriates freedom for a nationalist project that excludes so many. There is a referencing of Dr Martin Luther King or Nelson Mandela or John F. Kennedy to support this case, as recited by Hanima, from an Asian Muslim family, with US citizenship, living on the east coast: 'If I am free than everyone should be free, and I am not free until everyone around me is free.'[20]

For Hanima, her economic opportunities, credit rating and ability to rent improved after marrying her white partner, Mark: 'The freedoms that I have are also some of the freedoms by association to a white American male.' They met overseas on an exchange programme. As Mark and I continue to talk abstractly about freedom, Hanima intervenes, irritated with us, and noting that the conversation is 'such a privilege':

> Hanima: You were talking about rational thought, yeah, you can be rational about it because it's never affected you to give you any emotional response. Because you walk around looking the way you do. [...] I can't just talk about this. Like, it does affect me emotionally and personally and deeply. Because depending on how I walk outside and how I'm dressed and who I'm with [it] makes a difference.
> MB: It's not a theoretical exercise for you.
> Hanima: No. No. It's not an intellectual thing, which I think you both can have a conversation very intellectually about. It isn't. It's not that for me, sorry.

As Hanima highlights, trade-offs of freedoms are made not only on the basis of a cost–benefit analysis of external factors, such as environmental, economic or community impacts. Decisions are made based on how freedom makes us feel. And at the top of that emotional scale is feeling safe. For Hanima, safety and freedom go together, 'and there are a lot of times when I don't feel safe so I don't feel free'.

This was explicitly recognised by the MAGA movement, cloning itself into Make America Safe Again (MASA) as part of Trump's campaign to expel migrants, deemed en masse as threatening.[21] The rational, the material, the enumerated rights of freedom, the right to due process and free speech, for example, were weighed up against feeling safe throughout conversations in this book. It became a negative correlation: the less of one, the less of the other. As Cat, a community organiser and 'truth activist' involved in the medical freedom movement argues: '[T]hey're weaponising so many things against us in ways that can only be done with fear, that give people a sense of fear about their own security. So [people] are missing that freedom to feel safe.' Driving the sense of insecurity are rapid and profound processes of cultural change that have instigated doubt about what it means to be free in the USA today, and subsequently what it means to be American.

Change and feeling bad

If freedom is held to be part of 'America's DNA', then this underlying infrastructure is unravelling within a frenzy of social, economic and geopolitical change, accompanied by a raft of conspiracy theories. Fractious governance has overseen divisions along generational, gendered, class, racial, rural/urban and religious/secular lines, leading to a ferocious contest between different versions of freedom. There is shifting and buckling under the weight of history that will not lay buried, while contemporary geopolitical transformation threatens the sense of American exceptionalism and prosperity. Under such conditions of change, points of authority, including previously held values and beliefs, also begin to shift, and the ability to navigate the norms of everyday life becomes increasingly precarious. Something is 'out of balance'; there is no sense of 'control' or 'order'. These sentiments are repeated throughout conversations and the conservative media landscape in particular.

The result is an anxiety-inducing realisation that freedom can be contingent, random, luck of birth. As life shifts around us, others may gain the power to determine what our freedoms are and where the limits lie. We can change our own balance between freedom and safety, as well as have it changed for us by others. Responses to this rupturing and reshaping of a master narrative that was once taken for granted can range from psychological discomfort to murderous rage.[22]

For those who feel they have lost out, there are efforts to try to regain control of the narrative, and with it a sense of place and purpose. As a result, freedom is made concrete in a resurgent nationalism, feeding into exclusionary language with profound public policy implications, particularly for minority communities or those with a different view of freedom.

Anxiously imagined futures generate calls to 'save America', couched not only in terms of hate ('the other side') but also love (of country, of community). In social clubs, shooting ranges, workplaces, in living rooms and over dining tables, people name the threats to freedom against which it must be defended: Big Government, Big Tech, China, immigration, fentanyl, 'woke', 'gender ideology' and critical race studies, but most often, a nebulous 'globalism'. The USA, as with other countries, has faced a series of challenges in an age of globalisation. The concept of national sovereignty has altered, impacting on the idea of citizenship and whom the state grants freedoms to within its borders. Freedom of movement brings with it strangers that appear to threaten the comforts of familiarity as well as local livelihoods. Demographic shifts are transformed into anger directed at a Mexican border imagined as threadbare.

A democratic deficit and polarised dissent seem unable to find solutions to the anxieties of globalisation and rupturing social norms. The narrative of freedom embedded in consumerism and the promise of an affluent future is disappearing in the face of environmental collapse and successive financial crises. Deindustrialisation and the shift to a digital economy raises uncertain futures for coming generations. There is anxiety as the distinction between man and woman slips into the freedom to choose a gender and new pronouns, while the #MeToo movement hammered home ongoing gendered inequalities. Secular and Christian America argue over the line between freedom of and freedom from religion in society and politics. Temporal borders determining who gets to control history are fought over in public schools and libraries.

How we live together, and how we remember, has changed. There is anguish at the thought of being forgotten in this turmoil as the meaning of freedom slips between generations. If anyone did score freedom lower than a 10 in importance on my Likert scale, it was more likely to be Gen Z, university students, studying social sciences, leaning Democrat, recognising privilege and calling it out, much to the annoyance of more conservative voices. Jade, a university student and military veteran in Texas, makes a clear distinction: 'There's the conservative freedom and the liberal freedom.' She associates Trump and Black activist and academic Angela Davis with the different world views.

For these Gen Zs, equality, community and well-being are just as important as the idea of freedom. There is a questioning of established narratives, a feeling that 'they gloss over a tonne of history'. There's recognition that movements such as Black Lives Matter (BLM) have effected important changes. Questioning the 'stupidly strong' status of freedom, Tim, currently living at home with his family in Texas, regards it as 'an overinflated value'.

But there is a sense of precarity for this generation as well. As the conservative Gen Z commentator Isabel Brown describes it, they face 'a changing reality'.[23] They lack the ability to buy a house or pay for health care, have racked up student debt and have fewer economic freedoms as a result. The world feels like it's getting 'narrower', more 'restrained', there is a tightening 'noose'. According to Snyder,[24] if the future is lost, if there is no better time to aim for, then the present becomes repetitive stress sustained by endless threats and crises; this is something Ines, of Venezuelan heritage at university in Texas, feels:

> The generations that are growing up now don't know a world where there wasn't a school shooting every week [...] we were born into disaster and like our world is literally dying [...]. So it's like our generation doesn't know a time when things were safe and comfortable, and gas was $1.29, and there was literally no inflation and houses were dirt cheap. We don't exist in a space anymore like that and the policies have to change. [...] I can't speak for my generation, but I feel like a lot of the frustration is like, 'that's not how it is anymore, grandpa' [...]. There [are] so many things that have changed in America due to like safety concerns, and just the world changing, and so for the policies not to keep us safe.

The narrative of a generation no longer feeling safe threatens a reckoning for older generations as the young talk of 'ripping down that system and starting new'. This threat, along with calls for racial justice and greater equity, appears to have influenced the decision of some corporate leaders to switch from Democrat to Trump in 2024.[25]

Stereotypes and mocking rebound on all sides, only adding to the pain: from 'radical socialists' to 'red neck deplorables', and everyone is a 'fascist'. The image of 'BBQ man' in a 'freedom isn't free' t-shirt, reciting the Pledge of Allegiance with his hand on his heart, watching baseball and standing for the anthem, induces eye rolls. But to roll eyes at this man, to call others 'weak' who espouse patriotism, is to humiliate them. This becomes fuel for the nationalist populism of America First/MAGA.

Older generations speak of their sacrifices being forgotten. Back to Will and his fellow veterans at the community centre in Indiana: 'I really respected the freedoms we have and don't forget about them because other people died for that, and I think a lot of people, the younger generation has forgotten what it really means.' One of the community workers drops in to see how we're going and joins the conversation, giving honour to those who allowed her to have freedom: 'You made a sacrifice for my freedom. You've sacrificed for me, a lot, right? You did. Everybody in here sacrificed so that I can have freedoms to go to church, to vote, to live my life.'

For some elders, there is nostalgia for former points of authority like legendary American newsreader Walter Cronkite, who represented the trust many feel is lacking today. Travis, a retired businessman in rural Colorado, reminisces about television in the 1960s:

> You know it was Walter Cronkite everybody believed [outburst of agreement from friends, laughing]. We all watched the same news and we all believed the same thing, and it was a very focused, small world, I guess. I didn't realise that at the time. But now we have such a broad world because everybody has the freedom on the internet.

The rupturing of freedom as a master narrative across generations exacerbates the sense of social upheaval, reinforced for some by widely disseminated images of young people rioting. The murder of George Floyd in 2020 and subsequent uprisings in cities across the country is referenced repeatedly as a point of anxiety in more conservative conversations, even four years later. In 2025, it is anti-Immigration and Customs Enforcement (ICE) riots in California that are described as 'the early stages of a left-wing insurrection' by conservative commentators.[26] Cultural breakdown can be watched incessantly, on repeat and timeless, as we doom scroll on our phones.

'Big Tech', the concentration of power in Silicon Valley, also raises concerns across the political spectrum. Conservative and libertarian voices dislike the ability of social media companies to 'cancel' people, seeing this as a threat to freedom of speech. Those with more liberal perspectives raise concerns over privacy, surveillance and economic monopolies, as well as psychological well-being.[27] Toni, a 'liberal' in rural Colorado, feels the double-edged sword of this technology, 'pulling us out of our little rabbit holes and making us see the whole world is damned uncomfortable. It's wonderful for some of us, "oh, wow,

I really feel free to fly". Right! Other people say, "Oh my God, what's going on?"'

The speed of change contributes to the sense of dislocation. For all our imagination, human cognitive resources are limited, and we generally prefer evolution and predictability over randomness and rupture. We rely on patterns that can become biases that, at the extremes, can become conspiracy theories. We grab hold of something solid to manage the vertigo, filling in the gaps to explain our feelings and to maintain a sense of control.

According to the economist Amartya Sen, freedom is a measure of the agency we have over our own lives and the environment around us.[28] As Ines notes, 'freedom to me personally just means being able to be in control of my life and my decisions'. If a condition for freedom is feeling safe, then that is more likely when we feel in control of our world.

Claiming freedom then has also become a defence against change and part of regaining control through conforming to a particular sense of order. For the writer Sebastian Junger, 'the inside joke about freedom [...] is that you're always trading obedience to one thing for obedience to another'.[29] That thing might be a God, a constitution, a nation, other people, a leader. 'Sometimes boundaries give you freedom' is an idea repeated throughout the conservative ecosystem. Oren Cass, Director of the conservative think tank American Compass, notes that

> [w]onderful though the unfettered freedom to enjoy oneself may sound, millennia of civilization and even rudimentary familiarity with human nature teach that most people will struggle to live fulfilling lives without the *benefit* of constraint and the *opportunity* to fulfil obligations; for some, the absence of guardrails leads to great suffering [his italics].[30]

Similarly, the political theorist Patrick Deneen argues that liberalism's focus on individual rights has in effect undermined freedom through 'material and spiritual degradation' and left many Americans feeling they have little agency in the face of change.[31]

The backlash, the need to reassert control in the name of freedom in order to feel safe again, is inevitable, underpinning a shift towards conservative and populist politics. In Trump's 2024 election campaign, he focused on law and order, dystopian cities and out-of-control borders. He talked of the USA being dragged into Europe's

World War III. His allies raged across the airwaves: the world is scary, it is unsafe.[32] Negative feelings were reframed as grievance and displaced on to others: 'radical leftists', 'illegal immigrants', 'the Deep State', the trans-community. He offered his 'protection' to women, young men, Christians, the working classes. In announcing his presidential transition team, Trump prioritised a return to safety: 'The 2024 GOP Platform to Make America Great Again is a forward-looking agenda that will deliver safety, prosperity and freedom for the American people.'[33] Order would be restored and contradiction banished, despite the impossibility of removing inconsistencies.

In the face of instability, there is comfort in not changing, defending the status quo, reasserting order. There is freedom in knowing our place, staying put, feeling certainty. Such feelings are not reserved for older generations, as socially and politically conservative young people at AmFest clearly demonstrate, defiantly reasserting borders because if they don't, 'we won't be free anymore'.

These arguments indicate the tensions between freedom as personal autonomy and the simultaneous necessity, for safety's sake, to know where the boundaries lie, in other words, to limit freedom. Criticism by 'progressives' of this stance, sketching out 'the deplorables' and the 'stupid', neglects the pain some feel in managing change and the fears of being unsafe that go with it. What we have seen in America is more than just 'angry Trump supporters' suffering from the loss of a conservative hegemony.[34] The 2024 election results suggest there is a broad spectrum of people who felt uncomfortable to some degree with the direction of change in America.

Previous certainties are crumbling, at times papered over by nostalgia even among 'liberals'. Conversations are haunted by concern at the breakdown of community, that which is familiar and safe, due to digital technology and the arrival of 'strangers'. Political allegiances are shifting. There is a visceral sense that something is being lost over which we have no control; a shift in the master narrative of freedom that people cannot fully articulate, in a direction they do not feel totally comfortable with, that is related to a gnawing feeling that all is not right. As Bella, a university student in Indiana remarks: 'Freedom can be looked at as a very positive thing, but it can also be scary. Because too much freedom might not give you the stability of safety.'

As the journalist Adam Serwer argues, it is how such feelings of loss and uncertainty are understood that makes the difference in terms of how people respond: flexing borders to incorporate new freedoms if feeling more comfortable with change, or hardening them in defensive measures if not.[35] For some, the speed and depth of cultural change exacerbate the pain and fear of losing the beloved, a sense of community, the nation. America First/MAGA voices reiterate that now is a time of 'chaos', 'crisis' and 'disorder'; at the border, in cities, in a society grappling with shifting boundaries of race and gender. America has reached a 'critical point', a 'crucial juncture'. The nation needs saving as trusted points of authority fail. God has gone missing. We are a bit lost, and it hurts. Without that feeling of safety, more emotions tumble out: shame, fear, anger, hate.

Anthropologist Veena Das describes these reactions as stemming from the 'world-annihilating doubt', uncertainty and vulnerability that emerges when trusted categories, like freedom, lose their ability to help us interpret the world.[36] In a state of flux, the master narrative buckles under the weight of domestic and global transformation. It takes on new meanings, and life as it was known unravels, becoming bent or distorted by change. Even the body can no longer be relied upon as it remains open to the possibilities of transformation; this is potentially why transgender activism causes so much anxiety today, particularly in conservative politics.

A politics of pain develops, centred on claims of who hurts the most. Working-class communities speak of the pain of lost livelihoods as a result of globalisation, outsourcing and deindustrialisation. People of colour speak of the pain of being subjected to legacies of empire, enslavement and everyday racism. Women speak of the pain of being subjected to misogyny. Conservatives and Christian nationalists speak of the pain of humiliation in a secular world. Young men speak of their pain of rejection. Rural communities speak of the pain of abandonment.

Pain reframes our experience of the world, transforming lives and ways of being, shaping everyday practices and social encounters. Reconfigurations of power influence our ability to recognise our own pain and the pain of others, to invest in the stories we tell about pain, its cause and cure, and the willingness to inflict pain. Inflicting pain, according to philosopher Elaine Scarry, is bound up with making others manageable.[37] Stigma and exclusion coerce the strange and uncomfortable into forms that can be expelled. In Trump's America, that would include the immigrant, the queer and some women.

There is further discomfort at discovering that the long arc of history doesn't always bend towards greater freedom. Instead, it can take jagged turns towards authoritarianism as a solution to pain, the feeling of drift, of not feeling safe – the feeling of not being free any more. These feelings, along with structural inequalities that remain unalleviated by a disappearing social safety net, appear to be sending us collectively backwards into autocracy, in the USA, the UK and across Europe, at times, ironically, in the name of freedom. The master narrative is now a marker of continuity, carrying a sense of order and safety for some, but with painful costs for others. The result is that there is a widespread sense of discomfort across the political spectrum, as Veronica, a self-described 'liberal' retiree in rural Colorado explains: 'That's what's so disturbing right now was that we thought freedom was a good thing, and now sometimes it doesn't feel so good.'

But we can also engage in practices to manage pain through repairing social fractures, and re-imagining freedom is part of this process. If Trump's return to power in 2024 created the realisation for some that freedom needs 'guard-rails', then those guard-rails can be found in acts of care and community. There is always hope.

Acts of love, care and hope

The complexity of emotional responses to change and the potential loss of freedoms leads to a more speculative thread that quietly weaves its way through conversations. Can the intense emotional content of this current moment be re-focused into forms of care through a re-negotiation of freedom that breaks down 'sides' and generates safety for all, rather than pain for some?

Cultural theorist Sara Ahmed has argued that emotions are more than just psychological dispositions: they have agency, driving us towards or away from others, creating insider/outsider distinctions.[38] It is through jarring encounters with 'not like me' that we come to know difference, recognising those hated or loved, those who create pleasure or pain. As we arrange ourselves, where we live and whom we socialise with on the basis of how we feel, the end result at times can be a form of 'partisan segregation'.[39] Democrats and Republicans, for example, appear increasingly unlikely to live in an area where they will find someone with a different political view.

Beyond difference, however, in every conversation across the political spectrum in this book, there is a call to gather, to belong to something bigger, to care for something other than ourselves, to re-find safety in acts of community. There is a nostalgia for restoring economies of affection. Even at their most angry, the conversations indicate a desire to live in meaningful, caring relationships, with family, friends and workmates. There is a greater sense of safety and control over our lives when we are within communities of care.[40]

Without a doubt, gatherings can ratchet up emotions. Get 10,000 young people together at AmFest expressing love for their country, and expressions of intense hatred can follow, as we'll see in the next chapter. Too much love and the boundaries of community become hard, less adaptable to change, generating discomfort when faced with difference. Too much love and we easily blame others for the pain of its loss.

But as the following conversations explore, connection can also hold the potential to work against feelings of loss, ambivalence and fear of change through generating acts of care and empathy. Freedom, despite its complexity, remains a narrative around which people could potentially develop these connections, repairing social bonds and bringing people together to hold spaces of difference in a changing world. This was the opening gambit of the 2024 Kamala Harris campaign for the presidency, although ultimately it was not enough to defeat Trump.[41] But in speculating on practices of care and affection that run throughout conversations, perhaps America is not as polarised as widely portrayed. There is hope in the capacity to re-find points of connection, including what I refer to as 'bring out the cake' moments woven throughout the following stories. These are a starting point for empathy, or at the very least a momentary suspension of judgement.

As disagreement across generations and political affiliations appears entrenched, it is a difficult proposition to imagine de-polarising American society at present. Yet there are points of consensus that emerge across the divides: for example, that the current political system is broken and needs to change. There are moments of reimagining what the future of the USA might look like if the master narrative of freedom was rewritten with new seats at the table. In conversation, there is nuance and empathy, caring and love, and people just 'figuring things out' the best they can. In the cracks and inconsistencies it is possible to imagine an American future that looks and feels different, held together by a new version of freedom.

The following chapters will explore these themes in more detail, drawing on the lived experience of freedom, from El Paso to prisons, churches to classrooms, documenting the defence and re-imagining of freedom in the face of change, and how emotions such as love and hate emerge in the redefining of what it means to be free. I start with a range of voices and complex responses to managing change that have fuelled a nationalist populist politics calling for freedom to be defended. This 'playbook' shapes the world of America First/MAGA, creating the emotional landscape in which the conversations in this book are set.

2
Defending freedom, saving America

> I am Donald J. Trump. FEAR NOT! I will always love you for supporting
> me. Unity. Peace. Make America Great Again.[1]
>
> 14 July 2024

Phoenix, Arizona is a desert canvas of squares and rectangles, grid
lines, golf courses and air conditioning. The summers are unbearably
hot and getting hotter, but no one walks outside on the streets in a city
designed for cars. Even on a mild December's day, I am alone in the
suburbs, wandering on wide, shaded boulevards, past quarter-acre bun-
galows, finding my way to a tramline heading downtown to the city
convention centre for AmericaFest (AmFest), an annual rally organised
by the conservative youth organisation Turning Point USA (TPUSA).

It's 2021, and the Trump Republicans are still licking their wounds
from the loss of the 2020 election. But TPUSA, are combative, optimistic, seriously organised and clever. AmFest will be my first experience
of the American political rally as spectacle, and after four relentless
days and nights I'm convinced that it will be this America First/MAGA
wing of the Republican Party that will have the White House in 2024.

This is just one rally among many in a conservative universe that
ranges from Neo-Conservative, Commonsense Conservative, Main
Street Conservative, Freedom Conservative and National Conservative,
with some overlap and some disdain between them.[2] America First is
dominated by ideological strands of National Conservatism, libertarianism and Christian nationalism.[3] It gathers together a constellation
of organisations that agree on the need to 'save freedom, save America'

and, adding more recently, 'save Western civilisation'. This is a movement that proselytises a muscular nationalism, immigration control, small government, anti-socialism/pro-capitalism and Christian morality. Shoring up what it means to be American today, organisations like TPUSA seek to secure borders, cultural and cartographic, defend the Founding Fathers and an infallible Constitution, and assert a primary role for heterosexual families at the centre of social policy. Underpinning this work is an ecosystem of podcasters, influencers, community organisers, political action committees (PACs) and networking events targeting different demographics.[4]

At AmFest, a who's who of America First/MAGA politicians and commentators – mostly men, mostly white – build the foundation on which Trump's 2024 victory will be laid. It starts with cementing the fear that the freedoms at the core of American identity and exceptionalism are in crisis. The future is uncertain as a result. There is hatred directed towards those who are seen to denigrate freedom, and collective love of the nation demanded from the audience as a way to secure freedom in the future. This playbook consists of six key principles, on repeat not only at AmFest but throughout the America First/MAGA ecosystem, permeating political rhetoric and everyday conversations.[5]

Principle 1: Freedom is threatened by 'tyranny' and must be defended

It's a festival vibe in the convention centre when I enter. Thousands of mostly white, mostly young people are registering, milling around, checking out the exhibitors' hall, with some parents and supporters in tow. It's 'business casual' sports jackets, jeans and dresses, stilettos, chinos and sequins, some boots and Stetsons.

In the main hall on each of 10,000 seats is an A3 poster that reminds me that America is the 'Greatest Country in the History of the World'. There is a new poster each day ('Do Not Comply with Tyranny', 'Self Defence is a Human Right', 'Big Gov Sucks'). I take a seat near the stage and try not to look too conspicuous. A DJ plays an eclectic mix of music, warming up the crowd, including 'YMCA' (a Trump favourite) and Harry Styles (an interesting choice given the conservative antipathy towards gender fluidity). Popular dance tracks have people dancing in the aisles, and eventually a conga line forms. Chants of 'U-S-A' lead into the chorus of 'We Will Rock You.' The coded phrase 'Let's Go Brandon' morphs into its original, 'Fuck you Biden.' Bass rumbles through bodies as the clock counts down to the start.

If America is fragile, it will not be presented as such. The thunderous electric guitar riff that opens 'The Star Spangled Banner' is followed by a recording of Ronald Reagan's inaugural speech referencing the need to defend freedom. Confetti cannons and fireworks introduce Charlie Kirk, the co-founder and CEO of TPUSA, which has become, according to him, 'the largest grassroots freedom movement in the country'. The crowd roars its approval.[6]

It is the same for each of the headline speakers on the main stage over the next four days: a gut-thumping introduction, archival footage and voiceover on giant LED screens. Lights zig zag and pyrotechnics fire up. The room echoes to chants of U-S-A, 'lock her/him up', choruses of the national anthem and the Pledge of Allegiance. 'Stage craft is State craft', as former Congressman Matt Gaetz notes in his speech, and TPUSA do it well.

The stage craft creates the effect of an evangelical meeting, to match the messianic purpose of 'saving America'. Speakers such as Texas senator Ted Cruz talk of 'Revival'; for others, it is a 'Great Awakening' or 'Reawakening'. Kirk is often centre stage, and like other leading voices in conservative politics, his productivity is enormous: a daily three hour, nationally syndicated radio show and podcast, speaking engagements around the country on university campuses, as well as evangelical churches and other conservative rallies, running TPUSA with a growing number of affiliated organisations (TPAction, TPFaith, TPAcademy) and media platforms (e.g. Turning Point Tonight, on the digital channel Real America's Voice).[7]

Targeting Gen Z, TPUSA have built a socially conservative, Christian-oriented, pro-free market, anti-Big Government youth movement.[8] They claim to have 'a presence' in over 3,500 school and university campuses, with over 820,000 student activists nationwide.[9] Apart from AmFest, they organise similar rallies and conferences targeting specific demographics, such as the Young Women's

Leadership Summit, young Blacks (Blexit), Young Latino Leadership Summit and Student Action Summit.

My request for an interview is ignored. Kirk has Fox Nation and other conservative outlets such as Breitbart broadcasting daily on site, amplifying the message via multiple channels. The media corridor and exhibition hall are surrounded by backdrops and ring lights for live streamers, podcasters and YouTube channels. We receive texts throughout the day letting us know which celebrity will be at which backdrop at what time so people can queue for selfies, circulating AmFest further throughout social media and the conservative universe.

But what is all this noise and energy and money saving America from? Summarising a fusillade of speeches, workshops and digital content: 'TYRANNY'. An eighteenth-century-sounding word that gets a lot of use in twenty-first-century America where there is 'a battle for survival' against those tyrants who would 'corrupt and destroy her forever'. There is 'threat after threat to your freedoms'. The nation is 'broken', in 'danger'. There is 'chaos', 'crisis', 'chaos', 'crisis'. There is impending tragedy, despair, fear, uncertainty and a disappearing future. The nation is on a 'precipice', at 'a critical time', 'hanging in the balance'. 'Our enemies seek our destruction.'[10] The border is broken, elections are no longer 'free and fair', cities are rocked by disorder and violence. 'We don't have a country anymore.' There is inflation, lawfare, 'pride flags replace American flags'. 'The next generation is taught to hate their country and themselves.' The 'left' has created 'cultural disintegration', destroyed respect for laws, for history, for biology and 'truth'.

The narrative is repeated relentlessly throughout conservative media, often attached to requests for donations. Freedom has become a zero-sum game. 'Special' freedoms have been created for 'some' – fill in the blank with 'people of colour' or 'LGBTQi+ rights'. These 'collective liberties' have come at the expense of individual liberties, particularly freedom of speech. *They* (conservatives) are no longer heard, silenced by universities, Democrats, bureaucrats, liberal elites. Other branches of conservatism are criticised as complying with this hegemony. 'Neo-Cons' and their 'forever wars' 'are Trotskyites', according to Kirk.[11] Trump is lionised as a 'class traitor', rebelling against his elite status by supporting 'the muscular class', the ordinary working man of America.

There has been 'betrayal'. Attack comes from the enemy within, a 'fifth column', the unseen traitor corroding and corrupting. No longer recognising the country you love, no longer feeling at home; 'something doesn't feel right'. Those responsible, the 'tyrants' and 'traitors', are named: Big Government, China, Big Tech, the mainstream media, RINOs (Republicans in name only), George Soros, a pernicious 'wokeism'. But mostly it is an amorphous 'globalism' and 'the left', an 'angry, bitter, destroying' mob, subverting the Constitution and taking away people's freedoms. A 'Global Elite', 'is trying to control you'. There is a repeated general antipathy to being 'sheep' and a nostalgic yearning for a time when 'children can play outside, where criminals are locked up and where you don't have to wear a mask' (Jack Posobiec); when it was less 'chaotic' (Tucker Carlson).[12]

The left, socialists, fascists, Nazis are conflated into the tyrant: an authoritarian figure that must be defeated. America is going through nothing less than a 'communist revolution' according to Congresswoman Marjorie Taylor-Greene. To press the point, she refers to 'the communist Democratic Party of America'. If 'they' win, they will 'transform America into something we don't fundamentally recognise' (Sarah Palin). If America First loses, they lose 'a proper country' (Posobiec).

In order to restore freedom and America to greatness, to defeat the tyrants, it is necessary to engage in what the conservative writer Medford Stanton-Evans describes as a form of 'authoritarian freedom', adhering to a set of values to ensure freedom continues rather than trading freedom for material benefit.[13] These values broadly include 'keeping faith with our Constitution' and 'patriotic education'. As Trump will later put it, speaking at an event in 2022:

> We believe that the Declaration of Independence and the American Constitution represent the principles of human civilisation. [...] We believe the USA is the greatest and most virtuous republic in the history of the world [cheers]. [...] We believe in law and order and we know that the Constitution means what it says as written.[14]

There is a desire to promote the idea of 'human flourishing', although there is no clarification on what that might look like. There is clearer agreement on the need for strong national defence, strong law and order, less government and socially conservative lifestyles.

For Kirk, America 'is the last stand of freedom on the planet', 'holding the line'. There can be no queering of its boundaries, national or gendered. 'We have to draw definitive lines between what's right and wrong', and it is God who determines those categories and the values that underpin them.

Principle 2: The United States is a Christian country and must re-find its moral centre in order to be great again

It's Sunday morning, 8am, and we're in full evangelical mode. Worship leader Sean Feucht leads a rock music prayer meeting of several thousand mostly young people, all with their hands in the air, singing praises, exalting God. There are many incarnations of Jesus Christ in America, but America First/MAGA generally aligns with Christian nationalism: God is definitely a 'he', has a preference for the USA, for individual freedom, small government, free markets and absolutist interpretations of how to be good and, conversely, what is evil.

The word of God is presented as 'truth', and that 'truth', whether it's American exceptionalism, anti-abortion or gender norms, must be defended. Pastor Rob McCoy, following on from Feucht, re-states God's authority over man: 'There is a God and you are not him.' Nature is God's creation, and the laws of nature, such as man's inalienable freedom enshrined in the Declaration of Independence, are absolute. I catch the last ten minutes as I'm in a long queue for coffee, which I need before I can face others' damnation of my soul, but there is so much more to come. It is reaffirmed by speaker after speaker that America is a Christian country whose values are based on Judeo-Christian principles. They thank 'our lord and saviour Jesus Christ' and call on God to 'Bless America'. Succinctly put by former Congressman Madison Cawthorn, 'the most important thing we have to do is save souls for Christ. Atheists are idiots.'

In the myths of nationhood, this Christian heritage enabled American greatness, but in the reality of the present, it has defined America in terms of civilisational and religious chauvinism, at times incorporating support for white supremacy and replacement theory.[15] Today, so the story goes, American culture has become weak and emasculated through seeking pleasure rather than virtue. While God doesn't want us to have less freedom, that freedom should have a moral core, delaying the desires of the flesh to go towards a higher plane of existence. Kirk is clear that 'freedom is not being able to do whatever you want to do' but rather to live in a way that's 'meaningful' and 'beautiful' as defined by conservative ideals. It's not the freedom to have instant gratification, Tinder hook-ups, gender transition surgery or take drugs.

Reduced to 'good versus evil, darkness and lightness', 'spiritual warfare is raging'. The universe is on its head. 'So Much That Feels Deeply Wrong Has Been Elevated as Acutely Right.'[16] The current round of 'culture wars' is described as 'freakin' evil man' by the frenetic Chadd Wright, a former Navy Seal and 'man of God' who appeals to young people to 'read your Bible and give your heart to Jesus'. Wearing running shorts with wiry ultra-marathon legs exposed, fidgeting and roaming the stage with furious energy, his feelings about 'wokism' are clear. 'It's the intangible force that we can't see', but soldiers like Wright 'have seen it and it's called evil. It's not a liberal ideology. You can't negotiate with evil. You have to drive it back into the shadow. That's what you do with evil. Screw these people man.'

The reference to 'intangible forces' is a trope repeated throughout the America First/MAGA movement and highlights the act of faith required to believe that 'something unseen is happening, there's a spiritual dimension to this' (Tucker Carlson). We never have complete knowledge of the forces that shape our lives, but the unknown can be better handled by God, particularly when it comes to combatting the invisible hand of the 'Deep State'. Music icon Taylor Swift, for example, was supposedly involved in a covert CIA 'psy-op' to re-elect Joe Biden through influencing her millions of followers. Kirk 'could feel something was wrong', interviewing a former CIA operative to reassure himself that his feelings were valid and to reassert claims that Swift was deliberately planted as a disrupter.[17] Battling against the unseen, conservatives are urged to go on the offence to restore America's moral core, and the primary fields for this action are the family and education, ground zero of America's cultural wars pitting ideas and people against each other.

Principle 3: The family and education are at the heart of American freedom

Culture wars mark the pendulum of release and restraint within cultural change, and I have lived through several cycles in different countries. Faced with changing expectations of what is and isn't permissible in the nation, the street, the classroom, the home, there is a struggle to control the master narrative, the values and belief systems that underpin our cultural infrastructure.[18]

At AmFest, the culture wars are intensely focused on women's bodies as bearers of tradition and morality. A woman is responsible for reproducing the nation through ensuring the 'correct' upbringing and education of her children. Young people are told to abstain from premarital sex, 'get married early and have large families'. Young men must control themselves and are reminded that 'women want to be led' according to Kirk (with disturbingly loud cheers from the audience).

Speakers become role models while talking of their love for their families, bringing their children and spouses into the spotlight. Benny Johnson, TPUSA's Creative Director and podcaster, introducing his one-year-old daughter and later his pregnant wife, brings home the point: 'Libs don't want to procreate. They are not sexy [cheering]. We are creating the next generation of freedom. Make fathers great again. This is how we take back culture. We have great children. We love our wives.'

While women are busy reproducing the nation, raising children with the correct principles of freedom,[19] it's up to the ideal masculine warrior to defend the country at a time when nationalist populist and conservative commentators bemoan the emasculation of the American male and his falling testosterone.[20] Cawthorn is known for his publicly stated belief that American women need to raise their sons as 'monsters'.[21] His political career, however, did not survive a set of scandals that raised questions about his own morality.[22]

The 'warrior' narrative calls for a return to 'real' military leadership (i.e. men), and veterans feature heavily in the AmFest schedule, introduced as 'American patriots', 'lions' and 'heroes'. At Trump campaign rallies and other Republican events in the lead up to the 2024 elections, support for veterans and police ('back the blue') is foregrounded.[23] The US military is seen as being weakened by 'wokism', which 'steals the hearts of soldiers'.[24] Biden's withdrawal from Afghanistan in 2021 was repeatedly criticised as a 'retreat' and 'shameful'. That America is now seen as fragile by its 'enemies' (Iran, Russia, China) is on repeat at rallies and in the conservative media landscape. Former National Guard and Fox News presenter Pete Hegseth's appointment as Secretary of Defense in 2025 was seen as the remedy.

If you cannot join the military, then at least you can own a gun and defend your family. At AmFest, the apex of the 'American warrior' meme rested with Kyle Rittenhouse, accused of murdering two people during the Kenosha riots in 2020.[25] The 'independent' journalists who contributed significant material to the trial that eventually acquitted Rittenhouse are presented as heroic, standing up to Antifa and a tyrannical government that seeks to censor 'the truth'.[26] James O'Keefe, political activist and founder of Project Veritas, has his 'oppression' at the hands of the state depicted in a surreal interpretative dance. He later wanders around the main hall in his 'press' flak jacket, posing for selfies.

Women, on the other hand, fulfil their primary role of raising children as patriots and inculcating values of freedom. Love of children is motivation for attacking public education, ensuring they are not used as 'pawns to overthrow our society' and are protected from 'inappropriate' books, lessons and genders. Diversity initiatives and social-emotional learning programmes are seen as challenging the right of parents to instil their values in their children and dismantling the foundations of America by questioning 'true' history. Education should create 'a nation you can recognise', but instead, according to writer and podcaster James Lindsay, it is now part of a leftist system of control. He draws parallels between public school and 'Maoist' re-education programmes, arguing that the intention is to destroy families so that 'Marxists' can take over the country.

The argument lacks all nuance and evidence, but there is no space for shades of grey or critical debate. America is the GOAT (greatest of all time), and that should not be questioned. It is not a racist country, although white privilege is a racist concept, according to Kirk among many others. Heroes of the past, including the slave-owning Thomas Jefferson, 'allowed you to have freedom'.

Without irony, the term 'indoctrination' is used to describe attempts to introduce critical historical perspectives and diversity programmes into education curricula. But indoctrination clearly works both ways. At AmFest, just one rally among many in a packed calendar of America First and conservative networking events, there is no time for self-reflection, no time to think, no alternative perspectives presented. Sessions are back to back, with twenty- to forty-five-minute speaker slots interspersed with a selection of longer breakout sessions covering topics such as election integrity, how to fight against 'leftist media', conservative politics and pop culture, biblical citizenship, effective local activism, how to get elected, college financing and cryptocurrency.

To square the circle between calls to abandon public and higher education and the idea that we still need to know stuff, speakers emphasise that there is a difference between knowledge, necessary in order to 'hold tyrants to account' and available to anyone, and wisdom, that is, the understanding of knowledge. For Kirk, who says he learns something new every day, wisdom is eternal knowledge (i.e. it comes from God), sometimes referred to as 'common sense'. He reminds us that professors and teachers 'want you to be intimidated. Using big academic words to make you seem stupid when in fact you have wisdom.' This leads to a recurring theme of nationalist populist rhetoric: anti-intellectual, anti-elite hostility, with a dash of abject humiliation thrown into the toxic mix.

Principle 4: Elites have humiliated us and the nation and must be dealt with

'Elites', as defined by America First/MAGA, are a disparate group: a 'righteous ruling class', 'leftists', 'Marxists', globalists, academics, Big Tech, presumably excluding financial supporters such as Peter Thiel and Elon Musk. They generally reside in a big city (any mention of New York generates a pantomime 'boo' from the audience, although some of the attendees I speak to come from big cities) and are part of a shadowy Deep State responsible for bringing down Trump in 2020.

Donald Trump Jr reminds the crowd that the Democrats 'think they are better than you', and 'What do you think our enemies are doing? They are laughing.'

In his 2024 campaign rallies, Donald Trump will repeatedly state that the world 'is laughing at us' following foreign policy failures such as the withdrawal from Afghanistan. One of his first foreign policy actions in January 2025, forcing Colombia to receive a military flight carrying illegal immigrants, will be described by Kirk on his podcast as a return of 'masculine energy' to the White House and a rebuke of the US diplomatic corps, who were forced to 'bend the knee'. Trump 'made fools out of all of them'.[27]

Referencing anger and a sense of loss in this moment of cultural rupture, the pain of humiliation is clear and personal. 'They' (elites) hate 'you' (conservatives); 'they' have laughed at 'us', shamed 'us' for our faith and our patriotism. As Gaetz affirms, they are 'mocking us for accepting the word of God'; or as Carlson puts it, 'their only point is to let you know who is in charge; obey; it's not your country'.

Love of nation emerges as a means of resolving such humiliation, along with associated feelings of discomfort, vulnerability, anxiety, shame, eventually turning to hate. There is a line through American history repeating the same narrative: a resentment boiling just beneath the surface, as the following excerpt from historian Sarah Churchwell's research shows. This is from a 1926 Ku Klux Klan pamphlet, attacking 'liberals':

> Liberalism is today charged in the mind of most Americans with nothing less than national, racial and spiritual treason. [...] Nordic Americans for the last generation have found themselves increasingly uncomfortable, and finally deeply distressed [...]. We are a movement of plain people, very weak in the matter of culture, intellectual support and trained leadership. [...] [T]he opposition of the intellectuals and liberals who held the leadership, betrayed Americanism, and from whom we expect to wrest control, is almost automatic. [...] The assurance for the future of our children dwindled. We found our great cities and the control of much of our industry and commerce taken over by strangers who stacked the cards of success and prosperity against us.[28]

'Economic distress', the blaming of elites, protecting children, fear of strangers, the discomfort of change, a future lost, the humiliation of 'plain people', all converge into grievance in 1926, and it continues today. At times in my conversations, those leaning liberal/Democrat do express contempt and even pity for the 'uneducated', for the 'stupid', for those who 'don't think for themselves', who can't handle the riches of a digital life, those working class, not college educated. Those voting for Trump who are perceived as posing a threat to progressive lifestyles.

Years of research have taught me to never underestimate what humans will do to avoid feeling humiliation and shame, including defacing the humanity of others they perceive as the cause of those feelings. This is the bedrock of populist movements. It is global and universal. Love of nation becomes a justification for attacks on others to assuage the pain of humiliation. At AmFest, the rhetoric turns to retribution and punishment. MAGA will have their revenge, and on his return to the White House, Trump will deliver, adopting the 'move fast, break things' approach. He will go on to sign a slew of executive orders targeting diversity, equality and inclusion (DEI) initiatives, the LGBTQI+ community, immigrants and his 'enemies'.

There was always a whisper of violence at the edges of MAGA rallies, couched as self-defence, 'to protect ourselves from a government that wants to get out of control', keeping enough distance to ensure plausible deniability. As Carlson states at AmFest, violence is horrible but sometimes unavoidable. Pastor McCoy continues his sheep parable, noting there are wolves who 'want to take away your freedom, slaughter you'. Questions from the floor for Trump advisor and media commentator Sebastian Gorka include 'when should the Second Amendment be invoked', to which Gorka responds: 'God preserve us from another civil war. But if they try to take our liberty, I am not afraid of them.' Ted Cruz later emphasises the point: 'I think violence is wrong', but 'we are not going to let them persecute freedom loving people'.

There is a performative element to this staging of America First/MAGA: the pantomime boos, the macho rhetoric, the interpretative dance. But this makes it no less dangerous when the rhetoric is designed to inspire others to ignore democratic process or take up arms. Emotions have to go somewhere.

Principle 5: Express your love and hate

The anger veers at times into palpable rage, on repeat throughout the conservative universe, as the following e-newsletter from podcaster and filmmaker Dinesh D'Souza makes clear. It will be sent in response to the attempted assassination of Donald Trump in July 2024 (emphasis and caps are his):

> For years they've wished for President Trump to be murdered. For years, they've rioted across the entire country, laying waste to homes, and beating innocent Americans *to death*. For years, they've lied, and fed you propaganda while they label you a 'conspiracy theorist' and a 'terror threat'. They *forced* people to take their vaccines, and now all these years later, people are still *dying* from the side effects they claimed didn't exist. These people are **vicious** … they're **violent** … and they're **after you**. None of this has been a coincidence: it was **always by their design**. They call for violence in the streets, they call for open borders, they call for **you** to lose your job and livelihood if you speak up … This isn't about President Trump, our movement, or our ideas … This is about **destroying our way of life, and what they're doing is just *one way they're choosing to get there***. They **want you silent, broke, and *dead*. DESTROY THE VIOLENT LEFT.** They've allowed our country to be flooded with savages, shot our President, and they're just waiting to activate their mobs to burn our cities down once again, throw bricks at police officers, and beat down anybody in their path … Let's just hope it isn't **you** or **somebody you love** that gets in their way when it starts again. [...] Times are tough, I know … But if we can't get across the finish line this November, trust me … Things are going to get a **whole lot worse**. Sincerely, Dinesh d'Souza.[29]

As Naomi Klein found in her book *Doppelganger*, the America First/ MAGA world thrives on distress.[30] Age has made me more resilient to the barrage of excess emotion that comes with political dystopia, but do not dive into it just before going to bed. You may not sleep well.

Such extreme language serves a purpose other than to generate fear. In Sara Ahmed's writing on culture, it is through intensifying emotions that an 'other' takes shape. No longer ephemeral, the object of hate ('the left', in the case of the email above, or 'Globalists' or 'illegal immigrants') becomes something that can be felt and therefore made real. Sharing emotions, rage as well as love, creates bonds. The 'mob' coalesces around emotion and a leader.[31] For Trump, the 6 January

2021 (J6) attack on the Capitol has been reframed as an exercise in 'unbelievable love and patriotism', and the rioters 'love our country'. Throughout his election campaign in 2024, he will remind his followers: 'I truly love our Country and love you all.'[32]

The emotional intensity of AmFest, and similar rallies in the conservative ecosystem, cycles between hate and love and back again. Pumping music, pyrotechnics, jump cut edits on interstitials, strobe lighting, all generate a sense of restless energy associated with a stream of references to 'crisis', 'chaos', 'tyranny' and loss. The use of personal stories taps into our emotional core, such as Gorka's retelling at AmFest of his Hungarian father's torture under a communist regime.

In the confines of a conference centre in downtown Phoenix, 10,000 young people feel safe, exhilarated in the knowledge they are free to express their emotions: their patriotic love and anger. Protected by others, they have found their people. They belong. Benny Johnson's high energy, clever use of pop culture brings home the message that 'I love you, my people.' 'I love my wife. I love my kids. I love my country. I love all of you. I love my saviour.'

Sides are drawn using emotional indicators: 'the left' are 'angry', 'bitter', 'miserable', 'destroying not building', according to Kirk (ignoring just how angry most of the speakers, including himself, sound). Gorka is perhaps at the apex of anger: 'I'm not afraid of you,' he rages, pointing to an imaginary Nancy Pelosi, after announcing he has had his phone records subpoenaed by the Congressional Committee investigating the J6 riot.[33] 'I ain't afraid of you [Nancy],' repeats Gorka, to a huge cheer. 'You chose the wrong enemy [loud cheer, ovation, U-S-A chants].' 'We are not afraid. I declare right now, bring it [finger pointing forward, still shouting at his imaginary Nancy].' 'We will not be intimidated and we will win! [loud cheering].' Invoking more outrage at his current phone provider, he goes on to promote a new telecoms company that he is brand ambassador for. Never let rage get in the way of the free market.

There is no love in the collection of terms used by Donald Trump at rallies and on social media to describe his 'enemies': vicious, fascist, communists, menacing, thugs, extremists, resentful, weak, unhinged. The left 'hates all of you. Hates me even more than you but I'm just trying to help you out. What the hell did I do! [big cheers].' 'We have to fight some very sick and very evil people.'[34]

Yet it is 'the left' that is blamed for creating the conditions for violence through emphasising Trump's threat to democracy. Kirk will later stress the point in criticising CNN's coverage of the assassination attempt against Trump. 'You. Do not. Hate. These people. Enough. Trust me. You do not.'[35] There is no recognition of MAGA's part in ratchetting up the political temperature. For while the left is fuelled by 'hatred', according to Gorka, 'Our fuel is love. Love of country, love of the greatest nation on God's earth and that is why we will win!' Winning is important, and that requires action.

Principle 6: Fight back – the nation is not going to save itself. Sacrifice will be necessary but 'you are not alone'

If a price has to be paid for their activism, the audience at AmFest is constantly reminded that they are not alone. It's a numbers game. 'There are more of us than them' is on repeat. The personalised messaging emphasises that to belong is to take responsibility for tackling the loss of freedom. 'Don't let America slip away.' There will be danger and perils, but together 'we' will overcome. 'It's going to take all of us, so can we count on you? [...] Conservatives can restore a broken nation, but only if we stick together!'[36]

Speaker after speaker rounds out their speech with a motivational push, calling for young people to 'not be afraid', to get 'louder, stronger, tougher' (Matt Gaetz). Young people will need to let go of fear and sacrifice social media 'likes', family, friends and wealth for a more meaningful life. 'Stiffen your spine' and take those positions that you know are right (Sarah Palin). 'You are going to have to get comfortable being uncomfortable' (Marjorie Taylor-Green). 'Stop being sheep, stand up and be lions' (Madison Cawthorn). 'If you believe in those principles you should have the scars' (Ted Cruz). Freedom now becomes a rallying cry. Everyone in the auditorium is a 'force multiplier for freedom', fighting 'for what we love, which is the freedom we have'. 'We are the front line of freedom, we are the front line of liberty.' 'You guys are the front line of freedom, liberty and justice.'

In her investigation into the funding of libertarian and conservative movements, journalist Jane Mayer notes that from the 1970s there has been a drive to create a supportive group identity among university students as key to capturing the state.[37] With TPUSA, conservatives have succeeded, with much of this activism underpinned by donations, political action committees (PACs), and 'dark money'.[38] There is power in the collective recitation of the narrative, in the chanting, in the cultural cohesion of this group. After his inaugural address, Kirk asks anyone who has travelled on their own to put their hand up so that TPUSA volunteers can find and connect with them. No one is left alone.

TPUSA will be credited within Republican circles as being instrumental in bringing enough Gen Z over to Trump in 2024 to influence the final outcome. In the lead up to the election, they, along with other America First-aligned organisations, will deploy Democratic Party principles of community organising and fan out across the country in myriad formats.[39] Even love will become a strategy. Tyler Bowyer, Chief Operating Officer of TPAction, will describe on the *Charlie Kirk Show* how they engaged 'affectivity' in their 2024 field operation to turn out the vote in Arizona and Wisconsin, particularly among low propensity voters: primarily building relationships through multiple 'meaningful' contacts with people. Conversations with friends and family were key influences, moving beyond just leaving leaflets or sending texts to showing that they cared:

> We were building relationships having 5, 6, 7, 8, 9 meaningful relational contacts with these people and that's the difference. Bringing them cookies, offering to help, bring in their groceries, seeing them at the park, waving to them at the mailbox, being from their neighbourhood. That is what moves votes. That is how you get people to turn out who are not likely to turn out. That affectivity was able to get Donald Trump across the finish line.[40]

Back at AmFest, there is a constant call to action, even if that means starting small, by convincing family and friends, running for school boards or an election monitoring role. Hot button issues such as immigration, gender and education draw in those who have not participated in political activism before, particularly young people and women. An efficient pipeline, from TPUSA to other conservative organisations,

36

funnels young people into internships, training programmes and directly networking with power centres in Washington, DC. Young people can get connected to think tanks and media outlets, rallies and cottage meetings, study groups and community gatherings, further amplified through links with allied institutions such as evangelical churches and pastors. The network is supported by training initiatives on how to lead, how to run for office, how to organise and how to be a social media influencer.

Well-known conservative politicians, such as Cruz, extol the young audience to 'speak out, use your voice, speak out for freedom. Go find a campaign and volunteer. Find alternatives to mainstream media' (he recommends his own podcast of course). To counter 'miserable leftists', they are told to 'be joyful, happy warriors for liberty'. Despair, according to Gorka, is 'unAmerican'. 'We never give up. We never give in.' Wright tries emotional manipulation, arguing that if the audience don't leave the event and execute what they have learned, 'you are selfish, cheating your nation and cheating generations that follow you. Execute, execute, execute. That is what warriors do.' 'Negativity', especially any reflection on the legacies of slavery and racism, is perceived as 'unpatriotic' and designed to 'destroy' American freedom. This criticism also comes from high-profile Black conservative voices such as Ben Carson and Candace Owens.

There are plenty of opportunities to find a campaign in the exhibition hall, or even employment as anti-abortion activists. TPAction and Breitbart are looking to recruit. In 2024, TPUSA will hire over a thousand full-time 'ballot chasers', with Kirk exhorting his followers to 'work your ass off, work like hell'.[41] At the very least, the call to action is a call to disobey, and at this juncture it takes the form of a confluence of disparate voices adopting variations on the words of the Declaration of Independence ('That whenever any form of Government becomes destructive of these ends, it is the Right of the People to alter or to abolish it') and misappropriating Dr Martin Luther King Jr (e.g. 'One has a moral responsibility to disobey unjust laws', emblazoned on a Young Americans for Liberty poster).

People becoming politically active could generally be considered a good thing in a democracy, but the unremitting weight of conservative and nationalist populism, embedded in networks that extend from local school boards and churches to Congress, is having a profound impact on key democratic institutions such as the law, education and election integrity. Yet despite appearing as an all-encompassing take-over of American society, there are holes in the America First/MAGA playbook through which it is possible to see some light.

Re-considering the playbook

Stepping back from the America First/MAGA narrative, there are obvious contradictions and inconsistencies that are impossible to rec-oncile. There is the uncomfortable co-joining of authoritarianism and freedom; complaining about 'cancel culture' while calling for book banning; decrying indoctrination by others but insisting there is only one 'true' world view. Fears are expressed that liberals and 'globalists' are attempting to control conservatives, while conservatives attempt to control politics, education and women's bodies ostensibly as an act of self-defence and to assuage feelings of humiliation.

The relationship between capitalism and populism is a particularly fraught contradiction. In 2024, Kirk, for example, will begin embedding health messaging into his podcast, referencing the adverse impacts of pollution and heavily promoting supplements. The drive for a cleaner environment and healthier food will be taken up by organisations like Moms for America (MfA) as necessary for the development of young patriots.[42] With vaccine sceptic Robert F. Kennedy Jr becom-ing Secretary for Health in 2025, MAGA will clone itself into MAHA (Make America Healthy Again). Yet in all of this criticism, there is no recognition that free markets, car culture and environmental degrada-tion in the name of profit might have something to do with the USA's poor health indicators.

Conjuring an anti-urban, rural idyll, replete with myths of the frontier, Tucker Carlson calls for a return to arcadia, feeling sorry for the banker in his Manhattan penthouse in a crumbling metropole. We should be living in a log cabin in Montana with the snow falling romantically outside. Apart from the rationalisation of difference (you may not be wealthy in your cabin, but your life will have more worth), Carlson lectures that meaning is being stripped from our lives, and we should turn off our phones and listen more. Yet even as he's speaking, a glamorous influencer wanders through the auditorium with an entourage of GoPros in her wake. The movement relies on smart phones and the accelerant of social media to ricochet messages nationally and globally.

There is no reconciling the desire for unfettered capitalism promulgated by conservative and libertarian think tanks and the noise, chaos and stripping of meaning that capitalism creates. Many of the new conservative champions of the working classes, like Carlson, are themselves very wealthy. The disjunction has been noted by some conservative outlets, such as American Compass, who are attempting to rethink the impact of capitalism, acknowledging its negative effects on our social fabric. The free market, in their view, should be tempered by decent wages and the needs of communities as a whole. There is even talk of a role for unions (something Freedom Conservatives may reject as a lurch to the left).[43] From an impoverished childhood, J.D. Vance, picked by Trump to be his vice presidential running mate in July 2024, speaks to this form of populist conservatism.[44]

Former Democrat supporters describe feeling politically orphaned because of the party's neglect of working-class issues, while large corporations are criticised for virtue signalling racial and gender equity but ignoring inequalities in their pay scales and other working conditions. This has left a space clear for populists like Trump to reclaim the working class as well as Black and Hispanic communities that the Democrats once took for granted.

However, rather than alleviating economic inequalities, much of the nationalist populist rhetoric focuses on 'traditional' values ('guns, god and family') and reducing government interference in economic and social life. There can be criticism of global elites and globalism, blamed for causing pain in American communities through outsourcing industry and importing pandemics, but free markets continue to be promoted as the only model worth having. As Hegseth puts it at AmFest, three years before his elevation to Secretary for Defense, America wants 'patriots and capitalists'.

It is fair to say that few of us are wholly consistent. It is a trait of being human that we are very capable of simultaneously holding opposing views, although these are generally expressed at different times to different people. More problematic is how to develop bridging capital in order to cross political divides and find consensus. To not allow exposure to other ideas that may challenge our world view through naming them as deviant (e.g. 'grooming'), demarcating them as good or evil, is an effective means of maintaining control by keeping people apart.

The end result is a curtailing of freedom for everyone involved. It is worrying in terms of social cohesion that the America First/MAGA movement has built their own social, cultural, IT and economic infrastructure – 'uncensored' social media platforms like Truth Social, Gettr and Rumble, voter marketing and polling platforms, schools and colleges, financial and banking services. Affiliates within the constellation cross-promote 'patriotic' businesses. Red Referral, for example, a conservative business network, asks the question: 'Why give your money to people who hate you and tell others to hate you as well?'[45] In joining their network, conservative businesses can support each other against the 'crushing weight of disparagement from the left and the population in general' and 'be in a room with people who are just like you', with a 'traditional Judeo-Christian mindset that we've all come to believe in'.

This conservative momentum may cause sleepless nights for 'liberals' or 'progressives', in the USA and beyond, and even for those Republicans who feel their party has shifted too far into the morass of culture wars and authoritarianism. But closer inspection of how the playbook is evaluated reveals not only cracks in the rhetoric but possibilities for rethinking the divide. There is space for empathy and dialogue, hopeful but complicated, starting with small steps.

To begin with, the message is not unanimously received or uncritically absorbed, even among conservatives. In every conversation that is part of this book, there is dissent and disagreement, followed by some resolution. It may not always be pretty, but the effort is there. There are raging supporters who will attack the vulnerable (refugees, trans-children). Yet there are also articulate, thoughtful people voting for Trump who are not deluded by who he is, who express disgust at how he behaves, but who are also weighing up the trade-offs and moral choices they have to make in order to feel safe in an uncertain world.

Even at AmFest, the young people I speak to have a range of motivations and reactions to the event. There are favoured speakers, while others are criticised. Internal dynamics within TPUSA are discussed by a group of activists, and Kirk is called a hypocrite. One activist is upset about being labelled the wrong ethnic group. I'd suggest some diversity training but doubt it will be taken up. Similarly, not all conservative and Republican organisations would agree with the playbook or the way America First/MAGA-affiliated groups are carrying it out. A spokesperson for a prominent anti-abortion non-government organisation, for example, describes TPUSA as 'obnoxious'. Some Republicans are trying to wrest control of the party back from the America First/MAGA agenda, notably the Lincoln Project ('we're here to stop Trump, break MAGA, and save America').

Even Kirk occasionally broadcasts differing viewpoints, debating on his programme everyone from 'Marxists' to young people involved in the adult entertainment industry. Minor differences are tolerated within the organisation. Following the furore over Taylor Swift as psy-op, Kirk will be joined on his podcast by two TPUSA 'Swifties'.[46] Their response is clear: conservative men need to stop trash talking Swift and focus on more important issues, like immigration.

Lived experience and contact can counter generalisation and caricature. During several conversations, when participants begin to rail against professors teaching children to 'hate their country' with their gender studies and critical race theory, I gently remind them that I am one such person. There is usually an awkward pause, and then the phrase 'but I don't mean you'. If I had a dollar for every time I've heard that phrase over the years. 'Remove all Muslims if they don't accept the removal of their mosques' says the fundamentalist; 'it's nothing personal,' he adds. 'I don't mean you. I love you,' says the woman talking about how refugees are taking jobs, turning to her immigrant partner to reassure him it is those 'other' immigrants who are the problem. And so it goes on: the separation of the individual that is in front of us from the amorphous mass of others, the strangers who make us feel uncomfortable. But in a polarised America, this problematic response also gives me a sense of hope that in conversation a small door can open that allows the world to be seen differently.

Cognitive linguist and philosopher George Lakoff has argued that 'liberal' and 'conservative' differences in the USA, defined by moral world views, are hard-wired into thinking and perhaps becoming increasingly so.[47] According to a 2022 Pew survey, 72 per cent of Republicans and 63 per cent of Democrats now say that members of the opposing party are immoral, up from 47 and 35 per cent in 2016.[48] Similar increases are also seen in judging the other side as 'lazy', 'unintelligent', 'dishonest' and 'close-minded'.

But in reality, it's never such a clean division, as the conversations in this book illustrate. Moral world views, including how freedom is defended, can be an expression of other factors: managing change, feeling unsafe, wanting to belong. More importantly, our moral world views can be re-evaluated. They can shift, adapt, be re-prioritised and traded against other priorities. They can take on different meanings even in contentious spaces like the Mexican border, as we'll see in the next set of conversations, as different stakeholders re-imagine what free markets and free movement can look like.

In the meantime, post-AmFest, I find a craft brewery in downtown Phoenix with fire pits and vegan bowls and wait for my ride home to New York. Kirk may imagine me miserable, Vance may call me a 'cat lady',[49] but for now I'm happy drinking a beer in a bar with an open fourth wall, the inside and outside merging under canvas sails. It's perfect for a mild winter's day in Arizona enjoying my own company. People around me laugh, play on their phones, chat, flirt, talk about God and politics. The gay pride flag flies next to the Arizona and USA flags. No symbols are under attack here; they just hang together, gently waving in the afternoon breeze. The beer doesn't quite remove, however, the lingering feeling that AmFest is a preview of the love and hate that will underpin Trump's victory in 2024.

3

Re-imagining free movement: El Paso/Ciudad Juárez

A few months after AmFest, I am heading for the US border with Mexico. Driving across the fracking hell-scape of north Texas, I watch hundreds of trucks stream east and west along one of the country's busiest highways, to and from El Paso and its Mexican twin, Ciudad Juárez. They add to the thin film of dust already covering me from last night's storm. The Borderplex (El Paso in Texas, Ciudad Juárez in Mexico, and Las Cruces in New Mexico) is one of the largest manufacturing and distribution zones in the USA. US–Mexico trade is reported to be worth around $500 billion, and 20 per cent of it comes through El Paso. There are more than 1,100 manufacturing operations, producing everything from electronics to medical components, cars to clothing, shipped out by road and rail to the rest of the world.[1]

The border makes this economy possible with the cheap labour of the maquiladoras (mostly foreign-owned factories) on the Mexican side and the higher-value management and distribution functions on the USA side, supported by a foreign trade zone with tax and duty exemptions.[2] The region's population of some 2.5 million makes it, according to El Paso County, the western hemisphere's largest bilingual and binational border community. In their upbeat promotional video, showcasing economic growth, high-tech and knowledge industries, high-quality leisure and hospitality options, low cost of living and good weather, the region is described as an 'intersection of possibilities'.[3]

Yet in the America First/MAGA media landscape, this area is imagined as something far more dystopian. In shouting headlines multiple times a day, audiences are bombarded with stories of the 'millions' of 'illegal immigrants' crossing into the USA. A 2024 Pew survey found that 77 per cent of those surveyed perceived the influx of migrants at the US–Mexico border as a crisis (45 per cent) or a major problem (32 per cent).[4] This mobility has been linked to catastrophic outcomes: crime, violence, human trafficking, drug smuggling, including the synthetic opioid fentanyl implicated in tens of thousands of overdose deaths that have devastated communities in America.

In the run up to the 2024 presidential election, Republican politicians in the southern states of Texas and Arizona declared an 'invasion'. Asylum seekers were bussed or flown to New York and Washington, DC to make a point.[5] The murder of several women by illegal immigrants created a wave of toxic commentary, without adding statistics on how many women were murdered by American men during the same period. As Charlie Kirk repeated: 'Yet again the left embraces tragedy after tragedy as young American women are raped and killed at the hands of illegal immigrants in the most horrific stories you have ever heard.'[6]

The tradition of using violence against women to justify violence against others has been well established by politicians globally. In the first week of taking office in 2025, Trump will order mass deportations, hailed by his supporters as Making America Safe Again (MASA).[7] Running beneath this depiction of a violent, 'out-of-control' border are the rumblings of replacement theory and a conspiracy that points to Democrats allowing mass migration as a way of increasing their voter share (assuming that all Hispanic Americans vote Democrat, which they do not).

The hyperbole illustrates the capacity of borders to be more than simply cartographic lines. They represent a sense of safety. As the rhetoric at AmFest highlighted, imagined boundaries around a nation can become very hard when threatened, corralling not only immigration but also cultural change. Order, certainty and continuity, ensuring that the future will be the same as the past, is determined by the strength of a border, well defined and unambiguous, shaping what is and is not permissible within its perimeters.

As a master narrative, freedom is a key marker of the USA's borders, setting out familiar rights and expectations that demarcate the nation. America First's nationalist populism draws a clear, sacred line around these rights and expectations and all the benefits that having those freedoms entails. There is an assumption that there is only one version of freedom and that everyone within the border should share the same understanding of what that means. Their focus on sovereignty is an effort to maintain, reinforce and defend not only physical borders, between the USA and Mexico, for example, but also secure historical borders, created in the stories passed on from one generation to the next, and cultural borders, determining socially expected roles, for example how to be a man or a woman.

Yet despite all the efforts to maintain them, physical and cultural borders are inherently unstable and subject to change. There is an endless oscillation between release and restraint as societies cycle between hardening and easing borders. At these moments of change, cracks in the perimeter may cause anxiety but may also enable new opportunities, new freedoms, to emerge. There can be different ways of imagining the Borderplex, for example: not as dysfunction, not as an economic production zone, but as a living, dynamic, cosmopolitan port. For those living next to it, used to border crossing, who know and understand its history, a bit of flexibility, ambiguity, queering of the borders even, is generally fine. There may be tensions, arguments, but it is understood that a border can be porous, useful at times, ignored at others. It is a line of aspiration and curiosity about life on the other side. The border can be an invitation to transgress.

Traffic congests on the approach to El Paso as multiplying lanes divide and twist over and under themselves. On my left, a long, long train passes, heading southeast, weighed down with shipping containers. On my right, a 2.6-million square foot Amazon 'fulfilment' centre appears in a barren stretch of land. The El Paso business district emerges in front; a small collection of high-rise offices by day and bars at night. On closer inspection, it is surrounded by quiet streets of cheap electrical and clothing stores, boarded up shops and Bail Bond companies on most corners.

All roads, it seems, lead to one of El Paso's six international bridges, owned by the city but controlled by the federal government. These are the arteries that connect Mexico and the USA, with a constant flow of cars, trucks and human traffic. According to former local representative Peter Svarzbein, there are around 75,000 crossings every day by people who live, work and/or study on one side or the other. A family could have their home in Ciudad Juárez, shop in Walmart in El Paso, visit grandkids, take in a movie and return to Juárez in the evening. This movement, back and forward, intertwines the two communities. We'll hear more from Peter later – it takes me a couple of days to track him down – but in the meantime I find my own attempt to cross ending in a minor detention.

My imagination of the border from watching too much social media was that it would be a heavily militarised space involving intrusive identity checks. So it was disorienting to find I would just have to pay 50 cents at a toll booth to walk across Stanton Bridge into Mexico. At its crest, the Rio Grande appears below as a dirty, wide concrete canal, lined along the USA side with a rust brown metal barrier topped and bottomed with razor wire. On the other side, Mexican security aren't too bothered about identity papers either, so, accompanied by a British friend, Sophie, I wander into Juárez.

In a tiny vignette of everyday border-crossings, centred on a local fruit juice and ice cream kiosk, two Mexican women help us translate our order (mango chilli ice lollies are the best). They live in El Paso but have come over to see a dentist in Juárez, where it's not only cheaper but the dentist will drive to the juice bar to pick them up. A young student arrives, wearing a blazer from a private school in El Paso. He travels each day back and forth, studying with American, Mexican and Korean students. While El Paso has a majority Hispanic population (almost 83 per cent), it is a multicultural city with indigenous, white, Black and Asian communities. Immigrants from Europe have also added to the city's fabric. The reason for Sophie's visit is to find the home of her German grandfather, who lived in El Paso in the 1960s while training pilots at a nearby German air-force base that was only closed in 2022. Sophie grew up with pictures of Texas in her grandparents' home in Germany.

We spend an hour wandering Juárez's main shopping precinct, a neatly paved area that seems more active than El Paso. There's a busy market and restaurants. A patrol truck with a machine gun installed in the back is a reminder that drug cartels still cause trouble. We eventually head to Paso del Norte bridge, paying 30 cents to cross back to the USA. And now, of course, the militarised imagination of the border begins to appear.

At the crest, the dividing line between Mexico and the USA, two border officers check our passports. One is chatty, articulate and good PR: the border is easy, free flowing, he tells us, except on weekends when the immigration line can stretch back up the bridge. The other officer, in dark sunglasses, doesn't speak except to say goodbye. We head down to the immigration terminal and a relatively short queue, waiting about thirty minutes, making small talk with people around us: a Pentecostal pastor heading to Denver, a young woman with a puppy visiting family on the other side.

Sophie, with dual UK–US citizenship, eases through. As my turn arrives, I hand in my passport, visa page open. All fine until I'm asked for my SEVIS paper (Student and Exchange Visitor Program), which would be the one I left behind in New York. The material of borders is not only walls, bollards, razor wire and drones but still bits of paper. My freedom to move hits a secure room with several officers at desks, doing paperwork, questioning other detainees. Chairs around the walls and in the centre of the room dangle handcuffs. A cage at the end, door open, holds an unseen crying baby. I assume the mother is in the cage with the child. A woman in a white medical coat and another in scrubs attend to a young girl sharing the room with me: she is weighed; her arms are checked and measured. They say she is tall for a five-year-old and place a blue nit net over her hair. There is talk in Spanish about another case, a young Hispanic man in the room who doesn't seem to have the correct papers either.

I am told to stand, to sit, taken by a female officer into a side alcove, body and bag intimately searched, the latter taken away in a tray along with my camera while I go back to waiting time. Then the questions: why was I in Mexico (just looking), how long (an hour or so), what am I doing in El Paso (just looking). Apologising for my error and for making them do more paperwork I explain my nationality and trajectory, which causes some concern (Australian? British? London? New York?). After about ninety minutes (longer in detention than in Mexico), I am given a temporary form and told to get new paperwork on my return to New York, to be sent to Immigration within thirty days.

In reality, I know that as a white, middle-aged, professional woman, the worst that could happen is they cancel my visa, and at no point did I think that was likely. On the other side of that border, the Hispanic man and woman with the baby were taken away, and I'm guessing sent back to Mexico. As I'm escorted out, the young girl, maybe five years old, continues colouring with her crayons on the seats with dangling handcuffs. The next day, my university lets me know that Homeland Security has called to report my transgression.

As an act of control, the border is pre-determined by racial and economic categories and hardened in narratives of fear. Violence erupts around it, across it, through it. Cartels at times battle to control the flow of drugs and human cargo into the USA and weapons into Mexico.[8] But there is also that quiet violence embedded in the legal, global, economic structures that require the inequalities borders create. There is nothing spectacular about this structural violence for the media to dramatically portray: it just grinds away at both humans and the environment.

An inequitable share of both forms of violence has been borne by women. They have been murdered in the hundreds in Juárez since the 1990s, memorialised in the 'Ni Una Más' (Not One More) campaign. They also provide the majority of labour in the maquiladoras and are subject to exploitation and discrimination.[9]

Women in the Hispanic community on the El Paso side have also suffered. The garment industry was one of their main sources of employment, but as with other deindustrialised cities in America, jobs that once paid a decent wage have disappeared with the outsourcing of free trade agreements such as NAFTA (the North American Free Trade Agreement, in force since 1994).[10] According to the NGO La Mujer Obrera (LMO), forty years ago a garment worker in El Paso with minimal industrial skills could earn $11–$12 an hour. This enabled them to buy a house, send their children to school and to retire with some benefits. The Twin Plant Agreement in the 1960s allowed most of the production of clothing to be done in Mexico and then finished on the US side, so it could still be labelled 'made in the USA'. As a result, the El Paso garment industry began downsizing and shifting production to Mexico. Small sweatshops replaced factory work on the US side of the border, and NAFTA compounded the losses.

As a result, between 1984 and 2001, some 35,000 women lost their jobs, according to LMO. Two-thirds were heads of household, resulting in a devastating decline in income, the fracturing of communities and the shame that comes with being unable to sustain your family. While the federal government provided some resources for reskilling, investment on the USA side was primarily aimed at a younger, bilingual workforce. Almost half the population of El Paso is now under the age of thirty-four. The county's promotional material highlights fresh-faced, youthful innovation, highly skilled and entrepreneurial, in burgeoning technology, medical and hospitality industries.

According to the director of LMO, Lorena Andrade, once the calculations were made about who was worth investing in, former garment workers were told 'we're too Mexican, we're too old'. The better jobs that free trade was supposed to bring were not for these women, who found themselves surplus to economic requirements. In the spatial fractures and unequal entanglements of free trade, they were now loose ends, a residual population dispossessed of livelihood and increasingly displaced. In the same rhetoric heard the world over, the women were effectively told to go elsewhere and look for work.

Some did move away to jobs in industries like meatpacking or took on domestic and care work. There was a rise in temporary employment agencies providing casual work for minimum wage, and some small sweat shops remain in El Paso. However, nothing has replaced the garment factories as a source of employment. While NAFTA was renegotiated under the first Trump presidency, becoming USMCA (United States–Canada–Mexico Agreement), according to Lorena, '[i]t doesn't matter how much they negotiate it. [NAFTA] doesn't understand our world.' In an act of progress purposively blind to those left in its wake, the city, politicians and factories moved on.

In response, LMO have been campaigning since the 1980s for economic justice and indigenous rights for women in El Paso. Its workspaces are in a part of town that seems industrial but tidy. There are signs of creeping gentrification in the craft breweries, restaurants, clothes and cowboy boot outlets nearby. I see three Porsches, including one parked by LMO's café, so there is money in this city for some.

The café is part of their social enterprise work, training women in catering using local produce and traditional Mexican recipes. It is an alternative to the maquiladoras and sweat shops, creating employment that enables them to stay in their community. All the tables are full with a middle-class, slightly arty crowd, mostly Hispanic but with English as the dominant language. Ordering the day's special, red mole stew with black bean soup, I make the schoolgirl error of eating too many tortilla chips to start and forget to ask if the stew is meaty (it is, but I decide to ditch vegetarianism for the day in order to try the astonishingly good sauce).

Behind the spacious café is a large open warehouse decorated with murals, campaign posters, information on the project and a square of tables with separate meetings going on each side. Lorena, originally from California, has been working with LMO since 1998. She's learned 'on the job', organising with women in El Paso to get the attention of 'the powers that be' (local, state and federal government, factory owners). Tactics such as hunger strikes, marches, blockading a bridge, getting arrested, chaining themselves to machines, travelling to Washington, DC to lobby for resources have produced little change. Traditional labour unions have also not always been helpful, excluding women from top-down decision making.

LMO has instead embedded a different idea of freedom to that entrenched in global trade agreements. Starting with the question of whether women are there to serve the needs of their community or the needs of industry, with its desire for 'efficient and loyal workers', they resolved on the former. According to Lorena, it is 'our right to think, plan and implement our ideas, our vision for community', and that means focusing on education, health, culture and 'political liberty'.

Several times in the course of our conversation, Lorena repeats the statement 'we're not cheap labour', highlighting the struggle between economic structures and who we think we are as functioning human beings with free will living within a community. Rethinking identity in this way required the revalidation of forms of knowledge that have been swept aside by industrialisation. From the twentieth century, Western models of economic development have been rolled out globally, denigrating and discarding indigenous cultural knowledge systems. To repair this loss, LMO points out that women on the border have the capacity to create and sustain their own community. According to Lorena, 'because we've been in this box we have to convince each other that we have knowledge to share, and that my neighbour is a genius'.

Underpinned by their knowledge of the environment, plants and recipes, they started the café as well as a day care centre, and developed an indigenous women's cooperative network in Mexico, selling their products in El Paso. They have also generated creative spaces for festivals, art, music and poetry. In the process, they re-imagine their lives on the border not as 'cheap labour' but as defined by relationships with each other and with the earth, rather than a factory. When all you've done is sew the inseam of a pair of jeans every day, over and over for years, the idea that you know how to do something else of value can be a radical thought.

Their choice to focus on community highlights several points at which freedoms clash in the USA (and globally): a free market imposed without choice that is focused on the individual versus the desire for freedom to choose a cultural collective; the freedom for 'they' (politicians, factory owners) to move factories and employment across borders versus constraints on freedom to move or the freedom to choose not to move if you're an employee in those factories. For Lorena, it is clear: freedom is their right to live as an intergenerational community, in a healthy environment, that is not co-opted into economic structures they have not chosen.

This sense of community is very much connected to place, and actively choosing not to move becomes an act of resistance. There is a sense that as working-class Mexican women in the USA they would always be fighting no matter where they went, so they might as well stay and fight here, creating a home on the border for their children and their culture. Their activities, the centre, the café, the garden, sidewalk meetings are all an essential part of carving out and reclaiming their community in a physical location:

They want to determine what I do in my day, and how we use our creativity. They want to keep us in survival mode, right? But in this other vision, hey, we set the timeline. And we make our plans about how our day is gonna look like as well, right, at least part of our time, as much time as we can take. So that's why it's important to [think] how do we have a little bit of freedom, even if we're living in this chaos, right? And if that's a meeting, if that's an event, if that's us hanging out with the neighbours, if that's playing with the kids, us playing too in the dirt in the community farm [...] we taste a little bit of freedom.

Lorena stresses this is not a romantic notion of freedom. It's difficult at times; there are arguments and differences of opinion over social issues such as abortion in this largely Catholic community. Part of Lorena's work then becomes keeping the focus on what they have in common, the shared experiences of living in El Paso, and not judging others for the decisions they need to make. Their priorities are their relationships with each other and with the earth, which, as Lorena reminds me, is not only an indigenous way of seeing the world but has Catholic links as well. Pope Francis's cyclical *Laudato si*, a critique of consumerism and a call for environmental action, is one of the influential readings they discuss as a group, as well as works such as Mario García's *Desert immigrants*. The women have done their own research on the history of garment workers in the region and past labour strikes, highlighting how their present conditions are a continuum of inequality.

With this emphasis on place, the environment has become an active part of their work, centred on mitigating the negative impact of the borders' economy. Local schools, for example, have found themselves in the way of heavy vehicles, placed next to train tracks, behind metal recycling facilities, in front of a border bridge with trucks waiting to cross idling out fumes. Fighting against these problems seems like a never-ending game of whack-a-mole; fix one and another soon emerges. But Lorena somehow maintains her optimism: 'I think if you're not optimistic, then there's no point,' she laughs. 'So many things happen to us as women, like, we're not always in the best mood. But we can't lose faith in each other, or our families.'

The effort to stay optimistic includes creating spaces where they are not always in survival mode, where they can demand the freedom 'to be able to figure it out' (another phrase Lorena repeats several times), where they set the terms of the debate instead of being trapped in someone else's narrative that takes away the freedom to share their experience. In this space of dialogue, the women attempt to redefine freedom, redefine the American Dream, redefine what is 'opportunity', and in doing so, redefine the border.

Much has been written in the social sciences about the co-optation of every aspect of our lives by economic functions, particularly with the advent of neo-liberal economic doctrine in the late twentieth century.[11] We are witness to the commodification of leisure, the marketisation of education, even the commercialisation of religion. So this will to carve out space and time to 'figure things out', to be creative, to undertake that grave offence in a consumer society of spending free time doing nothing, being unproductive, also becomes a small act of everyday resistance.[12] That half an hour to hang out, to share stories, to cook together, that's already a little time that these working-class women have taken for themselves.

This vision of life in community on the border stands in marked contrast not only to Republican dystopia but also Democrat visions of the future. It is the problem of binary political systems where parties may disagree by a few shades on social issues but broadly agree on economic structures. Yet it is the economics, according to Lorena, that is destroying communities on both sides of the border.

Lorena's description of the impact of free markets and globalisation on her community, that 'break away the soul [and] tear the social fabric', is being recognised within some conservative circles courting working-class voters. American Compass, for example, has argued that if the USA wants 'strong families and communities', then there is also a need to support workers' rights, including the right to stay in place, in community, creating local industries that pay decent wages. They stop short of calling for alternative forms of economic distribution (socialism is still a dirty word in conservative networks). But there is some common ground with organisations such as LMO in the idea that capitalism needs to be recalibrated to balance the capacity for wealth generation, with its negative impacts on the human condition.

Walking back to the city centre, I have to wait, along with a few other pedestrians and cars, for a freight train to pass through the middle of town. Despite the impact of contemporary economic globalisation, El Paso is a reminder that while cross-border trade and mobility may have sped up in the twentieth and twenty-first centuries, it has a history. The free movement of goods and people has been creating cosmopolitan encounters for centuries in this region, along migration routes that still exist, as embodied by visual artist, former city representative and Mayor Pro Tempore Peter Svarzbein. His Jewish French grandmother survived the Holocaust and migrated to the USA after being rescued from a concentration camp by Peter's grandfather, Pedro Campello, a Spaniard who joined the French Resistance. Peter's father, Leonardo Svarzbein, migrated to New York from Argentina to study medicine and met Peter's mother, who was the head emergency room nurse at Albert Einstein Hospital. Wanting to live somewhere warm, with economic and cultural opportunities, where his bilingualism would be the norm, they moved to El Paso in 1978. Peter was born two years later.

Despite stints away for study, Peter felt the pull to return home. For him, El Paso is 'the ultimate all American city', representing the American Dream of a better life within a melting pot of diversity. He doesn't recognise the language of 'invasion', 'chaos' and violence spoken by those that 'don't understand and don't want to understand the reality here'. That reality for people living on the border, across the political and class spectrum, is knowing that it must be crossed, daily, for family, for work, for study, for life.

Instead, Peter reimagines the border as 'a blessing', 'a privilege' and 'an opportunity', something to celebrate rather than feel threatened by, imprinted with the idea that we're all interconnected. 'Opportunity', economic and cultural, is a word Peter mentions twenty-three times during the conversation, even more than he mentions 'community' (twenty-two times). Opportunity includes how the Borderplex's manufacturing and distribution hubs connect a much shorter production chain. This is a distinct advantage for the region when the importing of things from Asia slows down, as it did during the COVID-19 years. While skirting around questions about inequality and maquiladoras,

Peter describes El Paso/Ciudad Juárez as akin to a port city, with the everyday multiculturalism of such places entangled with economic activity that necessitates adaptation and flexibility.

He picks me up in his SUV, and we head out of town to Sunland Park, an outlying suburb of El Paso that lies in New Mexico, and one of its poorest zip codes. New Mexico is itself one of the poorest states in the USA, third behind Louisiana and Mississippi. Where there was once a chain link fence there is now a barrier, Trump's 'wall', a privately funded section paid for by a crowdfunded initiative, We Build The Wall Inc., whose founders will later be imprisoned for fraud.[13]

Serried rust red, angled metal pylons stand some 20-feet high, spaced a few inches apart to allow the Border Patrol to see through to the other side. The pylons are set in reinforced concrete going several feet into the ground. Smooth metal plates run along the top of the barrier to make climbing more difficult, with sections overseen by flood lights. Yet despite the obstruction, it is a foundational principle of life that if there is inequality, if there is upheaval, if there is unfreedom, people will move. This barrier is just one of many impossible projects by politicians across time who seek to harden borders that have always been porous. Trump may relish the art of creating a barrier for televised spectacle, but his wall is part of a continuum of presidents posing for cameras while erecting a useless fence.

There has been some kind of barrier along parts of the US–Mexico border since the early 1900s, and Trump in his first term simply continued plans for border wall construction that had begun during previous administrations. Biden in turn extended the Trump-era policy of 'Remain in Mexico' with what was known as Title 42. This allowed for the expulsion of asylum seekers back to Mexico, initially to control border crossings during the COVID-19 pandemic. It was reinstated in 2022 to control a surge in Venezuelan immigration.

Given the salience of immigration, Biden will harden his policies in the run up to the 2024 election, issuing an executive order making it more difficult for migrants who enter illegally to seek asylum and remain in the country.[14] Mexican authorities will also increase enforcement on their side. This will appear to decrease migrant crossings but not stop the America First/MAGA rhetoric of 'invasion'.[15] Early in his second presidency, Trump will begin deporting immigrants suspected of criminality, ignoring due process and at times sweeping up those with legal rights to remain.

For those that have made their lives on the border, wanting and/or needing to cross it, sometimes several times a day, this hardening of the barrier between the two cities will make life increasingly difficult. Up until 2008, it was possible for US citizens to cross between El Paso and Juárez without a passport, to visit family and friends, to party. Legend has it that as long as you had an American driver's licence and were sober enough to say 'American' to the border guards on the way back, they let you in.

Now, according to Peter, the border has become an integral part of people's lives, and they need a 'dignified and efficient' way to cross. These are two more words Peter uses regularly, with 'efficient' perhaps more problematic when compared to the stigmatising of some as 'inefficient' and therefore disposable within global production chains as noted by Lorena. However, within the context of the thousands needing to freely cross every day, for work or family or pleasure, a less hostile, more humane boundary would seem to be a virtuous goal, even if justified on economic grounds.

Throughout the few hours we spend walking this section of the border, patrol vehicles appear and disappear. Peter gives a friendly wave when we pass: he knows many people, and the afternoon is interspersed with 'hellos' from his car window. Border Patrol have an innocuous green insignia, like landscape gardeners, and have had to adapt vehicles to cater for the shift in demographics of people trying to cross: more women, more families and growing numbers from China and Africa attempting this route.[16]

Despite the height and metal plates, migrants still climb the wall, dropping over 20 feet to the other side (and now it makes sense why one of the young men I saw at a migrant charity in El Paso the day before was on crutches). We later find one of the wire contraptions used to hook over the top, hoist themselves up and drop down. Border Patrol drag tires to grade the earth near the wall to see footprints more easily, to track those crossing the barrier and to find people if injured.

The patrols are another part of the complicated relationship the local community has with the border. Just as America First/MAGA imagine this place as dystopian, so 'the left' and 'progressives' can project their world view here, including demonising Border Patrol as lacking humanity. For Peter, '[i]t might be easy to look at that when you're sitting in the Upper West Side, or in a flat in London [...]. But reality is more complex.' I suspect this may be a gentle admonishment of the irritated recounting of my time in detention. Point taken.

Over half the economy in El Paso is centred on the public sector, including border infrastructure, universities, schools and the military.[17] Peter, for whom the relationships are personal, sees a working-class community who have less freedom of choice in the employment they can take, particularly with the reorientation of El Paso's economy towards the young, high skilled and high tech. For the left behind, such as garment workers, options have to include Border Patrol, as well as police and army (nearby Fort Bliss is the USA's largest land base, home to almost 48,500 military personnel and their families). This reality requires a shift in the language used to describe those living in this community. Just as working-class women reimagine themselves as something other than 'cheap labour', migrants are not 'illegals' but 'asylum seekers' in the language of Peter and other campaigners in the region, and Border Patrol are fathers, sons, mothers and daughters.

Returning to the Rio Grande, Peter puts his truck into 4WD and we take a rough track along the river, opposite El Paso. Another random, disconnected section of 'the barrier that isn't' comes down to the river, cutting across a public access road. We simply drive around the metal pylons into no-man's land at the intersection of Mexico, New Mexico and Texas. A national monument, Mile Marker 1, indicates the easternmost point of the Gadsden Purchase and the beginning of the land border between the USA and Mexico (the rest of the border being the Rio Grande).[18] The barrier runs a short distance upwards but ends abruptly. The land above it is owned by the Catholic Church, who, in this part of the world at least, generally take Christ at his word and demonstrate a preference for the poor. A Mexican border patrol is parked nearby. We wave hello to each other.

As I straddle the boundary between the barrier and the unwalled Mexican side, standing in two places at the same time, it's easy to see the make believe. Peter stresses that 'a line does not separate people and families and culture and traditions and business'. This place is more indicative of Peter's reality and the shared past, present and future of these twin cities than anything we see in the media. Much like the spaces of community carved out by LMO, Peter has used this place-in-between as an opportunity to bring people together for community events from both sides of the border. It is a liminal moment that transcends barriers and expectations, perhaps a metaphor for the Borderplex as a whole, where two countries meet and a third space emerges that might allow for the freedom to see the world differently.

Back on to the rutted track, we pass another historic marker next to a trestle railway bridge: El Paso Del Rio Del Norte. At this point, a *camino real* (royal road) crossed the Rio Grande as caravans of travellers journeyed north from Mexico City to Santa Fe, the oldest state capital in the USA. Spanish colonists were in residence in this area from 1607, and indigenous communities for hundreds of years before that. The *camino real* has been a highway for over 500 years, and the Spanish were probably following already existing indigenous trade routes and crossings.

Markers such as this make it possible to re-imagine the USA's beginnings not in the colonies on the east coast established from the seventeenth century but in the deserts and trade routes of the southwest. Yet as important as this area and its residual markers are to understanding how borders are imagined in the USA, it is out of the way, not on any tourist maps, and requires some steady driving. We talk as we bump along and then get back on to metalled road and head across the Rio Grande again to El Paso.

Peter slows to watch a Pacific Union train cross the bridge on the New Mexico side of the river with the sun dipping behind it, a pleasure for him and me. Farther on, we pull off the highway on the other side of the Paso del Rio del Norte to inspect an older section of chain link fencing built in the 1990s. At this point, we're standing on one of America's man-made pressure points: in less than a few hundred feet, between mountains and the Rio Grande, train tracks, two highways and the border.

It's Friday afternoon and now gone 4pm, and the roads leading up to the crossings are busy as daily and weekly commuters and school students head back to Juárez for the weekend. Roads leading up to the main bridges of Stanton and Paso del Norte are in gridlock, with tailbacks several blocks long. Side streets are blocked off to enforce one-way traffic. An old pickup truck sits in the queue, precariously balancing a load of blue pallets. In the circular economy of these twinned cities, what is unneeded in El Paso can be reused in Juárez for something that may later find its way back to El Paso.

While admiring a mural next to the Stanton Bridge crossing, we notice an elderly man with a shopping trolley full of large bags of cat food and a super-sized plastic bottle of milk, heading to Juárez. A young man nearby explains in Spanish to Peter that the older man feeds the stray cats in both cities. I ask which side he lives on and suddenly realise what Peter has been trying to tell me all afternoon – 'it doesn't matter,' we both say simultaneously.

Looking at the tailbacks and a creeping sense of chaos, Peter again articulates his reimagining of the border: a space that is seen not as threat but as an economic opportunity for which mechanisms can be created to enable people to safely move back and forth, 'efficiently', with 'dignity'. In Peter's imagination, this ideally involves digital technology and an analogue streetcar. Starting in the 1880s and running for most of the twentieth century (ending in 1974), El Paso had a trolley line that ran between the two cities – one of the few international streetcars in the world, and more symbolic of this community than any wall. In 2018, Peter was instrumental in gaining support for a relaunch of the streetcar in El Paso, and he continues to work towards getting it once again across the border.

Rather than funding an international streetcar, the federal government in 2022 announced a $600 million investment in border security. In 2025, Trump will ramp up spending again and increase the military presence at the border, leading to a further slow-down in crossings. In past surges, El Paso has shown great compassion and support for migrants, receiving at times 1,500 to 2,000 migrants a day. City authorities have stated they are 'committed to providing assistance and support to all migrants passing through our community', but resources are stretched.[19] The resolution as Peter sees it is not to build a bigger wall but to support the economy in other countries where asylum seekers come from. 'If you could create 100,000 more jobs or a million jobs in Central America, then you don't need to worry about how big a wall you've got.'

The final leg of our conversation takes place during a drive up the Franklin mountains overlooking El Paso. Taking the scenic route, Peter points to what he feels is one of the best projects he was able to make happen: carving out a walking path from the verge of the winding road, with an incredible view over the two cities. It's the little local, useful things that mean the most sometimes. From the lookout, Peter points out various landmarks: the Bridge of the Americas, Chamizal Park. Other visitors join in and ask questions. In the distance, there is a large red X, prominent in a landscape of browns and greys. It's a sculpture by the Chihuahuan artist Sebastián. On the Juárez side, in large lettering in Spanish, painted on the mountain above the city: '[T]he Bible is the truth; read it.'

From this view point it's easier to see how the river as border moves, winding around paths of least resistance, picking up detritus, putting it elsewhere. In the past, it has literally shifted the boundary, leading to conflict then an agreement between Mexico and the USA to curtail its freedom by channelling the river into place. From this height, we ponder whether it would be better to build a wall around the twins and leave Washington, DC and Mexico City out of the lives of *fronterizos* (border residents) altogether.

We've been talking for four hours, and Peter's fiancée calls to check he's okay and ask can he please bring the groceries home that have been in the back of the car all this time. We swing by his house in a neighbourhood of Spanish tile and the occasional oddity: including a mini Statue of Liberty on a neighbour's front wall. It is almost 6pm when Peter, generous in his welcome and his time, drops me back at the hotel. In parting, he emphasises that for those who live here, 'we are not defined by the border. We are defined by how we cross it. [...] Because [crossing] is part of our culture', part of the 'DNA' of this place – part of its habituated everyday practices of freedom as people move back and forth over this arbitrary line.

Driving across Texas over the next few days, Sophie and I follow the border southeast, along straight, straight road. It's a landscape of scrubby plains with mountains randomly emerging along with checkpoints that highlight the privilege of free movement and being taken at your word, of being trusted. An officer pulls the car over and asks if we are American citizens. Sophie is. I say that I'm British, having learned that it gets too confusing to explain the co-presence of other nationalities and guessing that other characteristics may matter more. He comes out of the booth to look through the car window and without looking at our documents waves us on with 'have a nice day'.

As we approach Del Rio, the landscape becomes even flatter to the horizon. There are no landmarks, just gulches, hillocks, canyons to get lost and die in. We reach another random check point with an array of lights and several Border Patrol officers milling about. The same questions (where are we coming from, where are we going to, are you American citizens?). This time, I'm asked for my passport, but Sophie is still not asked to show any proof; they trust her when she says she's a US citizen. The officer doesn't question my temporary supplementary bit of paper (Form I-515A, replacing my DS-2019 that is held in conjunction with my I-94 admission form). He is friendly, mentions how beautiful the river drive is where we've come from and waves us on with 'y'all have a nice day'.

This taken-for-granted freedom of movement for some of us means that it can be easy to ignore the barriers others have to face, those who lack the requisite capital (financial, social, cultural) that eases border crossings. For those who fall foul of rapidly changing immigration law, the situation under the second Trump administration will become increasingly precarious. Immigrants with the right to remain will find themselves caught within the USA's sprawling carceral system, extending in 2025 to offshore mega-prisons in El Salvador. These actions of the state, while appearing extreme under Trump, are in fact a long-standing tradition of using the withdrawal of freedom as part of a political project to control change.

4

'Power and control, baby': Stories of (un)freedom and (in)justice

Alfonzo is quietly spoken, unassuming, a Black man in his fifties sitting opposite me in the foyer of Brooklyn Library as people around us go about reading, chatting, playing. He was a nineteen-year-old engineering student with no previous convictions or trouble with the police when he was convicted of murder under a law that allowed guilt by association: aware that a crime would take place but not in the vicinity of the crime or aware that it would end in a death.[1] He was sentenced to an above maximum term of seventy-one and two-third years to life, reduced on appeal to thirty-one years. When we meet, he had spent more time in prison than being a free man.

The conversation with Alfonzo, and three other formerly incarcerated, Jonel, Pamela and Sean, brings home the realisation that our fundamental expectation of a right to freedom is dependent on a fragile coalition of compliance and whim. The American prison system makes clear that there is no understanding freedom without a conversation about its twin, justice; a concept not so much blind as hitting its head against a wall of pettiness, cruelty, racism and fear while freedom is restrained, immobilised and disciplined.

With the eruption of MAGA violence on Capitol Hill on 6 January 2021, freedom and justice have also become mired in conspiracy: the defence of freedom considered necessary by a semi-organised militia and disorganised mob, caught up in a spiral of rage and lies. For those involved in defending the people imprisoned for taking part in the riots, there is a deep-rooted belief that they are protecting freedom from a justice system 'weaponised' against ordinary Americans.

The carceral system in the USA restrained about 1.8 million people at the time of writing, locked up in over 6,000 facilities operated by public and private agencies. This was the fifth highest incarceration rate in the world, and about 20 per cent of the global prison population, with a further 4.5 million on probation or parole.[2] The number of incarcerated has grown 500 per cent since the 1970s, the start of the 'War on Drugs', without a corresponding increase in crime.[3] Women have become one of the fastest growing prison demographics, attributed by some to the opioid crisis. Female incarceration is now more than seven times higher than in 1980.[4] In addition, those designated as illegal immigrants are detained in over 100 immigration centres, the majority managed by private companies working with Immigration and Customs Enforcement (ICE). In 2024, the number of immigrants in detention was 37,000, with ICE spending reaching $9.56 billion.[5]

Accompanying these numbers is the sound of 'liberty and justice for all' crashing against racial and economic disparity. According to the American Civil Liberties Union (ACLU), one in three Black boys and one in six Latino boys will spend some time in prison in their lifetime, versus only one in seventeen white boys. Black incarceration rates for drug offences are ten times greater than for white people, despite drug use being at roughly the same rates.[6] The War on Drugs saw lengthier sentences for related offences, including non-violent drug crimes, with racialised discrepancies disproportionately affecting Black and brown communities (e.g. longer sentences given for crack cocaine offences than those involving the more expensive powder used in the clubs of Manhattan and Mayfair).

Varying from state to state, criminal records and myriad restrictions on the formerly incarcerated become markers of unfreedom, extending punishment well beyond probation or parole and impacting on basic needs such as employment and housing. The numbers are magnified by other distortions in the system, such as an overreliance on plea bargaining, a feature of American justice widely seen as coercive. The rate of cases going to trial is falling: from 6 per cent in 2000, less than 3 per cent in 2010, to just over 2 per cent of federal criminal cases in 2022. Eight per cent had cases dismissed, and the rest pleaded guilty.[7] If you have no income, are in danger of losing family and/or a job, unable to afford bail, being housed for months in a local borough-based jail or, worse, Rikers Island awaiting trial, you'd probably accept a plea as well. Doing so possibly without understanding the ramifications of a conviction even for a lesser charge that can then affect the rest of your life.

Alfonzo did not take the plea bargain. As a result, he entered a system designed to maximise control through the removal of that which makes us human: not only freedom of movement and choice but markers of identity. The system now 'tells you who you are'. Jonel, an Akwesasne Mohawk woman whose territory straddles the US–Canada border in upstate New York, still remembers her prison number after thirteen years:

> The minute you get there, the officers are like … take all your clothes off, lift your tits up for me, open up your crotch, hold it there, flick your ears, let me see your tongue … It's like some kind of sexual assault the minute you get there … you're just standing there naked with all these other women being humiliated. […] I am no longer Jonel. I am X-X-X-X-X-X-X. That was my number. And you just get called by your number X-X-X-X-X-X-X. So you are no longer human. You are property of the state. You have no more rights. And that's the end of it.

Jonel disassociates at times during our conversation when we meet in a small town on the Canadian side of a border that runs through her community's territory. She switches between first and second person. 'Not all of me survived. Not all of you survived.' She had been convicted of a smuggling offence when nineteen, while moving goods across the Canada–US border, and placed on parole. She then found a job she loved working construction, gaining qualifications along the way. At twenty-three, she went out with friends one night, ending up at a property where a dispute broke out. Police were called, and she was charged with burglary, that is, 'entering a dwelling with the intent to cause harm and property damage', despite the fact she was in a house with people she knew and not involved in the dispute. Now in breach of probation, Jonel was sentenced to maximum security for 12.5 years.

The unsettled question of 'what is prison for' begins to make itself heard above the clatter of early morning diners in the café where Jonel and I talk and eat. What is the appropriate punishment for someone in the wrong place at the wrong time, who had been trying to get their life together, who had just lost her mother to cancer and whose three small children would now lose their mother? How to measure out the quantity of justice required to pay back a crime, and who gets to decide. What is the point of extreme sentences, like the one Alfonzo initially received, that extend far beyond life expectancy? According to the journalist Adam Serwer, who has written extensively on the US justice system, 'The cruelty is the point.'[8]

In jail, the idea of freedom is constrained to the smallest possible space, where the razor-thin veneer between this world and insanity becomes eroded by 'regret and guilt and shame' that has nowhere to go. Minor infringements, for example not buttoning up a shirt properly, could lead to solitary confinement. Describing the noise at night on her wing as women regularly tried to kill themselves, the only option Jonel could contemplate in her first year in prison was to follow suit. 'Can you imagine being in a place where your only thought of freedom is to die?' She brought herself back from that brink by the thought of her children, but the trauma is just below the surface, and she begins to cry.

It is a similar story of pain for Pamela, a Black woman in her fifties from Atlanta, Georgia, found guilty of a white-collar crime and sentenced to six-and-a-half years prison, while pregnant. She spent segments of time in solitary confinement that she describes as 'brutal', 'torture', 'invented to basically take a person out mentally'. Her thoughts went on repeat, replaying over and over and over again. On a shaky telephone line, Pamela also becomes distressed, and the full story of her loss emerges. After a fall while shackled (pregnant and shackled), Pamela began to miscarry. She was then shackled to her bed during the loss, enduring the miscarriage with two male officers standing nearby. 'They threw my baby in a trash can. They placed me in solitary confinement for about eight months.'

Navigating this unfreedom, the system, officers, other inmates and violence, generated exhaustion and a point of 'rock bottom' from which survival strategies emerged. Alfonzo, Jonel and Pamela developed the mental gymnastics to create spaces of freedom in incarceration. Further denting the great American myth of individualism, it was relationships, family on the outside and 'family' inside, that helped get them through, including replicating mother/daughter and intimate partner relationships. There were education programmes, sport, creative outlets and work.

Alfonzo never accepted he would not be going home, maintaining faith that he would find a judicial remedy. He volunteered in the Children's Centre and earned a bachelor's degree and paralegal certificate in a system where 28 per cent of federally sentenced inmates have never graduated from high school.[9] Jonel ran the prison's domestic violence circles and was paid the grand total of 25 cents an hour (she started out at 10 cents). Restitution for crimes meant the prison took half, so every two weeks Jonel made about $6 to buy food from a commissary to avoid eating the substandard meals provided.[10] She 'self-educated', reading psychology, history and spirituality, reciting positive manifestations every morning, visualising winning her appeal and going home. Despite the prison walls, she found a way for her mind to be free. 'My freedom was in my imagination, [...] being awake to yourself [...] that is freedom, be awake to who you are, and what you want, and you are free as a bird, you are free in prison, you are feeling all of this.' She gestures to the world around us. We have gone for a walk in a nearby nature reserve, Jonel's sanctuary, where we fall into silence and feel the land breathe.

Sean also disassociates at times when recounting his experiences, separating his sense of self from his conviction, living 'a lot of my life in that period of time in a third person'. While New York state had the physical possession of his body, they didn't have possession of his mind, 'and I was free. Even in the surroundings of incarceration, I found ways to still be free.' We meet in the New York offices of the justice institute where he's working at the time. Now in his fifties, Sean was arrested in 1995 for a murder he argues he did not commit and for which he spent over 24.5 years incarcerated. Being in the wrong place at the wrong time was a precarious position for Black men during the War on Drugs. Organisations such as the Equality and Justice Initiative would argue not much has changed.[11] Calling for racial equality and reparations, justice advocates draw a direct line between slavery's racialised oppression and the country's continued high rates of incarceration, particularly of Black men.

Like others, Sean found the law library. Starting with advice from inmates on his first day, over the course of his incarceration he gained a bachelor's and master's degree. He deciphered the opaque language of justice that is designed to keep people at a distance so we don't see the arbitrariness at its heart. He litigated at every court level available to him, and is on parole seeking exoneration when we meet. His appeals to overturn his conviction have never been successful, but he is one of the few to gain parole while still claiming innocence, having found evidence that was persuasive enough to convince a parole board.

Jonel also used the law and worked with her 'Black sisters' in jail to better understand the structural injustices that led to her being there. She found that 'knowledge gives you freedom because it gives you options'. Against the odds, she found a way to get a state-funded appeal lawyer, and she won. Her charges were modified and reduced to time already served, meaning she could be released after two years. Yet understanding the technicalities of this complex, capricious system is sometimes not enough. Returning to the court she was sentenced in, there was no apology for any errors in her original conviction, and the judge sentenced her to another year despite her lawyers arguing that she had already served her time. She was handcuffed again and taken to county jail. Her lawyers were only able to have her released after another night in a cell.

Jonel summarises the process succinctly. 'Power and control, baby'; a power equated with the control of others' bodies, lives and ultimately an entire population.[12] In many of the conversations in this book, there is a word that tends to be repeated, and for Jonel that word is 'accountability'. The system requires bodies to be subservient and disciplined, but there is no accountability, in Jonel's view, when the system gets it wrong. Remarkably, Alfonzo holds no anger at losing thirty-one years of his life, acknowledging his association with a crime and showing greater equanimity than I ever would in that situation. But the state shows no humility and takes no responsibility for decades of arbitrary over-sentencing that stretches the definition of justice out of all proportion, beyond life. There is no accountability from a system that has entrenched plea bargaining, cash bails and judges that take bets on who can hand out the most years before they retire. There is little accountability for unsafe convictions from a police precinct later investigated for corrupt practice; from judges who take it personally when an appeal overturns their decision; nor from governments that criminalise populations in return for popularity and the illusion of voter safety.

Accountability is not just about responsibility for mistakes but also recognising who counts and who doesn't, and how things got to be this way. For those seeking reform of the justice system, accountability is required for the structural damage of colonialism, slavery and policing the cultures of others. For example, over a dozen institutions, Canadian and American, from Homeland Security to Tribal Police, surveil Akwesasne Mohawk territory – 20,000 people on a patch of land 10 by 3 miles. Unlike a blindfolded statue, that is a lot of eyes on their community, along with judges and juries that Jonel feels are 'only trained to see them in some kind of way'.

Jonel, who admits to her earlier smuggling charge, places her incarceration within the wider context of indigenous dispossession in the USA and Canada. A treaty enabled freedom of movement across a new border, but the existence of that border now criminalises the movement of particular goods, including marijuana and tobacco:

> I didn't criminalise marijuana or tobacco, you criminalise that and you criminalise that because you want the taxes off of it. That's why we get locked up. [...] I'm like, 'Are you fucking kidding?' You took everything from us. You don't think that was tax enough? You taxed the shit out of millions of dead indigenous people. I struggle greatly with paying tax to any country that has graciously glorified the murder of my whole history. So trust me, yeah, that pain runs deep, but it's very real. It is very alive today.

I uncomfortably swallow the 'you'. Those scales of justice are not balanced yet.

The state gets to decide what is illicit, who is deviant and what behaviours need to be corrected in 'correctional facilities'. Criminalisation is predicated on the industrial-scale structural damage of racist and socioeconomic inequality. Some more than others are funnelled through a 'school to prison' pipeline: from poor neighbourhoods, poor education, the care system, juvenile detention centres, with addiction and mental ill health as added accelerants. Alfonzo, for example, didn't feel he had 'all options in the world' growing up in Crown Heights thirty years ago when it was not the gentrifying suburb of New York it is today.

Sean argues that institutional conditioning into systems of surveillance begins in schools that at times have the same dynamics as prison: the inspection of bags, metal detectors and CCTV. It could be argued that this enhances safety, but for Sean it raises the question of how the constitutionally protected freedom of the Fourth Amendment is being applied and to whom. No-one should be searched 'unless you have probable cause or reasonable suspicion'. Yet few talk about protecting the Fourth Amendment with quite the same passion as the First (freedom of expression) or Second (the right to bear arms).

On the outside, as a Black man Sean questions whether he is free, a sentiment repeated in many other conversations with people of colour. Pamela describes this existence for Black communities as being always on a 'leash'. Following the American Dream, she established a successful health care business but, lacking support and experience, failed to complete the proper paperwork on some twenty patients before billing insurance. She was audited and charged with fraud. The judge recommended she pay the money she owed (approximately $220,000) and receive home confinement, but prosecutors pushed for incarceration.

The cost of imprisoning people in the USA, including local, state, federal jails, juvenile and immigration detention centres, is now around $182 billion a year, according to the Prison Policy Initiative.[13] And yet prisons are seen as worthy investments: bringing jobs, visitors and inflated census population numbers into towns and regions that then draw in more resources. This economy has given rise to the criticism that the USA has developed a prison industrial complex: a form of black box economics that takes no account of the cost to the 'inputs', the incarcerated, or the cost of 'outputs', the telescoping of pain into future generations. The benefits of investing that money into poorer communities directly, into education, health care and social services, does not enter the equation.

It likely cost more to incarcerate Pamela than if she had paid back what she owed from a business that had been successful. It was a yanking of 'the leash', and a reminder that the American Dream is not for everyone. From the investigation, then court proceedings, then prison and home in 2013, it was ten years of Pamela's life, plus a further five years of parole restrictions, for the sake of poor paperwork with no malintent, according to Pamela. 'You want me to feel like I'm free and that I'm in the home of the brave, land of the free, all the equality. No, I'm not. It may be that for somebody but it's not there for me. Or anybody that looks like me.' Given these conditions, it is unsurprising that the moral compass guiding the state's authority to make judgements on others is regarded as 'hypocrisy'.

The opioid crisis in the USA cracks open the issue of race and justice more overtly. Pamela now runs a social enterprise that lobbies for reform of prisons. She argues they have had more success recently in changing legislation relating to the care of incarcerated women because of the changing demographics of the prison population. America's opioid crisis, and associated criminal offences, is predominantly white.[14]

Parallel to these conversations that highlight the malleability of freedom within a structurally damaged society are the stories of those imprisoned for taking part in the J6 riots in 2021. A question emerges: whether to apply structural explanations to MAGA supporters charged with related offences. The evidence of the J6 Congressional hearings and federal trials have shown that there were militias present (for example, members of the Oath Keepers and Proud Boys).[15] Some people were expecting and potentially organising violence. Media vox pops created before the attack included statements such as 'freedom is paid for with blood', and 'I fight for freedom and democracy.'[16] But according to a New York Times investigation, there were also people who had never been in trouble with the law before who suddenly found themselves taking part in a violent affray, swept up in the momentary vortex of a mob.[17]

Within the America First/MAGA ecosystem, the narrative has been reworked to suggest that J6 was a 'celebratory' event, a coming together for a rally to ensure 'that our voice still matters'. It was a 'day of love' according to Trump.[18] The Republican Party National Convention in 2022 declared J6 was 'legitimate political discourse'. J6ers are 'political prisoners to the cause of freedom and justice', jailed in 'Deep State gulags' for their beliefs, and denied their constitutional rights, persecuted for defending their 'traditional' values.[19] Trump referred to them as 'hostages', within a media landscape focused at the time on negotiations to release hostages held by Hamas in Gaza (2024).

Randy is a co-founder of Citizens Against Political Persecution (CAPP), an organisation set up to support J6ers. He was also a member of the Proud Boys. We meet in a lower Manhattan mall surrounded by Christmas shoppers, copious tinsel and the ambience of seasonal carols. His organisation was one of many that sprang up post-J6, mostly in the recesses of the internet, with varying degrees of support. All zealously defend freedom from the perceived 'tyranny' of Biden's administration, a compliant media and the corruption of 'the Deep State'. CAPP's particular focus is the 'weaponisation' of the justice system and its institutions, the police, the FBI, the CIA, the Department of Justice, in order to silence 'half of America'. According to Randy, 'there's still a lot of Americans that have no clue what's going on because a lot of it's still kind of hidden'.

The argument for conspiracy rests on the belief that 'bad actors', that is, agents of the 'Deep State', were planted in the crowd to incite a riot. There are claims to 'truth' and 'eyewitness accounts', purported video evidence of people changing clothes in bushes and emerging with MAGA caps on. There is a refusal to believe that the justice system has looked at this evidence or that of voter fraud in the 2020 election. 'The very institutions that were put in place and empowered to make sure that there is justice actually did the exact opposite,' according to Randy.

The disillusionment, the sense of hypocrisy and corruption, becomes at least one point of shared feeling between supporters of J6 prisoners and those demanding wider reform of the carceral state. There is common ground in a lack of trust in institutions and the realisation that freedom can be revoked at the whim of a system steeped in arbitrariness. For Randy, the realisation that justice is based on inter-pretation instead of rock-solid principles is disenchanting and fuels the sense that America is in decline:

> One court judges this way and another court judges this way. Precedent sets a particular decision that's completely disregarded in another court. When you begin to analyse why is that being disregarded here, it's just taken upon themselves to interpret the law however they want. How's that justice? There's a subversion of justice there somewhere along the line.

There is the assertion of a 'two-tiered justice system', a familiar descrip-tion for Pamela, who compares what Trump can get away with to her incarceration for poor paperwork. Randy uses the example of Hillary Clinton's emails.[20] Both in the same room would probably agree that people with money can influence outcomes in their favour.

The experience of deprivation felt by the J6 incarcerated is some-thing they now share with the millions of others who have become prison statistics. J6 Patriot News condemned 'the damage this govern-ment has inflicted on these men and women', their families and com-munities.[21] In a 'Letter to the American people from the D.C. Gulag', released by J6 prisoners in 2022, familiar deprivations are emphasised, with that uncomfortable 'you' in this instance accusing America of forgetting them:

> It is you, America, that has tolerated this injustice and allowed it to prevail. The blood of those four innocents [killed during the riot] is on your hands as the result of your silence. The responsibility is yours alone for permitting us to remain incarcerated. [...] Since our abduction we've had our civil liberties violated. We've been beaten, maced, malnour-ished, held in appalling conditions, been medically neglected, mentally abused, held in solitary confinement. Our food is often inedible, the water tainted with rust, the air contaminated with black mould from improper maintenance.[22]

The reality for hundreds of thousands of incarcerated are now con-ditions faced by 'patriots', and the injustice in the justice system is now theirs to bear as well. The partisanship of SCOTUS justices, and the seemingly indiscriminate use of pardons, by Biden as well as Trump, further eroded trust in justice. Randy calls for a system where 'everybody is treated the same', where 'nobody gets a free pass' – a state of equality that social justice organisations are also campaigning for, so that Black and brown and poor communities are not penalised for being Black and brown and poor.

Yet despite the mirroring of calls for justice, these conversations run on parallel tracks, failing to recognise a common interest in reforming an unequal and dysfunctional justice system. There is no reflection in Randy's narrative that justice and its institutions are already weaponised against some communities. Instead, he sees a two-tier justice system that now treats 'patriots' unfairly.

Grievances are entrenched through comparison with BLM. Over 1,400 people involved in the J6 riots were charged with various offences relating to the attack on the Capitol, ranging from obstruction to sedition, although most have now been pardoned by Trump.[23] On the other hand, there is a widely disseminated belief in nationalist populist channels that few involved in the 2020 BLM protests have been arrested. Fact-checking media sources counter that in reality somewhere between 10,000 and 17,000 people were detained, mostly for low-level offences such as violating curfews and obstructing roadways. Other reports suggest 'hundreds' of arrests for more serious offences such as burglary and looting. Despite repeated descriptions in conservative media of cities burning, less than 4 per cent of BLM events in 2020 involved property damage or vandalism.[24]

The facts, however, as seen repeatedly in conversations across America, are not as important as how we feel. Nor are facts as important as the narratives which structure those feelings, make sense of them and make the pain and discomfort go away. The kernel of common ground, bringing together opposing voices for a reappraisal of justice and prison reform is hampered by a fundamental problem. According to Randy,

> there's only one truth. And I think the same thing can be said of justice. There's only one justice. We can try and fight it all we want, we can change it, we can corrupt it, and or have an attempt at corrupting. But at the end of the day, there's only one justice.

To accept that the 'truth', which underpins a master narrative like freedom, can be reappraised is an existentially difficult position to be in. It implies for Randy 'the assassination of America'. The Constitution, founded on Judeo-Christian principles, is the source of his truth and the bedrock that removes ambiguity – 'that's the only way to restore any sense of justice, and the sense of freedom [...], this is what sets and defines what's right and what's wrong'. But as many argue throughout these conversations, the Constitution needs updating. Freedom and justice for all may be foundational to the political thinking that established the USA, but some of 'we the people' have always been left out.

There is also truth in the realisation that release doesn't necessarily equate with freedom. The deprivations of unfreedom can be carved on stigmatised bodies, and the trauma is dragged back into families and communities as a wrecking ball forged in the institutionalised violence of incarceration. They are not the same people anymore. Both Jonel and Pamela were scarred by understanding how precarious freedom is, and the fear that they may be arrested again at any time. They were often overwhelmed by stimulation: touching, smells, taste, textures. Pamela fears she had lost social skills and prefers to stay home. Supervised release meant she was still 'on the leash' for five years, unable to use credit, get a loan or spend more than $500 at one time.[25] She was on the outside, apparently free, but still constrained, with the added stresses of finding accommodation and paying bills.

Jonel suffered panic attacks. For a while, she refused to leave her house because the outside world was too unpredictable: 'I didn't trust it anymore.' For almost two years, she could not shut her bedroom door because of the regime of 'lock ins' and wake-up calls to make sure inmates are alive. Now working in community justice programmes, Jonel sees how women come out and find an abusive relationship as a new normal that mimics prison. It is 'violence that you end up meeting the world with because the world's been violent to us'. She excoriates the parole system:

> They expect you to come out of a place like that with no resources, no support, they've taken everything from you, you're in financial debt because all the financial commitment you had when you went in [...]. How are you even free after they lift you out of the institution and then they find more ways to incarcerate?

Sean also felt little elation on his release, recalling walking out of the cellblock as people cheered but feeling guilty for leaving them behind. Only Alfonzo expresses a sense of 'excitement' and 'joy', 'having a new chance at life, a new chance to live', when he was finally released in January 2019 after a clemency application was granted. From working as a paralegal, he became a director of paralegal services at the Legal Aid Society, and is studying for a law degree. Now freedom means

> the ability to walk around without permission, to be free to breathe, not being under the control of the carceral state, [...] to participate in society, to wear the clothes that I want to wear and not those that are chosen for me, within my abilities to live where I want to live.

After George Floyd's murder and the rise of the BLM movement, some Democrat state Attorney-Generals attempted to reform aspects of the justice system, for example removing cash bail and dropping prosecutions for lower offences. However, in the constant roiling between release and restraint, there has been a backlash against these changes, amid fears of increasing crime rates that belie actual statistics. For populist politicians, the USA must be made safe again, requiring the implementation of harsh penalties and performative punishment. Modest ideas of redemption have been replaced with narratives of retribution.

Alfonzo, Jonel, Pamela and Sean, on the other hand, are all involved in acts of repair, of themselves, their communities and the system, reimagining what justice and freedom could look like. Alfonzo speaks of the capacity for people to change and wants a 'total transformation' that decreases the emphasis on imprisonment. He sees hope in talk of prison abolition, which is up there with defunding the police as a dog whistle for conservative pundits to pile in on. Sean is not an abolitionist, but he argues that 'we need to make sure that when we take someone's freedom it is the last thing available to do, not the first thing'. He calls for a system where data, rather than 'the public's emotions', guides judgements and for more investment in communities that need it rather than the state relying on the withdrawing of freedom as a means to fix society.

Pamela maintains legendary amounts of courage and defiance. 'I'm gonna break that leash. I'm gonna snatch it out the wall or whatever it's connected to and throw it in the trash.' Her social enterprise drafts legislation advocating for the rights of incarcerated and formerly incarcerated women. Some battles she wins, some she loses. A big win was lobbying for legislation to ban shackling and solitary confinement of incarcerated women and petitioning for the 'Dignity for Incarcerated Women Act' (2019), passed at federal level and adopted in twenty-one states.[26] She worked on a bill, passed in 2021, that will allow people in Georgia to come off probation in three years under certain conditions.[27] She has also worked on registering the 80,000 formerly incarcerated people in Georgia who are eligible to vote. 'We formerly incarcerated people can control the vote here in Georgia, we have the numbers to do that. It's just a matter of getting folks motivated and mobilised and engaged and registered.' Power and control, baby.

Jonel sat on Akwesasne's restorative justice council and community parole board. She is the co-creator of a 'welcome' circle, building homes to enable those formerly incarcerated to transition back into community. Working with victims of domestic violence, Jonel also advocates for disrupting the relationship between an idea of justice and incarceration, capturing the psycho-dynamics best: 'I think everybody is really just like wounded five-year-olds running around here.' There is a concomitant need to heal the hurt kid inside us as well as the kids running around outside. She is referring to her own community's scars, but the prevalence of rage within the America First/MAGA movement in particular, the stomping of feet and cries of 'it's not fair', suggests that stories of loss and pain are also implicated in the road to prison for some that took part in J6.

I make no equivalence between the suffering of different communities and individuals, but it is clear that the justice system in the USA today, with its emphasis on the physical deprivation of freedom, is no solution to the pain of historical legacies or contemporary cultural ruptures. Instead, this system of industrial incarceration, created in the name of safety, wreaks havoc on individuals and communities, wasting human life and all its potential for freedom.

Along with the justice system, three other institutions have become key sites of contested freedoms in the USA. The family, school and church are immersed in competing narratives of the future. Intense emotions of love and hate are generated as different stakeholders seek to control the direction of change through shoring up their own versions of freedom.

5

Let's hear it for the girl

[J.D. Vance] is a mascot for manhood.
He is a mascot for America.
This is manhood versus Kamala. This is Americanism versus Kamala.[1]
Charlie Kirk Show, 17 July 2024

In today's volatile politics, nothing seems to generate as much love, hate, shame and suffering as navigating gender, sex and sexuality. So much so I'm going to argue that changing expectations of gender are a key force driving the shift towards authoritarianism and the rolling back of freedoms. 'Woman', 'man' and 'family' are load-bearing terms, carrying the weight of identity and social order. Doubt and uncertainty are removed as long as the parts we play remain clearly defined. This has particular implications for women, as we literally reproduce the nation.[2] As bearers of tradition, we are tasked with ensuring values like freedom are passed on to the next generation.

Given the centrality of gendered roles and expectations in holding cultural infrastructure together, any attempt to reshape them is asking for trouble, as the philosopher Judith Butler has noted.[3] Contemporary debates on gender and sexuality are feeding a muscular nationalism globally, reinforcing support for authoritarian leaders.[4] In Agnieszka Graff and Elzbieta Korolczuk's work on the link between gender, politics and the rise of the right, they argue that what we are seeing today is not simply a continuation of the 1970s anti-feminist backlash. Emerging out of 'the anxiety, shame and anger' caused by economic disparity is an ultra-conservative cultural movement that threatens the values of liberal democracy.[5] These values have become equated with sexual freedom and queerness – 'weaknesses' that have allowed for population decline and lax immigration policies. It is the duty of women then to reproduce and re-populate, and authoritarian leaders incentivise this through 'pro-family' policies.[6]

In the USA, a configuration of nationalist populists and Christian nationalists are likening what they call 'gender ideology' (primarily feminism and LGBTQI+ activism) to 'communism' and 'totalitarianism'. These groups agree on key points: that the 'traditional' family is under attack; that children are being 'indoctrinated' to become queer; and that gender is dangerous, threatening to destroy families, cultures, Western civilisation, God and men in general. In this world view, shifting gender roles and expectations have transformed what is permissible, restricting the freedoms of others through 'wokism' and cancel culture. Women are responsible for DEI programmes and weak border regulations because we are too 'emotive'.[7] We have been fed a lie, 'hustled' into the workplace 'with the false promise that wage work was the only way to be independent and self-actualized', killing off the 'family wage', according to the American Conservative writer Helen Andrews.[8]

In 'going too far', feminism has also pushed masculinity into a crisis. The central question that politicians have answered in recent election cycles is not really 'what is a woman' as much as 'what is a man'. The nation must not be emasculated. Cultural borders must not be queered. On his podcast, Charlie Kirk regularly catastrophised the threat of shame that men now face: 'They are trying to emasculate this entire country. They're trying to castrate you so that alpha men do not stand up against injustices, bullying, or a terror campaign against women. They are trying to metaphorically castrate an entire society of men.'[9]

To explain the ongoing beat of mass shootings committed by young men, conservative voices point to absent fathers and women who have 'cultivated a culture that emasculates boys by classifying manliness as "toxic"'.[10] The Patriot Post ran a series of blogs and editorials following the mass shooting at a school in Uvalde, Texas, by an eighteen-year-old in 2022, noting that 'there are bad expressions of machismo, but millions of boys are being raised by women to be less than the men they need to be'.[11] As the British conservative commentator, and now USA resident, Douglas Murray argues, men have been made to suppress their true selves. 'There must be consequences to telling men that their instincts are wrong, that their behavior is wrong, and that all their intentions are tainted by dint of their chromosomes.'[12]

Boosting masculinity has become prevalent in the conservative media landscape, with Republican politicians such as Nick Freitas discussing, for example, 'the importance of restoring traditional masculinity and the role strong families play in America's renewal'.[13] Republican Senator Josh Hawley, in his book *Manhood: The masculine virtues America needs* (2023), argues that 'a free society that despises manhood will not remain free'. Trump's 2024 election campaign targeted young men leaning conservative in interviews with influential male podcasters such as Joe Rogan and Theo Von.[14]

A conservative solution to the supposed crises that feminism has caused appears to be to roll back women's freedoms. The self-proclaimed Christian nationalist Joel Webbon, who 'despises democracy', advocates as a Christian position the repeal of the Nineteenth Amendment, which recognises women's right to vote. Allowing individual women to vote has led to households divided against each other, something antithetical to Christianity in his view. His concept of family is steeped in male headship. Where do women get their vote from then, you might ask. 'From their father, from their husband. If they're not married, it's from their father, if they're not married and their father is dead it's from their brother, it's from their uncle. It's the men in their lives that love them.'[15]

Another conservative British export to the USA, Calvin Robinson, ordained in the Nordic Catholic Church, has argued that if society takes away the expectation of male headship, somehow threatened by Drag Queens and women having control of their bodies, then our cultural edifice 'crumbles':

> They are worse than the WEF [World Economic Forum], the WHO [World Health Organization], the UN, the EU ... they are worse than the Mohammedins and the Jews put together. It is the white, middle class, liberal women who have destroyed western society. Feminism has been our downfall [...] The men have become more effeminate, the women have become too masculine that they are now having mental health issues and everything else crumbles.[16]

It is difficult as a woman to hear these views and not feel a sense of discomfort. But it is even more disorienting to hear that, while a degree of autonomy for women has apparently caused so much distress and disorder, it seems we also need to be protected. The 2024 Trump campaign deliberately used violence against women and girls as a campaign strategy to stoke fear and hatred, presenting Trump as the means of our safety:[17]

> I am your protector. I want to be your protector. As President I have to be your protector [...]. I will make you safe at the border, on the sidewalks of your now violent cities, in the suburbs where you are under migrant criminal siege, and with our military, protecting you from foreign enemies of which we have many today because of the incompetent leadership that we have. You will no longer be abandoned, lonely or scared. You will no longer be in danger. You will no longer have anxiety from all of the problems our country has today. You will be protected and I will be your protector. Women will be happy, healthy, confident and free.[18]

Brutal stories of rape and murder are retold and retold and retold. A twelve-year-old, a thirteen-year-old, a young mother, a young nursing student, all now grist for the MAGA mill. The message is repeated in the conservative ecosystem by commentators like Kirk:

> Every day we highlight another American who's either been raped, kidnapped or murdered by Biden's boys coming across the southern border. [...] allowing the third world into America to disrupt society, to create chaos, anarchy, confusion, disorder, disarray. [...] It is anarcho-tyranny [...]. The plan is to invade. The plan is to overwhelm. The plan is to change the fabric of the country. [...] If you are a female, buy a weapon, learn how to use it and do not leave your home without [it]. Period. It is open season on America's females. It is open season on American women. [...] Do not leave the home alone.[19]

This fear drives the statistic that women are now the fastest growing demographic of gun buyers in the USA.[20]

It is impossible to square this circle. Women must be protected, but we're also responsible for the downfall of society. Our skirts should not be too short or too long. Our sweaters not too loose or too tight. Meanwhile Trump is on record for making misogynistic remarks (2016); he has been found guilty of sexual abuse (2023); and he has made obscene comments about Hillary Clinton and Kamala Harris on his social media platform, Truth Social (2024).[21]

In addition to stories of brutality, there are the ordinary, invisible acts of everyday denigration women experience, compounded by class and race. Conservative calls for family-friendly policies ring hollow for Jonel, sitting in the wreckage of her matrilineal community at the northern border with Canada, where the safety net of 'mother law' was broken by colonisation. On the southern border, Lorena names those who are sacrificed for the potential economic advantages of transnational trade: 'It's usually women and children, right?'

The combination of misogyny and everyday violence constitutes what social geographer Anindita Datta describes as a landscape of hate that women must walk through.[22] It seems that in the conservative universe, freedom as autonomy is 'natural', 'inalienable', only for some. For women, our 'natural' state of freedom is only possible when subsumed into the relationships of family: wife and mother. As Oren Cass, Director of the conservative think tank American Compass argues, it is the height of 'decadent liberalism' to assume child rearing is a matter of personal preference. Instead, it is a moral duty to procreate.[23] For the good of the nation and the Republic, for the very survival of Western civilisation, the (heterosexual) family must be returned to its sanctified position at the centre of American society in order to restore and maintain freedom.

Saving the family, saving freedom

The family is America's 'bedrock', its 'foundation', its 'moral centre' passing on the baton of freedom. According to conservative commentator and founder of the American Cornerstone Institute Ben Carson, God set the 'original boundaries' around the family in order to benefit everyone.[24] But that holy institution is now under attack. 'An all-out war is being waged against traditional family values and godly principles in this country.'[25]

The virulence of this narrative is already impacting on the lives of women and queer communities that are regarded as threatening family values. Transgender rights, for example, have faced a fierce backlash as

Christian conservative organisations stress repeatedly that there are only two genders. In Kirk's words, there is 'a God-given order: men and women. It's a biological truth.' He references the false story of a school washroom rape case to support his argument.[26] But even among those I spoke to who identify as 'liberal', there is at times softly expressed concerns. They seek out reassurance that they won't be cancelled, particularly in their responses to trans-activism and worries relating to shifting pronouns and language such as 'pregnant people'.

The family became a central motif of the 2024 presidential race, discussed widely across both campaigns. Conservative and Christian nationalist commentators, think tanks and media urged women to marry (a man), have more children and push back against LGBTQI+ rights and reproductive freedoms.[27] From the National Conservative statement of principles, 'traditional families' as 'the source of society's virtues' are 'built around a lifelong bond between a man and a woman, and on a lifelong bond between parents and children, [it] is the foundation of all other achievements of our civilization'. This position stands in opposition to what is viewed as 'ever more radical forms of sexual license and experimentation'.[28] Anything but abstinence before heterosexual marriage is outside of the bounds of purity; all other choices are condemned.

Libertarian agendas join with conservatives in a preference for family as the centre of decision making. The Freedom Conservatives' statement of principles notes that 'the best way to unify a large and diverse nation like the United States is to transfer as many public policy choices as possible to families and communities', in order to decentralise the federal government.[29]

Against such standards, freedom of choice becomes limited, with boundaries patrolled and policed. The choice not to marry, for example, has created, in Vice President Vance's imagination, 'miserable, childless cat ladies', the stuff of a thousand social media memes, including most famously by Taylor Swift.[30] His messaging is simple: '[W]e should invest in American families in this country. If nothing else, we should be about healthy, stable families.'[31]

The depiction of miserable cat ladies is nothing in comparison to the at times harrowing attacks on the LGBTQI+ community.[32] Multiple states have legislated bans and proposed bills to criminalise gender-affirming care, including Alabama, Arizona, Louisiana and Texas.[33] In opposition, other states, including California, Connecticut, Minnesota and New York, have introduced legislation to offer refuge for trans-children and their families.[34]

The presence of trans-people makes real the idea that cultural borders are inherently imaginary. It is a painful space of difference to stand in. So while Butler asks us to consider what difference it makes to our social worlds if we disconnect 'the sex assigned at birth from the life that follows',[35] Kirk, among others, rails against proposed changes to Title IX protections.[36]

> BIG GOV wants boys in girls' showers and locker rooms [...] and they want deranged men who dress up like girls to be allowed to abuse real women and girls on the playing field. [...] The takeaway here is that progressive ideology hates women, hates young men, hates due process, hates fairness, and hates you.[37]

Steph, an evangelical Christian in Colorado and listener to the *Charlie Kirk Show*, whom we will get to know better in later chapters, agrees that there must be a definitive border between man and woman but shows a higher level of compassion. Talk of non-binary identities is softened to 'gender confused', although God should not be humiliated by the suggestion he might have got it wrong:

> God did not create them that way. [...] He created the male and female period. [...] I mean if you want to be a man, and you're a woman, you're messing with the natural order. You're trying to play God. You're saying God, you don't know what you're doing. [...] I think it's a tragedy not to celebrate the way you were created. I think it's a bondage. [...] It is [bondage] because they're not free to be the way they were created to be.

For Lionel, a long-time activist for queer rights in the heavily Christian state of Indiana, the ask is straightforward: the freedom to not be 'pigeonholed', to not have dignity denied. The freedom to walk down a street, to go to a nightclub or a bar 'without being attacked by boys in pickup trucks with baseball bats'.

The fear at the heart of opposition to the freedom to choose singleness, a same-sex partner or many partners is the impact these choices would have on families as the centre of child rearing, and consequently, nation building. The choice not to have children, in Kirk's imagination, has created a civilisational crisis, 'directly linked to the rise of authoritarianism, depression, addiction, malaise, and misery'.[38] His urging of young women to marry early and have more children segues with a 'wellness industry' that has increasingly focused on 'alternative' health and 'natural' contraceptive solutions.[39]

The Heritage Foundation's Kevin Roberts argues that it's time for a 'family first conservatism'. Republicans should be a party for 'moms, dads and kids', with every issue understood through the lens of family. 'Happiness', 'flourishing' and even 'national survival' depend on America's families. A family focus in government 'could solve problems as diverse as porn addiction, mental health, and climate change,' according to Roberts.[40] He is a little short on detail as to exactly how that would happen but suggests pro-family policies including making it easier 'for young couples to get married, buy a home, and have and raise kids. Lots of kids.' A January 2025 memo from the Department of Transport has institutionalised this push towards family under the Trump administration, directing funds to communities with higher marriage and birth rates.[41]

Roberts goes on to ask the question many a woman has asked over the years: 'What if we treated stay-at-home moms like the invaluable, full-time workers we all know they are?' I'd be excited by any politician suggesting that women should be paid for the housework we do, but this isn't what the Heritage Foundation is suggesting. There is a disconnect between the rhetoric of supporting women and families and policies that actually do this work for all women, not just the heterosexual and married.

The disconnect is also evident in the juxtaposition of men at the head of the conservative household and the plethora of women's organisations doing the work of saving the family. From the 1970s, the National Organization of Women campaigned for the Equal Rights Amendment (ERA) to the Constitution. Their counterweight was Phyllis Schlafly's Eagle Forum, who opposed the ERA and advocated socially conservative positions. Today, nationally there are organisations such as Moms for America (MfA), Moms for Liberty, Concerned Women for America, USA Women of Action and America First Women, as well as many more issue- and place-based organising committees and action groups at state and local levels.[42] Much of their work centres on 'saving' or 'protecting' children through advocating for parental rights, particularly restricting access in schools to sex education and material referencing race and queerness, as we'll see in the next chapter.

MfA, supporters of America First/MAGA, are 'on a mission to reclaim culture for truth, family, freedom, and the Constitution, to raise a new generation of patriots, and to heal America from the inside out through the homes and hearts of the mothers of America'.[43] To do this work, they have created extensive online resources, podcasts and study groups. 'Cottage meetings' around the country gather women in their homes to talk about what matters to them. Calls to action are made, keeping their national network of 500,000 moms informed about how they can get involved in campaigns such as school choice and elections.[44]

I sit in on their '28 principles of freedom in America' online study group, based on a structured text, with around fifty other women from across the country reading along with the facilitators.[45] I confess, as in my student life, I may not have gone to all ten lectures. Each week begins with a prayer and the Pledge of Allegiance, the flag posted on the screen. Supported by references to Enlightenment philosophers and the classics (Cicero, Aristotle and Plato, who 'was wrong'), the twenty-eight principles are presented as 'a solution to an ailing society', and we are encouraged to memorise them. The overarching theme is that, with the guiding hand of God, if you give people freedom it will unleash prosperity. Reiterating American exceptionalism, we learn a version of history through this lens, invoking the principles of freedom, how to raise the next generation of patriots and how to love America.

I would not prioritise the values nominated in this class (although I recognised them in my own Protestant, immigrant, upbringing), but these women care. Lectures are informal, like having a chat with friends in your living room. There is discussion that veers towards conspiracy at times (e.g. J6 was a 'joyful' protest; there was election 'chicanery'), and some fire and brimstone (the 'fruits of ungodly law rain down terror on the nation'; 'the enemies of freedom want to incite chaos in our country'). But there is also reflection, thoughtful questions and discussions after each lesson. Someone wonders if parts of the Constitution, maybe 15 per cent, do need repair. A woman feels an internal conflict over wanting less government but also recognising the need to address poverty, in the USA and internationally. There is a question about whether we need regulations to keep the rich from abusing the poor, who might have fewer education opportunities and be exploited as a result. Racism is acknowledged, but role models are given as examples of 'rising above it'.

To alleviate these questions, MfA offers a clear set of values rooted in the word of God and cultural nationalism, designed to offer moral guidance in the face of a fluid, ambiguous world. People are diagnosed as 'confused' about their rights, but the key message for moms is that they should be 'morally strong and virtuous', self-reliant, not asking the government to solve their problems. The role of government is only to foster and protect the family.

The strong commitment to moral order and stability embedded in these lessons aligns with Lakoff's summary of conservative values in America: hard work, thrift, industry, individual effort leading to social mobility, as opposed to what are perceived as divisive concepts such as structural inequality, CRT or government welfare. The facilitators repeat these key differences between liberal and conservative, emphasising that the latter operate on the basis of 'God's law' while liberals are ruled by 'feelings' (a point of criticism on repeat throughout the conservative ecosystem). It would be more accurate to say it is particular kinds of emotions that conservative commentators don't like: empathy, for example, directed at immigrants or trans-children. America First/MAGA politicians and commentators are okay expressing other emotions such as hate and anger, as documented at AmFest and many other rallies and podcasts noted in this book.

'God's law' in these lessons is the source of inalienable rights and provides the benchmark for permissible action. If something is not God's law, it is not a right, and this includes reproductive freedoms that impact on the sanctity of the family. Abortion is one of the most divisive topics in the country, with most conversations shifting into open argument when it is mentioned, split broadly liberal/Democrat in favour versus conservative/Republican against. The freedom for a woman to choose to have a child or not has become a bitter debate on what freedom means, its limits and who has the power to constrict the freedoms of others.

Debating reproductive freedoms

The constitutional right to abortion in the USA was founded in the 1973 Roe v. Wade decision and for half a century was generally considered as settled law. But the anti-abortion movement has been patient, strategic and effective. A raft of organisations, over time, have put legal pressure on the weak points in the original decision, particularly the question of viability, pursuing it through various ad hoc cases until it came before the Supreme Court (SCOTUS) again in Dobbs v. Jackson Women's Health Organization (2022). A conservative majority on the court found that the Constitution of the USA does not confer a right to abortion, and Roe v. Wade was overturned.[46]

Some states had trigger bans in place so that as soon as the law changed they could automatically introduce abortion restrictions. Other states have since brought in tighter restrictions. Florida, in 2024, enacted a near-total abortion ban, prohibiting the procedure after six weeks. Wisconsin has some of the most restrictive abortion laws in the country, with an 1849 law prohibiting abortion care including for rape and incest, except cases where the life of the mother is at risk. According to Annie Laurie Gaylor, co-founder and co-President of the Freedom From Religion Foundation (FFRF), 'this is parting with reality and is so cruel'. Four clinics closed in Wisconsin after the Dobbs v. Jackson decision and opened up over the border in Illinois. 'It's a crisis here,' according to Gaylor. 'We are starting to see people suggesting runaway slave laws.'[47]

An array of conservative think tanks, organisations and politicians, mostly aligned with fundamentalist Christian perspectives, continue to lobby for restrictions on abortion. Opposition to contraception access has also resurfaced. Alabama went further, restricting access to IVF treatment.[48] Some in the anti-abortion movement believe Trump would not have won without this hot button issue (John Seago, introduced below from Texas Right to Life, being one of them).

However, the controversy is not easy for Republicans. In the 2022 election cycle, their mid-term results for Congress were not as good as hoped, with speculation that 'suburban women' were unhappy about restrictions on reproductive freedom. A survey found that those who were morally opposed to abortion would still help a close friend or family member seeking the procedure.[49] Referenda in 2022 and 2024 enshrined the right to abortion in some states, countering the loss of Roe v. Wade at the federal level. Trump, while taking credit for the fall of Roe v. Wade when it suits him, has also performed contortions to try to appease both sides, kicking the ball to the states to keep himself away from the controversy, while evangelical and conservative organisations simultaneously pressure him to bring in a federal ban.[50]

If legal challenges are not enough, there are also the blunt instruments of funding cuts and disinformation.[51] The Trump campaign throughout 2024 continued the myth that the Democrats 'support abortion up to and even beyond the ninth month', much to the aggravation of abortion activists such as Aimee.[52] It is difficult to combat a myth once it gains ground:

> When I testify at the legislature, I get asked, 'Why do I approve of 39 week abortions', and when I say 'that does not happen' they don't believe you. [...] [T]he other side has done such a great job of co-opting the word abortion, and then filling it in with their lies. [...] And they've been unafraid to spout these lies for the past two decades.

Aimee is part of We Testify, an organisation that uses storytelling to support women who have had abortions, as well as campaigning to improve access to abortion care.[53] She is all too familiar with the violent side of the abortion debate. Her dad was a doctor who performed abortions: they lived in a gated community, he wore a Kevlar vest and carried a gun. He was threatened 'quite a bit'. 'We got some phone calls that were like, "We're gonna blow your heads off", and stuff like that.'

Aimee had an abortion after finding out she was pregnant in 2003, knowing that she would not be able to care for a child at that time because of health issues:

> I didn't talk about it ever until 2017. That's how deep the stigma was in me. And I found that ever since I started telling my story, people come out of the woodwork to talk to me about it, because they're like, 'oh,

I have a very similar story'. I think it's just so important so people know they're not alone.

We meet in a strip mall in the northern suburbs of Austin. This city is hipster central in Texas: a 'blueberry in a cherry pie'. Home to the sprawling SXSW Festival, there are food truck squares, BBQ masters, craft beer, coffee and kombucha. Austin is also the capital of a state that established a new form of anti-abortion law: the Heartbeat Act. The law's genius was to create a civil cause of action, rather than criminal, allowing a person to sue anyone they think performed or aided an abortion or intends to perform or aid an abortion, after the detection of cardiac activity (approximately six weeks).[54] In other words, it isn't the state enforcing the law but private citizens. The person suing doesn't have to know the person and doesn't have to have suffered any damages. The minimum fine is $10,000 plus court costs. 'So it's pretty, pretty heinous,' according to Aimee.

Since the passing of the Act, clinics in Texas have continued to provide care, but Aimee estimates that 85 to 90 per cent of abortions are post-six weeks. Those women now have to be referred out of state, with all the associated costs.[55] In addition to the Act, there are already numerous restrictions in Texas that Aimee surmises most women won't know. These include a twenty-four-hour waiting period between first and second visits and mandated information via a 'women's right to know' booklet, full of medical inaccuracies and biased information, according to Aimee. Women must also navigate around 'crisis pregnancy centres' that can be fake clinics attempting to persuade women not to have an abortion. These can provide free sonograms and medically inaccurate information, including telling women they are past the six weeks cut off.[56] Abortions are not covered by medical insurance unless specifically underwritten, which makes costs prohibitive for some.

Aimee is unapologetic about using the word 'abortion' rather than the euphemism 'reproductive freedom'. She argues that poll after poll shows that the majority of Texans support access to abortion care, something that comes through strongly in my discussions with 'liberal' and Democrat-leaning young women. The question then is why conservative politicians continue to use it as an election issue. Aimee makes a link between voting freedom and reproductive freedom. Abortion restrictions impact hardest on people of colour, marginalised communities, low-income and rural communities. Even pre-Roe v. Wade, 'white wealthy women have always been able to access abortion care, and that will still be the case'.

Texas, like other parts of the USA, is heavily gerrymandered, so electoral choices become less effective at reflecting the wishes of the majority, exacerbated by low voter turnout of those communities who are most affected – the poor and women of colour.[57] Gaylor makes a similar point, arguing that the overturning of Roe v. Wade was a symptom of the erosion of democracy in the USA.

The second reason for abortion's use as an election issue is the continued stigma, and the consequent reluctance of women to speak about it. Aimee comes from a Catholic family. 'People don't want to talk about abortion, or the fact that one in four people will have an abortion in their lifetime, or that many people that they love and know have had an abortion. People don't like to talk about it.'

We Testify use personal stories to reclaim abortion, highlighting that it affects people we know and love and care about. They say it loudly, as often as possible, to remove shame and to create a sense of safety, and they do this with a fraction of the resources of the state-funded 'alternatives to abortion' programme or Texas Right to Life's many thousands of donors and fundraising galas.[58]

Sub-zero temperatures overnight turn Austin's roads and sidewalks into ice rinks. I slide carefully into the Texas Right to Life office, conveniently located in the block next to the Texas state parliament. John Seago, 'the other side', is well dressed, well spoken and probably the most reasonable anti-abortion advocate I've ever engaged with. In his mid-thirties, a PhD in bio-ethics, articulate and sophisticated in his thinking, he bases his position on what he argues is rational medical science that determines 'viability' – that is, the start of life. The central ethical question centres on whether abortion is 'something that leads to human flourishing, that leads to a just society'. For him, the answer is 'no'. 'Elective abortion', as he describes it, is an act of injustice, as a stronger party taking the life of a weaker one. However, he advocates for civility, moving away from shouting 'murderer' at women to allow for 'a larger cultural conversation about the humanity of the child', our obligations and what we owe the yet to be born, including their freedoms.

Throughout our conversation, language stutters and gets tangled: 'elective', 'choice', 'anti-abortion', 'pro-life'. We switch and stumble between 'unborn child' and 'foetus' in discussing competing freedoms. I use 'foetus', and John says he is not offended by that. We continue.

Texas Right to Life is the oldest and largest anti-abortion organisation in the state. Like Aimee's work, they focus on education and advocacy, 'to promote the sanctity of human life, from fertilisation until natural death'. They run educational events for adults, get involved in political campaigns and elections, working on everything from 'elective abortion' to biotech research, patients' rights and programmes to support pregnant women. In particular, they target students, offering a scholarship programme that trains them in how to lead pro-life groups on college campuses. John's vision is a 'pro-life state' with 'efficient' systems in place to support women. 'If we say we don't want this woman to go to another state to have an abortion, and we want to convince her it's not a disability to have a child in Texas, we're going to need to build a more pro-life state.'

As head of the legislation department, John was instrumental in the creation of the Heartbeat Act. He is pragmatic, preferring 'legally prudent' legislation that has a greater chance of success, that can't be challenged by legal intervention and that 'at the end of the day, save lives'. Texas courts appear to have practised restraint in reviewing the Act and allowed the law to stay in effect at the time of writing, largely due to its specific civil enforcement mechanism. John argues it is reducing the number of abortions by about 60 per cent per month.[59]

In the realm of moral trade-offs, John agrees that a woman's right to bodily autonomy, to possible career and education opportunities, is 'temporarily' violated by forcing her to have a child, but this is necessary in order to 'balance the right to life of another moral agent'. While he recognises there is nothing abstract about the choices women have to make, abortion is 'not an abstract freedom, but a freedom that is being asserted that actually has deadly consequences on another moral agent'.

Referencing moral philosopher Peter Singer, he sketches the different moments that point to human development: communication, self-awareness, social connections. Based on that reasoning, people are not members of the human community until we're about two years old. At the other end of the age spectrum, the markers of being human can decline with diseases such as dementia. Morally, we do not ignore our obligations to elders who might be robbed of the capacity for communication or self-awareness as they age.

Therefore, for John, the most intellectually consistent, and morally defensible position, is taking the point of fertilisation as the start of life, when an egg cell begins to act like 'an individually self-motivated, self-protecting organism'. Referencing recent research by neurobiologists, he argues we become moral agents at this point of cell development, signalled by reacting to pain and the release of stress hormones.[60]

In this argument, morality emerges with suffering, signalling a lifetime of learning via painful feedback loops, including shame. But the logic is free from social context, the reality of poverty, sexual violence and mistakes. Choices that Peter Singer and John will never have to make. He concedes 'life of the mother' exemptions, but not for victims of sexual violence. In these cases, while the woman 'needs as much [assistance] as society can give her', 'a just society punishes the perpetrator. It doesn't punish the child.'

In the midst of this abstract moral argument, a ten-year-old girl, a victim of sexual assault, was denied abortion care in Ohio, a state that outlawed abortion after six weeks within hours of the fall of Roe v. Wade, with no exemptions for rape or incest.[61] She had to travel to neighbouring Indiana for the health care she needed. Yet John supports the overturning of Roe v. Wade as a policy outcome that enables the establishment of 'a more just society where moral agents are appreciated'.

When I ask if it's possible for a foetus to have 'freedom', and therefore moral agency, the conversation becomes stuck again. For John, '[i]t's too vague. I don't know what we're talking about', which is the first time I feel that he's avoiding the discussion. Aimee is clearer. To make the case that a foetus has freedoms discounts the freedom of pregnant women and their ability to make these decisions for themselves:

> Freedom doesn't just mean, you know, waving your flag. Freedom means having access to all the rights that are promised, by virtue of being in this country. If I don't believe that a foetus is a child, and I don't want to be pregnant anymore, I should be able to have that freedom.

The use of the term 'elective' also negates the question of how much choice women actually have, as Aimee points out:

> I do think that one of the reasons why our side needs to stop using the word choice is because choice isn't something that is afforded to everyone that is seeking abortion care [...]. Is the choice between living in poverty and not being able to care for the kids that you already have? That's not a choice at all.

John hears the argument that Aimee makes. His vision of a 'pro-life state' requires getting involved in public policy debates to advocate for social services, including counselling, parent and employment training. He envisages policies such as protecting students' scholarships and college housing should a woman at university need to take time for maternity leave. He wants tax incentives for companies that create pregnant-employee-friendly environments.

But these things cost money, and Texas Right to Life have avoided becoming involved in economic policy, strategically choosing to 'stay out of some fights' and keeping their focus on 'health care'. While they have lobbied for medical insurance coverage for up to a year after birth as part of Medicaid, they haven't tackled parental leave yet. Despite the emphasis on family as the core unit of American society, it is estimated that only 12 per cent of Americans have paid parental leave (falling to 5 per cent for low-income families).[62] John agrees it's an area the anti-abortion movement needs to address.

Expansive health care for women requires economic intervention. It's 'freedom to' (positive freedoms, the opportunities) as much as 'freedom from' (negative freedoms, the absence of constraints). John recognises that the pro-life agenda has to expand beyond prohibitions, and they are breaking ground into areas that are making some conservatives 'very uncomfortable'. He knows he will get pushback from Texas Republicans on anything that looks like providing welfare for women, but he pushes on regardless.

The professional grace of our discussion is the polar opposite of the threats of violence made by some anti-abortion groups. I took part in a Women's March pro-abortion rally in Washington, DC in the summer of 2022, following the fall of Roe v. Wade.[63] A small group of male Christian activists with megaphone followed the march, holding banners depicting an aborted foetus and castigating as 'murderers' the hundreds of women walking to the White House to protest. It was annoyance rather than threat, but more seriously, the National Abortion Federation has documented a marked increase in attacks against abortion providers since the overturning of Roe v. Wade.[64]

While anti-abortion debates are framed by Christian morality, and Texas Right to Life is officially a Christian organisation, compassion and non-violence can be sorely lacking. Inconsistencies are also evident when comparing the attention given to abortion by conservative politicians and commentators, with, for example, the low level of interest shown in combating childbirth mortality.

John is not happy with the polarisation, although he has had some success at building consensus, working occasionally with Democrats on issues such as social service programmes. 'It really is just becoming the party of the pro-life movement or the party of the pro-choice movement, and unfortunately, I don't think that's helpful at all.' He prefers to focus on 'changing hearts and minds' rather than hurling threats and sees a shift on college campuses where they operate. Activists talk to people, rather than 'just shaming them'. He is hopeful that 'a common morality is attainable, that there are some principles we can agree to'.

The movement to support reproductive freedoms can feel overwhelmed at present when faced with the weight of law, God and organisations like Texas Right to Life. Follow-up emails from the Women's March, for example, although not offering much in the way of constructive strategy, captured their mood: 'Hate, hate, hate. Double hate. LOATHE ENTIRELY!'[65] The 2024 presidential election highlighted that even the mythical 'suburban woman', whom Democrats had been relying on for support on the basis of ensuring abortion rights, will trade off this freedom for other needs – perhaps priorities like the increased prosperity promised by Trump. It is also these women who are having to navigate a changing classroom, and Democrats were unable to counter the pervasive narrative from America First/MAGA commentators that public education is damaging children. Schools became a site containing multiple anxieties as parents, politicians, teachers and students tested ideas about freedom, truth and the best way to pass on values to the next generation in order to secure the future.

6
Teaching freedom: The (mis-)education of America

In 2021, Republican Glenn Youngkin unexpectedly won the governorship of Virginia, relying heavily on a platform of supporting parental rights in schools. As a result, education became seen as a path to electoral victory for Republicans, who attempted to ride a wave of parental concern precipitated by the anxieties of COVID-19 and racial justice. As parents listened in to online classes in their living rooms and kitchens during the pandemic, they heard schools struggling to address systemic racism and inequality following the murder of George Floyd.[1] Schools soon found themselves having to contend with fears that children were being taught 'to feel guilty for their race'. The #MeToo movement, trans-activism and new approaches such as social-emotional learning, designed to improve mental health outcomes for children, added fuel to the growing bonfire.

From kindergarten to university, the controversies highlighted an interminable question. What is the purpose of education? To sow the 'seeds of a deep, unifying message of American citizenship', as the Hoover Institution would like,[2] generating synchronicity in the present and connecting the past with a predictable future where America is still the GOAT? Singing the anthem, saluting the flag, e pluribus unum, building the nation in the rituals of education? Is it to create 'freedom-loving citizens', forever 'passing the torch of American exceptionalism to the next generation' as the Ronald Reagan Foundation & Institute would like?[3] Should schools hold public trust to teach 'the truth', even when that challenges established narratives, or focus on creating the virtuous and like-minded?

And should freedom be taught as a master narrative that holds it all together?

All over the country, parents, students, free speech lawyers and think tanks, from across the political spectrum, engaged in conversations to unpick these questions. But always in the middle were the teachers trying to navigate around politics and the need for a curriculum that reflects a changing world, influencing how the master narrative of freedom is passed on from one generation to the next.

Battles over education ebb and flow as part of the 'culture wars', as the historian Jill Lepore notes in her history of America. A prescient SCOTUS ruling in 1943 found: 'Probably no deeper division of our people could proceed from any provocation than from finding it necessary to choose what doctrine and whose program public educational officials shall compel youth to unite in embracing.'[4] And so it continues today, fuelled by political expediency.

In conservative circles, a special venom is reserved for diversity, equity and inclusion (DEI) initiatives and critical race theory (CRT), both viewed as a fifth column 'dividing the American people'.[5] America First/MAGA commentators repeat claims that in classrooms across America children are being taught to 'hate our country' thanks to 'radical', 'leftist' philosophies and teachers. State schools and universities are seen as attacking the Christian family, 'grooming' children, and dismantling the foundations of America and its freedoms by erasing its 'true' history.

According to Lepore, since 2020, while seventeen states have tried to introduce anti-racist teaching of some description, thirty-six states have tried to restrict it.[6] For the Heritage Foundation, public education has been infiltrated by this 'perverse and wicked ideology'; it is a 'virus' and an 'existential threat against the American way of life'.[7] Conservative commentator James Lindsay, at AmFest and on various podcasts, cannot contain his outrage: '[C]ritical race theory is the end of our country if we let it continue. It's calling everything that you want to control racist until you control it.' On the other hand, activists like Lindsay call everything related to sex education 'grooming', until it's so toxic it can't be touched by educators. 'Queer theory is the gateway to hell,' according to Lindsay. 'People who do this belong in prison. It's psychological child abuse.'[8]

The legacy of the Cold War seeps into the diatribe, with Moms for America (MfA) describing DEI and CRT as a 'communist plot to destroy this country, happening RIGHT NOW.'[9] Public education is compared to 'Maoist re-education' camps. The 'left' or 'Marxists' are destroying 'common respect' for history and for values, posing an existential threat to the nation. At the intersection of culture and policy, 'Marxists' have orchestrated the shaping of not only the curriculum but education policy, teacher training and school cultures, 'slowly taking over our educational institutions step by step'.[10]

Invoking the Italian theorist Antonio Gramsci, leading campaigners such as Christopher Rufo talk of hegemony and cultural capture by 'the left', not only of public education but libraries, social media and Hollywood, in order to produce 'Marxists'.[11] Ben Carson, former cabinet member in the first Trump administration and founder of the American Cornerstone Institute, says without irony that 'if you want to fundamentally change a society, you have to indoctrinate and manipulate, so you gain control of the educational system and you gain control of the media'.[12]

Spending any time in the company of self-described Marxists would soon dispel any caricature of their alleged influence. Nor, as an educator, could I turn my students into Marxists in ten weeks of teaching critical theory even if I wanted to. But there is little space for shades of grey in the criticism of education policy. The argument reflects an emotional truth felt by many: that something has changed, and someone must be blamed, and in this case, it must be education. Where else could children be learning something different from the values held by parents?

According to Rufo, educators and unions 'are betraying taxpayers and parents' by including within lessons 'intolerant, racially discriminatory pedagogy'. More importantly, 'America should be defined as a nation that offers freedom and opportunity for everyone, regardless of the color of their skin.'[13] History would suggest otherwise. Notably, in the 1960s, the federal government had to intervene in the desegregation of schools, while facing opposition from those wishing to maintain segregation under the slogan of 'school choice' or 'freedom of choice'.[14] Alabama only removed a statute that enabled the segregation of schools from its state constitution in 2020.[15]

Amid the hyperbole of book banning and attempts to restrict what teachers can teach, in contravention of free speech, there is concern that children and students are vulnerable, 'being manipulated and brainwashed', open to indoctrination and 'false narratives', and used as 'pawns to overthrow our society'.[16] As former Vice-President Mike Pence argued in fundraising emails, 'children are brainwashed by these radical ideologies and refuse to carry the legacy of freedom into the future'.[17] According to the Heritage Foundation, 'young Americans today are easily indoctrinated with evil ideologies like critical race theory in their schools, through the media, and even corporations once they enter the workforce'.[18]

From criticism of formal education to conspiracy theories like QAnon's Pizzagate, the message is that children must be protected from uncomfortable histories and Drag Queens.[19] Parents and grandparents that I spoke to worry about their kids. Suzy, a Republican-leaning grandmother to two sixteen-year-olds and a nineteen-year-old in rural Indiana, believes her grandchildren 'absorb a lot of stuff, whether it's good or bad', and that 'these kids are not mentally prepared to [look at both sides and make their own choice]'.

Public education is no longer a safe proposition; it is no longer guaranteed to reproduce cultural coherence, continuity, 'the like-minded'. Synchronicity is fracturing. The malaise extends from kindergarten to universities, the latter described by conservative Gen Z commentator Isabel Brown as 'institutions of indoctrination' that have rejected 'objective truth'.[20] Campus protests in 2024 against Israel's bombardment of Gaza led to an outpouring of vitriol and grief. The Heritage Foundation summed up the problem:

> If [students] aren't fully indoctrinated by the time they graduate high school, college professors and administrators finish the job by pumping their brains with intellectually childish lies about American history and denying basic facts like men can't be women. This toxic leftist indoctrination is what created the shocking protests across America's elite universities. We must take back control of American education from these Marxists who want to destroy our country. [...] And with your support, we will not stop until the good-for-nothing, left-wing Department of Education is abolished. [...] [Will] future generations of American children grow up as America-loving patriots or vicious Marxist ideologues?[21]

99

Charlie Kirk was a fierce critic of universities, describing them as a 'scam', paid 'thousands of dollars to teach woke falsehoods that teach our nation's young people to hate America'.[22] He proudly acknowledged he was a 'college dropout' and campaigned ceaselessly for parents not to send children to university. I would agree with his argument that the level of debt young people have to incur is debilitating, but he appeared more concerned about what is being taught there than the cost. University education is 'playing Russian Roulette with your kid's values'. TPUSA set up Professor Watch (Education Watch in the UK) to name and shame 'woke' professors.[23]

Concerned parents, particularly mothers, are encouraged to 'take back control' by running for school boards or homeschooling their children. TPUSA and the Heritage Foundation are relentless in podcasting about the ills of public education and its 'progressive agenda'. Organisations such as Moms for Liberty and MfA offer support 'to return our public schools to local communities and end the tyranny of government mandates for education'.[24] Not only is the 'health and safety of our children under attack',[25] but in the reassessing of the nation's founding, 'it's hard to know what is truth in this landscape of lies'.[26] And without the truth, there can be no freedom.

Establishing the truth

Beyond the 'three r's', and the endless argument over who is indoctrinating whom, education is above all else part of the cultural infrastructure that disseminates 'truth'. It is this 'truth' that is at the heart of the struggle for freedom in the USA. Truth must be incontrovertible for some, like Randy in our conversation on the incarceration of J6 rioters. There can be only one truth, for it is the foundation on which all else is built.

It's at this point that postmodernity unexpectedly appeared in my conversations, and in the conservative ecosystem generally, as the root of 'leftist' attempts to undermine the truth about America's freedom. The concept has been resuscitated as the straw man of 'cultural Marxism', but the fundamental idea of postmodernity is that master narratives have reached the end of their usefulness as explanations for why the world is the way it is. Grand ideas like Marxism or freedom can be understood from different perspectives, and each of these perspectives is meaningful; everyone has a story, and they do not have to align.

This is a shaky foundation for some on which to build a future. Postmodernity makes 'truth' feel subjective, determined by lived experiences rather than objective, quantifiable or falsifiable evidence. CRT, for example, according to MfA, is underpinned by this 'new epistemology' that doesn't use empirical evidence. The ambiguity is too much. 'This is just wrong! How can mums protect their kids from this?'[27]

The challenge is exacerbated by a digital age: we are drowning in information in which it's difficult to find THE truth. Never in human history have we had so much capacity to create and disseminate stories. There is too much choice, too much data, on repeat. Tech companies as new points of authority compete with the government and religious institutions to control the truth. The ability to discern what is true becomes increasingly difficult, even for Gen Z digital natives like Anne, an engineering student in Indiana:

> A lot of people now are just like, well, if you look it up on this website, it says this, if you look it up on the other website [it] says almost the complete opposite. Yeah, how are we supposed to know? We're not gonna figure this out. It just takes a lot of mental energy. There's a lot of people now who are just like ... we don't know how to figure out what's the truth.

The problem of misinformation becomes evident in false narratives circulating throughout conversations and the media. Linda, an executive assistant living in a mobile home park in suburban Denver, mentions a local school that was going to start providing litter boxes in the restrooms because children there identified as 'furries' (kittens). 'Their parents have actually allowed them to go that far, and they don't relieve themselves unless it's in a litter box. [...] And they are petitioning the school districts to put litter boxes in the restrooms in school [banging table].' Despite having no evidence for this, Michael, a rancher and father to two children in a neighbouring county, heard the same rumour through other parents. 'There's some kids that identify as a cat. A cat! so they're requesting kitty litter put in the bathrooms.' The rumours also made their way to the UK.[28]

Heuristics such as 'common sense' are used to try to sort through the glut of information. Trump adopted this as a key part of his rhetoric in the early days of his second presidential term. Ron, a retired army veteran in suburban Indiana, relies on his common sense of what has gone before and the muscle memory of ritual in order to cope with the demands of a saturated present:

> A lot of it is just common sense. You know, you got it coming from everywhere. We are just overloaded, totally overloaded with information. So you have to pick out what you believe. And I'm just an old country boy. I stand for the flag. I stand for the national anthem. And I stand for all that stood before me. It's a belief in this country. I've started saying the Pledge of Allegiance ... what ... since ten years old. I've said it all my life and I believe it.

While Trump has promised to restore 'common sense' to education, including axing the Department of Education, Carson has his own podcast called 'Common Sense' and promotes a 'commonsense pledge'[29] to manage 'a rapidly changing society' where 'sometimes it feels like common sense is slipping through the cracks'. He believes that

> [y]oung people need to be taught why we love America, and what our country represents. [...] This [Gaza protest] is shameful. Parents, grandparents, and teachers of young children are watching this and thinking: [...] 'How do we instil our shared love of country into future generations?' [...] Something must be done if we want to ensure that the days ahead will look different.[30]

'Looking different' in this instance is a return to the familiar, a past before young people took over their campuses. For the Heritage Foundation's Kevin Roberts, 'we are fighting for the very foundational principles that made America great'. What should be taught in schools according to the Heritage Foundation, and private education providers like Hillsdale College, are Judeo-Christian values and the 'classics'. This will create a 'virtuous citizen' in a 'flourishing' society.[31] Education should encourage an appetite for things that are 'good and beautiful and true', cultivating an 'intelligent patriotism'.

There is no agreement on what a 'virtuous citizen' looks like, but Enlightenment philosophers, Roman history and Cicero often appear as the epitome of a virtuous republic. Such 'principles of nature and eternal reason' sit in juxtaposition to 'mindless revolutionaries trying to overthrow the government and sow chaos'.[32] Swathes of inconvenient classical history are ignored, including the complex queer social histories of Greece and Rome that some conservative organisations might regard as not so virtuous.[33]

Contested histories, mis- and dis-information, have increased distrust between parents and the education system, something noticed by Danni, a teacher in Indiana:

> There's definitely parents that don't trust me to take care of their kid every day. And that's unfortunate. They're full of ... I don't know ... of me doing the wrong thing for them, and that's not what I would ever [do]. [...] [W]e don't know what to trust. The media, even the internet, it's so saturated with stuff. [...] It's almost too much, like you don't even know what's real or what's not, what's true or what Joe Schmo put on there [...] it's so scary to think ...

Fear is conveyed repeatedly. Fear of the unknown if things go on like this. Fear that 'truth' and therefore America will be 'destroyed'. Fear that children and therefore the future will be different. Fear that 'something' is being 'lost' ... on the tip of the tongue ... that can't quite be articulated. It just feels wrong. The comfort of certainty, of being in control of the future, is slipping away, along with our grasp of the truth. As one of the Democrat-leaning Indiana university students describes it:

> You start being afraid of ... how free am I, can I control any of that? And if I don't then am I really free? It's also, like, scary how attainable misinformation is on the internet, and how people can get sucked into these rabbit holes of conspiracy theories and just lies [...]. And it just leads to scary stuff.

In an overwhelming rush of information, we can at least reach out for familiar narratives that give us a sense of comfort. But in the context of the USA's contested past, this has also fuelled the 'history wars' as different stakeholders grapple for control over founding myths and fairy tales.

Debating historical truths

Across a broad spectrum of conservative organisations, there is concern that young people don't know the 'truth' about their history and therefore will not be able to defend freedom. A Ronald Reagan Foundation

& Institute study in 2024 found that young people are 'faltering in their understanding of our nation's core principles and the values that have propelled us as a global beacon of liberty and freedom. Shockingly, only 18 per cent of America's youth expressed extreme pride in being Americans.'[34] For Carson, '[k]ids today aren't learning the true history of America, and we want to change that. America is the greatest country on earth, and people should feel proud to live here.'[35]

To generate the truth requires both the banning of 'woke' books, self- and systemic censorship of sex, gender and contested histories and the development of new resources such as the 'Heroes of liberty' series, in order to 'regain control of our children's bookshelves and bedtime reading', so that 'a great nation can pass on its values to the next generation'. There must be continuity; giving children 'the values that we grew up on'.[36] To have something different may be too painful.

Truth is particularly embedded in the stories of 'the Founding', passed on through generations and projected into the future. For those leaning conservative, difficult subjects such as slavery can be addressed, but only in 'the right way'. The USA is an example of freedom for the world; slavery didn't originate here, 'it came', passively showing up. It's still happening elsewhere but not in America, which can take credit for ending it, so the narrative goes.

If only it were so easy to 'move on'. The trauma of enslavement and segregation is a scarifying mark running the length of American history into the present. Those who would co-opt the narrative create new fairy tales. In 2023, Ron DeSantis, Florida governor and former Republican presidential candidate, was reported to have claimed that Black people benefitted from slavery, for example by having the opportunity to learn new skills.[37] To move beyond the shame of slavery has at times reduced history to an act of avoidance so that children are spared potential discomfort rendered by the past.[38] In reproducing the nation, there shall be no guilt or humiliation for past actions. Children should be protected from uncomfortable ideas, although not so much from school shootings if that infringes on Second Amendment rights.

More bluntly put from those leaning towards progressive politics, there is a suggestion at times that the removal of critical approaches to understanding the past is aimed at preventing children finding out that their parents or grandparents were the ones throwing words and/ or stones at Black children trying to go to school. The visitors' centre at the Dr Martin Luther King Jr National Historical Park in Atlanta holds an exhibition on the history of the Civil Rights movement. In one section, there is an installation on segregation, and on loop, there is footage of opposition to integration from the Ku Klux Klan and other parents. The 'n' word is said out loud by white folk opposed to school desegregation, who add that 'they' 'cannot learn like white folks'. A Black mum with two young kids, maybe five to seven years old, stands next to me in a room of mostly Black visitors. She says to the air 'I don't think this is suitable for my babies', and I asked myself the question: how do we teach this to children? We walk away at the same time, me a little in front, and I hear her explaining to her kids that 'there was a time in the past when these things happened, and there are still some things like that today, but your education is important'.

In everyday conversations, there are many sentences that trail into silence, pauses and euphemisms when race and enslavement are mentioned. Some parents and grandparents speak with concern about 'what they're shoving down these kids' throats', and that teachers 'have torn apart' the history of the country. This is countered by others who see 'history has always belonged to the victor', so that 'what was in the textbook wasn't always right'. 'We just trusted what was in the book was true', and that is no longer the case. There is recognition by some parents that something is 'missing', and that we don't as a society have the right to choose the version of history we like best or make the uncomfortable go away by calling it 'untrue'.

Yet the debate rages and pivots around a moving centre. How far to go to re-write or efface history? To tear down statues or use them as a teaching point? To add lessons informed by CRT, but not so much that 'we don't have to make it like white people are bad'. Removing the discomfort, like Confederate statues, means removing having to think about the past.

Teachers are caught in the middle. Sally and Malcom, now retired, are hardly radical Marxists. They are friends of friends who met on an education exchange programme decades ago in Australia. We have lunch in their suburban backyard outside Denver, Colorado. They describe how fast the classroom has changed in the last ten years to reflect social transformation – the inclusion of gay families and shifting pronouns, for example. But the history wars have created a sense of foreboding for Malcolm: 'If we don't teach this critical thinking or teach students about the blemishes in our history, and we just sanitise it and have this idea of exceptionalism, we're a bunch of lemmings. And that's scary.'

Presenting a counter-narrative to the exceptionalism, the *1619 Project* became a lightning rod for the history wars following its publication by the *New York Times* in 2019. This body of research, led by Black writers, historians and journalists, called for the USA's history to be rethought, shifting 'the Founding' from 1620 and a Protestant settlement of people seeking freedom from persecution, to a story that begins a year earlier in 1619 with the arrival of enslaved Africans in Virginia. This reframing of history aimed to place 'the consequences of slavery and the contributions of Black Americans at the very center of [America's] national narrative'.[39] The project, and its editor, Nikole Hannah-Jones, were openly vilified by nationalist populist commentators such as Charlie Kirk.

In response to contested histories, a range of conservative organisations are now also providing resources, from kindergarten to university, in formal and non-formal settings, 'to educate people' (subtext, 'in the right way'). TPUSA established its own academy in 2024 – 'an educational movement that exists to glorify God and preserve the founding principles of the United States through influencing and inspiring the formation of the next generation'. It's three 'r's are: Reclaim. Revive. Restore. Reclaiming children's education, reviving 'virtuous education focused on truth, goodness, and beauty' and restoring God 'as the foundation of education'.[40]

Carson's American Cornerstone Institute (strapline: 'Faith, Liberty, Community, Life' as the four cornerstones of America) has a partnership with TPUSA, touring college campuses with them, promoting their Executive Branch and Executive Sessions for America programmes for 'conservative minded college students'. For kindergarten to 12th grade, they created the 'Little Patriots' programme of animated history lessons and established 'Celebrate Freedom Week' in 2024, for kindergarten to fifth grade.[41]

The Heritage Foundation are 'working to build the next generation of conservative leaders',[42] targeting high school and colleges with a Young Leaders Program and High School Fellowship. The aim is for young people to be able to 'defend their values against leftist indoctrination' and 'drive change in their communities'.[43] Organisations such as Patriot Academy provide resources for anyone who would like to become a 'Constitution coach: to take the message of the Constitution to people in their community', promoting the 'biblical foundation' of the Constitution.[44] They also offer gun training on their purpose-built range. MfA run courses on 'biblical citizenship', 'Healing America' and from 2025 a cottage meeting programme designed for teenagers.[45] America First Works offered a 'Bootcamp for Boomers', to 'equip patriots like you with the knowledge and resources needed to safeguard our constitutional freedoms, defeat the extreme leftist agenda, and save America!'[46]

The conflict feels intractable and exacerbated by calls for 'education freedom'. While centred on 'choice', this movement also appears to have the capacity to reintroduce forms of segregation and institutionalise educational inequalities through removing Department of Education control and giving states and parents more freedom to decide on how their children are educated. Conservatives and libertarians join ideological forces on this issue.

Education freedom and the virtuous citizen

Libertarian approaches to education, as advocated in think tanks and lobby groups such as the Cato Institute and EdChoice, frame education as a 'human capital problem' that can be addressed by schools competing for students.[47] This has the added benefit of overcoming disagreements on what education is for, as parents can have the freedom to find a school that shares their values. As Neal McCluskey, Director of the Center for Educational Freedom at the Cato Institute argues:

> How do we shape the newest generation to be the way we want them to be? [...] [T]hat is a fundamental problem, because people don't agree on what constitutes a virtuous citizen. But that's one of the reasons that public schooling's promise in the abstract tends to fail and have lots of unintended consequences.

The next generation might have something to say about 'the way we want them to be', but from an education freedom perspective, it would be left to parents to decide what 'virtuous' means and how it is achieved through education. Funding would follow pupils directly rather than being controlled by the Department of Education.

The argument has its roots in the politicisation of centralised education. As industrial society segmented, urbanised and became more complex, it required people with diverse values to use one system. This was a recipe for conflict, according to McCluskey, 'forcing people into camps to fight with each other'. It also results in a hollowing out of education as teachers dodge controversies. High school biology teachers in some states avoid teaching evolution or include 'intelligent design', for example, to remove potential sources of offence or discomfort for some Christian students. 'We shouldn't want a system that requires people to negotiate and potentially lose on things that are really important to them.'

At its worst, differences in values and the strength of feeling among parents has seen school boards erupt into heated arguments, threats and even violence. Disagreement is also being settled through legal processes. The virtue of fairness juxtaposed with racism and inequality has become exposed in court room battles over admissions policies. For example, Thomas Jefferson High School for Science and Technology, a selective school near Washington, DC, based its admissions on standardised testing. In 2019, its student body was composed of 71.5 per cent Asian heritage, 19.5 per cent white and small percentages of African American and Hispanic students.[48] The school changed policy to include new criteria, such as socio-economic background, a move that was unsuccessfully challenged by a coalition of parents in 2023.[49] But the backlash to changes in admissions policies in other states has led to ongoing clashes between parents' groups and education officials.[50]

In my own sector, higher education, battles over academic freedom, free speech and cancel culture have riven departments and campuses, costing jobs and reputations. It has been exhausting. A challenge by Students for Fair Admissions led to a 2023 SCOTUS decision to outlaw affirmative action policies in universities such as Harvard.[51] Debates on academic freedom have also invoked free speech principles that have ended in the courts. The non-partisan Foundation for Individual Rights and Expression (FIRE), engages in direct advocacy for students, students' groups and professors, across the political spectrum. Zach Greenberg is a senior programme officer in individual rights defence, and a First Amendment attorney with FIRE. He grapples daily with the contested boundaries between individual free speech and our collective responsibility to the public sphere:[52]

> We're seeing a lot of professors that are being targeted for their research, their advocacy and their teaching. We're seeing organisations that are opposed to professors teaching many different topics and issues in their classrooms and we're seeing universities punish their professors by suspending them, terminating them, or taking their teaching privileges away based on their protected expression.

To defuse these conflicts, McCluskey argues it's better to allow people the freedom to live as they think is right, including deciding what their children are taught. If we're not happy with what a school teaches, we should not be forced to go into political combat with other people. We should be able to go somewhere else where we find teaching 'more acceptable'. His research suggests that letting people choose leads to more of the outcomes that people generally say is what we want in terms of 'shaping citizens', including higher levels of political literacy, being more likely to volunteer in the community and being more tolerant of diverse viewpoints.

Some states already allow for education freedom. In 2024, Louisiana became the twelfth state in the USA to adopt this policy, while introducing an Education Savings Accounts for all parents.[53] Louisiana state governor Jeff Landry also passed laws ensuring transgender students be referred to by their birth gender, allowing public schools to employ chaplains and placing the Ten Commandments in every public classroom (the latter was stayed in the courts as of November 2024).[54] Louisiana has also classified abortion pills as dangerous controlled substances.[55]

My argument back to McCluskey is that if a primary purpose of education is to generate cultural cohesion, *e pluribus unum*, how is that achieved through school choice if people are, in effect, self-segregating?

Danni, the teacher in Indiana, for example, values the experience of living in different communities (suburban Ohio where she grew up and rural Indiana where she now lives and works) and wants to re-create that for the young people she teaches:

> [Parents] want to be involved in their curriculum, which is absolutely fine. But it's getting close to the point where they can pick and choose what their child can know and not know. And to me, that's detrimental because you can once again have your child know what you view instead of allowing them to have some sort of open mind to life. [...] But it worries me that say, somebody in Columbus [Ohio] can teach this curriculum and they know nothing about the other parts, and then someone here can teach this curriculum they know nothing about other parts. So what is that child going to grow up doing? Are they going to have a choice to be who they want to be? And if we don't teach them everything, then we're not giving them that choice.

Choice, as we have seen in previous conversations, is a central motif of freedom in the USA. There is an argument that education freedom can result in less conflict between parents and the education system but also less choice for children in terms of exposure to different ways of being in the world. The latter can be a difficult proposition for some if those different ways of seeing the world are perceived as 'wrong' or threatening.

Danni's husband, Peter, also a teacher, emphasises the point. 'We start to divide ourselves more and more and more and more, because we're not seeing the other viewpoint ever at school.' Sally agrees, emphasising the 'scary' consequences of segregation:

> There really could be a threat to the whole democratic system, you know, if you can't have open dialogue, and you can't learn about different viewpoints, and then come up with your own viewpoint and defend it. Where else would you learn to do that if you don't learn it at home. [...] You know, you have to have an opportunity for that dialogue to happen otherwise, we're pretty doomed. [...] That's pretty scary. That's not a road we want to go down.

McCluskey doesn't agree that segregation is inevitable, but his response is somewhat circular. If people don't agree on what or how they want their children taught, then don't force them to go to school together, but as there is widespread agreement on American values, for example free speech, it shouldn't result in segregation because all schools will embed those values.

As every conversation in this book demonstrates, in reality rather than theory, there is little agreement on American values, including what the master narrative of freedom means. Education Department statistics suggest there are already entrenched divergences based on race and class. Sixty-five per cent of white students attend private schools, with 62 to 72 per cent attending schools with a Christian orientation.[56] Only 6 per cent of Asian students, 10 per cent of Black students and 12 per cent Hispanic students attend private schools. Some Christian schools are explicit in stating they won't teach CRT or address gender fluidity. Others use coded language, for example 'traditional' or 'classical' education, denoting their approach. Hillsdale College, a 'Christian, classical liberal arts college', with ties to TPUSA, is explicit in providing 'education for liberty'.

Other structural inequalities temper McCluskey's optimism. Unequal access to education resources drives trade-offs, as parents seek to reconcile contested priorities, personal values and hopes for their children's futures. There are particular levels of unfairness between rural and urban schools, but most school choice programmes are in urban areas, and parents do not always have the option to move. McCluskey argues that opportunities can be equalised by alternative provision such as online learning, homeschooling cooperatives and 'micro schools', providing options even in rural areas.

Post-COVID-19, there has been an increase in enrolments in home-schooling, with potential implications for the breadth of viewpoints young people have access to.[57] It is promoted across conservative organisations, including the American Cornerstone Institute, MfA and TPUSA. The decision is driven by different motivations that loop back to the question of what education is for. AJ, a Texas libertarian, homeschools her children because of her concern about rote learning:

> I think it's important that I have the freedom to communicate to my children anything that I find of value. They do not go to public school because I don't like what public school has to teach them. They're just teaching children to guess, to pass a test, to fall in line. They're taught to regurgitate information and listen to instruction without questioning.

I teach my children the exact opposite. If you are given an instruction I
want you to know why, I want you to understand the importance of it.

Elizabeth, founder of a parent support group in New York, sees homeschooling networks developing in upstate New York and imagines joining them. While her children attend a school in the city, she argues she
is already homeschooling to unpick the damage that mainstream education ('not real school') is doing to her children, whom she describes
as 'freedom machines':

The work that I have to do now every time they come home from school
is three times as much as it was three years ago. Conditioning and reor-
ganising and reorienting and asking questions and regaining critical fac-
ulties. The work that I have to do now is so much more because what
happened in school today is bullshit times 11.

'Real education', for Elizabeth, was never a set of multiple-choice
options. 'That's indoctrination.' How to think about what questions
to ask within a pedagogy that centres freedom is her idea of real education. 'But we don't have the capacity in the schools to actually bring in
educators who educate towards freedom and liberation.'

Steph, in rural Colorado, homeschooled her children, concerned not
only about discipline but that the internet has created 'too much to
choose from'. Choice is good, but there should not be too much of it,
and there should be the right kind of things to choose from:

I didn't want my kids to be in classrooms that were chaotic. [...] I noticed
that the academics had gone down drastically, what was expected of my
kids compared to when I went to high school, day and night difference.
The difference was [my daughter] had the internet, and the distractions,
and the teachers couldn't get the kids to do the same amount of work.

'Chaotic' in the sense Steph uses it refers not only to a sense of undis-
ciplined behaviour but also disorderly ideas: too much information,
too much difference, definitely too much sex education. The teaching
of history was again particularly problematic. 'We wanted to just have
that freedom to, you know, I don't want to say indoctrinate, but to just
protect our kids from lies, basically.'

Steph corrects herself. It wasn't so much 'lies' as 'withholding information' about the role of God in the USA's history that troubled her,
and there's more on that in the next chapter. Concerns about sex

education grew in imagination. Steph had 'heard' that a new sex education programme introduced in the county 'was very graphic starting in kindergarten'. Michael, who earlier registered a concern about 'furries', also mentions parent protests at attempts to introduce a new sex education curriculum. 'The part of it that I had trouble with was learning what sex you are in kindergarten. There's a lot of mind play there. [...] So just where do you say ... Where's enough?'[58]

Michael raises the anguish of cultural change: when do we say 'enough'? Where's the line? The definition of what is right and good has shifted, and decisions become even harder when they have to be made for another human being whom a parent might want to grow up with the same values as them rather than step into an uncertain future with new ones they do not agree with. For McCluskey, analysing education through his libertarian values, the benchmark is that parents should be able to make their own decisions about what is the right way to educate their children. Responsibility lies with them, not with government.

This idea of education freedom could be reappropriated to allow for alternative visions of what education could look like. I would add a side bar that it is often women as community organisers who provide these alternative visions. Jonel, for example, on Akwesasne Mohawk land, sees education as a way of reconnecting children with community traditions:

> I would like to see children back on the land, you know, connecting with nature, getting a better understanding of the elements, the waters, the scientists inside of them. Like there's so many aspects of them that gets stifled because they're not exposed to natural environments that actually are designed to keep them healthy.

Elizabeth, who used to run a forest school, has a vision for education that doesn't fit within the state model or 'classics' but is instead influenced by the 1960s counter-culture that questioned the basis of modern life:

> For me, education is to support freedom and to support spiritual development and to support goodness or a good life. Not a fake good life where you have things, an actual good life, where you live harmoniously, [...] you honour the cycles of nature, including your own cycles, and you

have an appreciation for life, and for other people's freedoms, and for community and for nourishing your body well, [...] where there's greater meaning in life than all of the challenges that we experienced during the day because there's something that is brightening and timeless and eternal that is in each of us, and we recognise that in one another. That's a good life.

This is a vision for education that may not mesh well with the needs of a digital future, or perhaps it is one that is needed more than ever because we have a digital future.

Despite the criticisms of public education from conservative organisations and the belief that it would be better without government interference, studies have found almost 90 per cent of children in the USA attend public education and about eight in ten parents are happy with that choice.[59] This is supported by research from the progressive NGO We Make the Future, as part of their 'freedom to learn' project, which found that 'by large margins', Americans support funding public schools so that 'every child gets an accurate and honest education, providing them with critical thinking skills and the freedom to pursue their dreams'.[60]

We ask a lot of our education system, our teachers and schools. Public education was designed as a means to smooth out inequalities, but it is now implicated in holding together the nation, reproducing it, representing 'truth', trying to create links between a past people argue over and a future no one can agree on. At the same time, it has to equip young people with the skills they need in a world that is rapidly changing, economically and socially. It reflects the contradictions and inconsistencies in parents' decision making: perhaps trading off dislike for Donald Trump for the promise that education may become a place where they won't have to worry about pronouns or having their children learn different values from their own. For Sally, as a teacher, 'it is mucky and as messy as it can be', but 'I still have faith in the public education system'. It is still a place that at least allows for the possibility of finding enough common ideals that enable us to live together.

There are other forms of faith and other sources of truth, however, that are having a profound impact not only on education but on politics and social attitudes, to gender in particular. America's future is being shaped by the tensions between freedom of and freedom from religion.

7

The many incarnations of Jesus Christ's love

God who gave us life gave us liberty. Can the liberties of a nation be secure when we have removed a conviction that these liberties are the gift of God?

Thomas Jefferson memorial, Washington, DC

Only two in all of history ever died for freedom all over the world: Jesus Christ and the American soldier.

T-Shirt slogan

Sunday morning, 9am, the First Presbyterian church in Dallas, Texas, and the service could not be farther in spiritual distance from the evangelicalism of AmFest in Arizona. There are some fifty people sitting on wooden pews, mostly older, mostly white, a few families with children. Everyone's hands are by their sides, and God is not demanding retribution for anyone's humiliation. Bell ringing marks the start of the service, followed by a classical music recital and morning announcements.

This is mainline reformed Protestantism, 'a tall steeple' church. Within its 160-year-old Grecian columns are stained-glass windows, a domed sanctuary, balcony and floor seating, with space for choir, organ, piano and pastor. There is also a preference for 'the marginalised and forgotten, the bound up, the oppressed, the put upon'. A social justice ministry serves the houseless, homeless and left behind. The church has gradually taken over its city block, with spaces for community and cultural activities, and plans for a café and recording studio. An old warehouse is being renovated as a small open-air amphitheatre where Sunday yoga is about to start after the church service.

Presbyterian doctrine directs its congregation to be 'the hands and feet' of God, with an ethic of service to the community. In a sermon designed to generate some discomfort with the world as it is, Reverend Amos Disasa reminds the congregation that our salvation comes with the salvation of others. The poor are 'weighed down by the pain of waiting' not just for equality but for everything: a bus, health care, decent schools. The slow grind of poverty while wealth races past. Yet the 'beat down', in Reverend Amos' world view, should demand the same dignity from us as they receive from Jesus Christ. The sermon ends with the Lord's Prayer, learned forty years ago and rarely spoken since, yet still it comes out word perfect from memory. 'Our father, who art in heaven …'

Across Christianity's varying manifestations, freedom is a universal theme. The bonds that hold us down may look different today, but they are still bonds; there are still those with power and those without; there are still states of unfreedom, now and forever more. Amen. In the doctrine of redemption and salvation, the enslaved will be liberated by the word of God, and that word is truth.

Yet this theology of freedom has diverged into separate canyons. Faint echoes of an opposing argument may occasionally seep through but quickly dissipates in the existential logics of who gets to own Jesus. Personal salvation, broadly evangelical, is pitted against the collective redemption of social justice approaches to Christian practice. For proponents of the latter, the Bible is read as divine but recognised as a product of the social context in which it was written. They know that its words are not infallible but trust that its message can be discerned in community.

For a range of Christian nationalists, on the other hand, America's freedom has been divinely ordained by the infallible word of God, and that transcendent truth determines what or who is or isn't permissible within the cultural borders of the USA. Purity is enforced within the public realm and private homes. Pastors and conservative commentators restate God's authority over a 'natural order' created by him, where laws, including man's inalienable freedoms, are absolute.

In the world view of Christian nationalism, the story of freedom in America can only be told in tandem with Christianity; one could not have happened without the other. The USA is the chosen land, the chosen people, ordained by God to bring freedom to the rest of the world as part of its manifest destiny. The narrative is transferred to the sacred texts of America's founding, the Declaration of Independence and the Constitution, now proxy for the word of God.[1] To battle the intangible forces of evil, it is necessary to 'destroy' enemies, an action that also appears at times as an attempt to assuage a sense of shame for practising faith in a supposedly secular country.

Contortions are required to reconcile Jesus 'the lamb of God', who takes away the sins of the world, the archetype of compassion, with Jesus the 'warrior', who brings divine retribution in a call to arms against those who have inflicted humiliation on his flock. The narrative goes something like: 'Good Christian people have been busy looking after their families and putting food on the table. We have turned the other cheek, but it's gotten us nothing. So we need to go on the offence to restore America's soul and save the country.'

There are now explicit calls for the ending of what separation of church and state remains in the USA, as the borders between secular and religious become borders between chaos and order.[2] If the USA is perceived as weak, it is because it has strayed from its path, and only by re-finding its moral core in the restoration of Judeo-Christian values will it 'heal' and be 'great' again. 'Only the church can save America', according to Charlie Kirk at TPUSA, who also argued in 2024 that it would be 'a desecration to the Lord' for a Christian to vote for Kamala Harris.[3] Former Vice-President Pence has explicitly stated that '[w]e must embrace that we are a Christian nation'.[4] For Ben Carson, founder of the American Cornerstone Institute, 'core biblical beliefs led our nation into unprecedented freedom and prosperity, and abandoning those beliefs led to the social decline we see today'.[5] Politicians, especially America First/MAGA aligned, must acknowledge their Christian faith in rallies and political advertising, thank 'our lord and saviour Jesus Christ' and exhort God to 'Bless America.'

Faith is required to reconcile God-given inalienable freedoms with the need to prescribe a God-given morality that curtails freedom. Conservative commentators square this circle by arguing that secular, liberal values do not produce freedom, and freedom in itself is not the purpose of our existence.[6] Instead, freedom is found in submission to God's will. The idea of moral limits is reflected in psychologist, author and political commentator Jordan Peterson's philosophy of responsibility. He argues that individual freedoms should be restricted in order to find salvation, and those restrictions can be guided by Judeo-Christian values:

> Freedom without responsibility is what a liberal West has adopted as its ideal, where any restrictive obligation is seen as preventing one from 'self-actualising'. Well, what the hell is left to actualise? What is left of you! You don't have a wife. You don't have any friends. You don't have any children. You don't take care of your parents. You don't have a job. Oh, now you're free are you? You're not free, you're lost. Well, you're free when you're lost, I suppose, because you can wander stupidly in any direction. *But that's not the sort of freedom you want.* [...] You can't have an autonomous Western individualist liberalism without the underlying Judeo-Christian conservatism surrounding it [my italics].[7]

It would seem contradictory for Peterson to dictate the 'sort of freedom' someone else might want. I have the freedom to make up my own mind. But this tension between freedom and restraint was widely debated among Christians I spoke with.

Steph lives in a cosy wooden A-frame on the western slopes of the Rocky Mountains. Seventy years old, an evangelical Christian and supporter of Trump, she is widowed and lives alone but has friends nearby. There are chocolate biscuits and tea for me on the table. At a nearby desk, genealogy charts set out an origin story tracing her family back to the *Mayflower*. 'They were Puritans,' she tells me, and there are the beginnings of tears to emphasise the importance of this connection. Tracing her family tree has been part of a wider project to discover 'the truth' about America, including its Christian heritage and her place in that story. 'I wondered why. Why was I a Christian and other family members weren't? And why did I have the more conservative viewpoint and others in the family [don't]?'

A little nervous, and unnecessarily apologising that her notes aren't well organised, Steph has prepared sheets of paper with quotations of freedom taken from the two books on the table: *The patriot's handbook of American liberty*, a version of the Constitution as a Christian history of America, and *The Founders' Bible*,[8] which links biblical passages with quotations from the Founding Fathers. Both texts emphasise that the Constitution is profoundly influenced by Christian teachings. For Steph, much of America's system of governance originates in the Bible: the book of Isaiah, she points out, establishes the USA's system of checks and balances.

Steph holds a sense of moral absolutism through her obedience to God's laws, with the Bible and Constitution (from the hand of God) as her guardrails. Yet the world still feels in flux. She refers to a popular John Adams quote circulated in the media landscape of Christian nationalism: America will only be good for a moral and religious people. Yet Steph notes, sadly, that 'we don't see the same kind of morality today'.

'Sadness' at the transformation of America is repeated throughout our conversation. Familiarity and tradition break down under the weight of alterations recited from the conservative playbook that Steph regularly hears on podcasts such as the *Charlie Kirk Show*: freedoms are being infringed upon, families are breaking down with divorce and gender fluidity. There is 'a lot of chaos', 'a lot of confusion' and 'complications'. There is a perceived lack of respect for former points of authority such as teachers and police, and nostalgia for days when education was 'more orderly'.

For Steph, the rules, based on the Constitution and the Ten Commandments, are being broken, 'and those people that want to reject those laws and be lawless, they are causing a lot of conflict in this country'. In her depiction of the moral decay of America, it is Antifa, BLM and fentanyl that have racked cities with 'more and more killings, more and more crime in general'. At the border, there are 'terrorists', 'drugs' and 'sex traffickers', undermining America's stability. In universities, nothing makes sense. Her daughter was an English major, 'and she started talking to me about ... I don't even remember the name of the ...'

I can guess what's coming next and venture ... 'postmodernity?'

> Oh yeah! [...] And I don't know where it all comes from. I think it comes from just the craziness of our world that there aren't absolutes, there aren't moral absolutes! That man can determine what his own truth is? [...] Moral absolutes are for our protection, not to make our lives miserable.

Once again, it's strange to hear postmodernity, this abstract academic theory that's been critiqued to within an inch of reality, becoming a topic of conversation in rural western USA. However, Steph's description of the decline of moral absolutes is a good synopsis of what French philosopher and postmodernist Jean Baudrillard argued:

> The liberated man is not the one who is freed in his ideal reality, his inner truth, or his transparency; he is the man who changes spaces, who circulates, who changes sex, clothes, and habits according to fashion, *rather than morality*, and who changes opinions not as his conscience dictates but in response to opinion polls. This is practical liberation whether we like it or not, whether or not we deplore its wastefulness and its obscenity [his italics].[9]

But while it possibly rankles to have a European academic calling out American culture as superficial, Steph's criticism of postmodernity, along with that of conservative commentators such as James Lindsay and Christopher Rufo noted in earlier chapters, is misplaced. Postmodernity doesn't bring an unruly world into being, it just describes it. For the record, I would argue it is hyper-capitalism that deserves much of the blame for the state of the world we have today.[10] As a theory, what postmodernity attempted to capture was an idea that our communities are shaped by the interplay of different ways of being in the world: different values, different belief systems. Texts, including Christian scripture, can only ever be products of their context and interpretations that potentially support different perspectives, including non-binary world views, porous borders and hazy ideas about purity. To be expansive in this way, to go beyond the pale, to allow more truths and more freedom after the death of master narratives, shifting moral boundaries in the process, can appear threatening. Those who have historically had power, may not want to lose it, share it or even budge up a bit and let others have a seat at the table.

With the removal of moral absolutes comes the placing of choice in our own fallible, sinful, hands; a reality discomforting for Steph. In order to navigate it she expresses a deep faith that God has a plan, set in the bedrock of an immutable truth that divides the world into those who accept it and those who don't.

Atheists, humanists and secularists may be mystified by this belief that as humans we are incapable of discerning what is good or right without the intercession of a deity. For Steph, however, it is a rational choice to turn to a God she has every faith will protect and provide for her. Decades ago, seeking solace and a way out from a life that, in her words, 'wasn't good' (relationship breakdown and general heartache), faith in God eased the pain. It was not an easy option. 'It was scary, because I didn't know what would happen. But I knew I didn't really have any other options here other than to trust God. It's a leap of faith. It takes a lot of faith. [...] So far he hasn't dropped me.'

Blessed are we for believing without having to see, for life cannot be assumed to happen randomly, especially when it causes pain. The dissonance of 'invisible', 'intangible' forces, disappearing borders, economic crises, foreign policy failures and cultural transformation, must have a cause. We must fill in the blanks as best we can with faith: in God, in family, in myth, in conspiracy, in the invisible hand of markets. A rational response perhaps when living in a time of too much information; to just follow the plan is a relief. As Annie Laurie Gaylor, co-founder and co-President of the Freedom from Religion Foundation (FFRF) puts it: 'It's kind of a frightening time, and when people don't feel in control they often want to cede that control to a deity.'

However, in submitting to God's laws, Steph sees change in her own life as a story of salvation: widowed, in her fifties, in debt, with no savings, 'God took care of me.' Her family's own hard work and planning may have contributed (an insurance policy, an inheritance, business success, work, loans, scholarships), but God gets the credit as a catalyst that enabled these things to happen. She still struggles with the idea of submission, but in her own experience it gives her 'a future and a hope'. 'Why would we think that we know more than God?'

Across the political spectrum of conversations that make up this book, there is a chronic lack of trust in government, media and civic institutions. So perhaps there is a degree of sense in Steph holding on to a God she trusts more than the seemingly arbitrary decisions of the state. 'I can put my trust in the government, or I can put my trust in God, what is the choice? [...] I don't want to have my freedoms infringed on okay.'

Placing trust in a moral order to protect freedom can be comforting when compared with the anxiety of a rapidly changing world, facing climate change, cycles of financial failure, artificial intelligence and so on. Anne, a member of a Catholic student association at an Indiana university, outlines the pessimism of her generation: 'I think part of that is uncertainty, like, just this anxiety floating there [...] because we don't know what's right.' The end result is ever more stressed students unable to cope, and a set of statistics well cited in the conservative landscape: that Gen Z appear to have more mental health and addiction issues.[11] Perhaps then some boundaries are a good thing. Anne reiterates that 'you can't do whatever you want. Like, doing whatever you want, is it necessarily like the best exercise of freedom you have?' In reconciling freedom with moral absolutism, having limits prevents us becoming a 'slave to sin', making us better people, more 'virtuous' and therefore more free.

What a relief then to have Steph's moral clarity. Her faith is rooted in a theology of freedom that sees humans as inherently sinful, 'wicked and desperate', in need of fixing, but with the grace of God available to us to set us free. 'So we have a choice of serving God and being saved for all eternity or serving the creature which is Satan or evil. We have the choice. That is a freedom, isn't it?'

I could say yes, but there is also the choice to get off our knees, to not believe in God, or to believe in God in such a way that the guilt of original sin is not front and centre in governing our lives. I do not say this to Steph though. At this point, nine months into my road trip, I had become used to the presence of God in conversations. Sitting in front of someone, with tea and cookies, moral absolutes could be held with grace in an effort to understand where they come from and what function they serve in someone's life.

But beyond the kitchen table, the seemingly incommensurable ways of experiencing faith have had profound political and social impacts. As Pastor Jessie Light-Wells from the First Presbyterian Church in Dallas puts it: 'I think we've gotten ourselves into a really sticky situation where I don't know what the way out is because we're reading scripture completely differently, with completely different authority placed in it.' She approaches me after the service that opened this chapter as I loitered in the airy, marbled foyer with a cup of Mardi Gras King Cake-flavoured coffee. It is part of her role at the church to welcome new people to the congregation, even those just passing through. We catch up later for a longer conversation, where she expresses the familiar concern that it is increasingly difficult to hold space for people with differing moral world views in the USA: 'What makes me probably the saddest is that freedom should be freedom to hold different understandings of the world, different understandings of God, different understandings of what it means to be in relationship with one another, but we're utterly failing at that right now.'

Believing theologically that evil is real and God is good, Pastor Jessie also believes that freedom is a large part of the way in which Christians should operate in the world. Aligning with Steph's views that we have free will, she argues that 'we are not beholden to a God who picks and chooses every single step of our lives, because a divine being would not deliberately lead us into suffering'. For Jessie, this means that freedom is a verb; it's something we do. We have the freedom to choose good, mercy, forgiveness and justice, but we also have the freedom to exploit and desecrate. The choice is ours.

There is divine, numinous, human contrariness to contend with in this exaltation of free will. Betty, a librarian and atheist member of a Free Thinkers group, believed she was raising her children to think critically, introducing them to different religions, but they converted to a Baptist church anyway. Betty also has to manage the guerrilla activism of church groups who steal books from her library, but she is defiant. 'I bet they read every word to see what to be mad about and they probably learned quite a bit, so I'm going to buy it again.'

Nathan, also a Free Thinker, was raised in a Catholic family and educated for three years in Catholic schools before he stepped away from the church on realising that 'this is not me'. Yet he married into a staunchly Catholic family, and his children attend Catholic schools. He is sceptical about the existence of free will when we are reduced to our fundamental biology but recognises that 'it's such a strong illusion, I'll live that way anyway'.

This begs the question if there is any difference then between faith in free will and the faith that Steph has in what the sceptics would regard as the 'strong illusion' of a God. To be atheist and sceptical about free will is to suggest that we have no real control over our lives; we are only the sum total of a network of electrical impulses racing across fatty tissues. We respond in nano seconds to the stimuli around us before consciousness kicks in to give some comfort that we have a degree of control.

The Free Thinkers can be found in Evansville, Indiana. The state itself is very rural, very red in the Republican sense and very Christian. The surrounding landscape is dotted with anti-abortion billboards and white wooden steeples. The city is so 'middle America' that many companies have market-tested products on its residents, assuming that if it works in Evansville it will work in the rest of the country. God is simply part of everyday conversation, starting with the questions 'which church?', 'which pastor?' when introduced to new people. In a diner, where I become 'hun', 'honey', 'sweetheart', 'sweetie', 'sugar', the chef has just returned from a Christian women's retreat and 'today is the first day of the rest of my life'. The story of her salvation is repeated to different customers as the lunch crowd ebbs and flows.

This overwhelming presence of God in daily life is the driver that brought together the Free Thinkers. Meeting in a library on the out-skirts of town, fittingly set like a bunker into a grassy bank, they feel somewhat under siege. Seeking fellowship with like-minded atheists, agnostics, humanists and sceptics, this group holds as an article of faith that 'the individual should neither accept nor reject ideas proposed as truth without recourse to knowledge and reason. Opinion should be formed on the basis of science and logic, without being influenced by authority, tradition, or any other dogma.'[12]

For holding this view, Betty feels they have to live 'in the shadows'. To be openly atheist is to invite segregation, for example children no longer being allowed to play with the neighbours when it's revealed they don't go to church. A mum was shut out of her daughter's gradu-ation because she didn't want to see the recitation of Christian prayers in a public school.

According to Gaylor, 'atheists are a little afraid to come out of the closet. Either they don't want to offend a religious neighbour, or they're afraid of retribution, or losing their job or business.' Along with her husband, a former pastor and now secular activist, Gaylor and FFRF have been campaigning since the 1970s against the encroachment of religion into the public realm. They educate about non-theism and defend the separation of church and state, debunking what they argue is the myth that America is a Judeo-Christian nation.

The national census points to an increasingly secular country, which might provide some comfort for atheists. From 2011 to 2021, the share of the population subscribing to a Christian faith fell from 75 per cent to 63 per cent.[13] A 2025 Pew Research Center study suggested that this share may have levelled out and remained stable over the previous five years (2019–2024), hovering between 60 per cent and 64 per cent, although eighteen to twenty-four year olds are less likely than older adults to identify as Christian.[14]

Yet while other Christian denominations have shrunk, the population identifying as evangelical has remained stable. A study by FFRF found that while the majority of Americans of Christian faith agree with the separation of church and state, white evangelical Christians are the least supportive. This is the group that Trump courted, along with young men, to pave his way back to the White House. The Gospel of Jesus Christ has been co-opted to suggest that he has a preference for nationalist populism.

It's important to note that not all evangelicals are Christian nationalists, and some evangelical churches are attempting to reclaim their faith from its association with that label.[15] However, the understanding of 'evangelical' is also shifting. A 2022 study highlighted that Republican Party supporters were identifying with the label even if not regular churchgoers, so closely has the party become associated with the term.[16] In addition, an increasing number of those with no attachment to Protestant Christianity, for example Catholics, Muslims, Hindus and the Church of Jesus Christ of Latter-day Saints, were also identifying as evangelical. Non-protestant evangelicals appeared more religiously devout, and to be religiously engaged and politically conservative equates with being evangelical, with or without belief in the divinity of Jesus Christ.[17]

This shifting set of alliances would suggest that while the USA is becoming more secular on paper, there's a strident conservative configuration with undue influence over politics. A loose coalition forms a moral cohort, consisting of religious and non-religious, fiscally and socially conservative supporters. This at times also includes an uneasy alliance with non-aligned voters on issues such as government overreach (e.g. the medical freedom movement).

This bringing together of differences in religious practice and doctrine, unified politically around ideas of Christian nationalism and National Conservatism, is a good example of how a common project can overcome the challenges of diversity. However, there are serious implications for US politics. Some Democrats, for example, were concerned during the 2024 election campaign about losing the largely Catholic Hispanic vote due to what was seen as their socially liberal policies. In the future, this could see the Democrats' support base in states with large Hispanic populations such as Texas and California dramatically shift.

The influence of the moral minority is highlighted by Gaylor, who argues that even as increasing numbers of Americans describe their belief as 'none', social acceptance of atheism has not improved. In their research, 'nones' tied with Muslims at the bottom of America's social hierarchy. The lack of influence is potentially linked to the largest percentage of 'nones' being younger people who have historically been less likely to vote. There was, however, some hope for change in their study, as a slim majority of Americans would now consider voting for an atheist, or agnostic at least, president or vice-president.

Despite the political influence of Christian nationalists under Trump's presidency, the shift towards increasing numbers of 'nones' fuels Christian nationalist claims that they are 'a persecuted minority'. Gaylor rolls her eyes at this one. 'Persecuted, how?' She has a good understanding of persecution, given that she has personally received death threats and harassment from those wishing to exile atheists like her. 'The typical thing we get told is you should leave. And we've been told that for almost fifty years [...]. We're being told we're not true Americans because we're not Christian.'

The breaking of God's laws, be it abortion, LGBTQI+ rights or promoting secularism, is felt as an existential threat by some. Making clear the strength of the binaries, Pastor Jessie notes that to disagree is interpreted as hate: 'It's either you hate God and you hate babies or you love God and love babies and those are the only options.' Sides are entrenched in the oft-quoted lines from Revelations 3:16–18: '[B]ecause you are lukewarm, and neither cold nor hot, I will vomit you out of my mouth.' Take a stand one way or the other. If you're not with God, you're against him.

To keep from giving or taking offence, atheists talk of avoiding the topic of God in 'mixed' company, but this is only a temporary solution to feelings of discomfort. Borders are being reset. The establishment of a conservative majority on SCOTUS, with three new appointments during Trump's first term in office, has caused the border between a secular and Christian nation to slip further, subverting the checks and balances between government branches.

Conservative organisations such as Advancing American Freedom, the Alliance Defending Freedom and the America First Policy Institute have used the law as a strategy to drive change. In 2022 and 2023, SCOTUS made several decisions on cases with national ramifications, with the result that Christian belief now has primacy over the right to not be discriminated against, particularly affecting the queer community.[18] These decisions have impacted on where God gets to appear in his proxies of prayers and flags, brought private religious practice into public spaces such as schools, and emphasised a Christian God in a public realm of many faiths and none.

While conservative media hailed these SCOTUS decisions as a 'resounding victory', Gaylor describes them as 'heart-breaking' and 'disastrous'. At least half of the 2,000 to 5,000 complaints FFRF receive a year refer to religious practices being carried out in public schools (e.g. prayers at assemblies), but their ability to take action is being eroded. Gaylor reminds me that the USA was the first country to adopt a constitution that's godless, with a preamble that begins not with investing sovereignty in a divinity but in 'we the people'. 'There is no God in our Constitution, and that was deliberate.' But as Steph's *Founders' Bible* and Christian nationalist organisations make clear, while God may not be named explicitly in the founding documents, there is widespread faith that the Founding Fathers' hands were guided by him.

For the Free Thinkers, the result of these changes has been the institutionalising of a regime in which Americans live with 'freedom of religion, but not from religion'. Free Thinker Nathan sees no problem with people wanting to pray on a sports field, for example, if it's personal practice – 'say hi to your imaginary friend, it's none of my business'. But it's the requiring of non-believers or non-Christians to participate that is problematic. That 'requiring' may not be an explicit demand, but there is a need to be a strong swimmer to go against dominant cultural currents, to stand out in a crowd that is kneeling.

The influence of Christian nationalism has grown in the time between Trump's terms in office. As a movement, it is laser-focused, well funded and patient. The overturning of Roe v. Wade was decades in the making. But organisations like the Southern Poverty Law Center (SPLC) and FFRF argue that the political resurgence of Christian nationalism is a threat to freedom in the United States.[19] The push back against the separation of church and state is more than just a theological argument but aligned with social transformations that would impose a moral world view restricting freedoms, particularly for women and the queer community.

It is a difficult task then for a counter-balancing form of liberation theology, working to measure faith in acts of justice and equality. Pastor Jessie feels 'an ongoing, semi-conscious state of dread triggered by witnessing the local and global demise of care for neighbours'. It has become much clearer to her that 'freedom is increasingly a privilege and not a right'.

Some weeks after the service in Dallas, I manage to catch up with Reverend Amos online. His father, raised by Presbyterian missionaries, brought his family to the USA from Ethiopia, and Amos was raised in the church. There was never a time in his life when he wasn't Presbyterian. 'Yeah, it runs in the blood for me.' His faith centres on the idea that God is less interested in a personal relationship but instead calls on all of us to participate in the work of repairing broken systems and the people they break. In holding this theological view, he wants us to reassess the assumption that we are all born sinners:

If you were to go back and say 'actually we are an expression of the divine', God cannot create something that's inherently tarnished, then how would we situate ourselves? How would we choose to relate to others? How would we structure our economic markets? To what degree [would] we protect the vulnerable, right, if we saw them all as, not sinners yet to be redeemed, but we saw them as little gods walking around everywhere?

In Reverend Amos's teachings, 'God is political, Melissa.' This is more my kind of God. I was brought up in a mainstream Protestant tradition, but God and I have parted ways, except for a lingering belief that Jesus was a political radical who sought the overthrow through non-violent means of an oppressive system of religious and political power. Not the sentimental shepherd of my Sunday school, perfect and blameless, but a community organiser actively engaged in political speech, speaking truth to power that ultimately led to his assassination. According to Amos, this sacrifice 'was a model for us to liberate ourselves from the death and darkness of empire', that is, power and inequality. Or, more simply, we should not forsake our freedom for the convenience that empire offers.

There is a convergence at times with TPUSA in this language of sacrifice, but different kinds of losses are called for. Charlie Kirk and other conservative, Christian nationalist commentators want us to delay gratification, give up the booze and sex, but submit to free market capitalism as well as God. For Reverend Amos, the sacrifice is more total: 'If we want to liberate people from poverty we've got to change the way in which we live' and address the systems that create inequality.

This call is also taken up within Baptist traditions. Friendship-West Baptist Church (FWBC) sits in the southern suburbs of Dallas, at the end of a long drive through suburbia marked by expressways and endless sprawl: strip malls, convoluted flyovers and four-leaf clovers, hoardings for accident lawyers and election candidates. A mega-church with a congregation capacity of 12,000, FWBC stands surrounded by dry, empty fields and a mammoth parking lot. BLM and other Black activist banners hang from the roof. Images of Frederick Douglass adorn the foyer. Operating an 'early voting' station (there are local and state elections in Texas at the time), the armed security guard lets

me in and guides me into the back offices to meet Reverend Danielle Ayers, Pastor of Justice. She is passionate, articulate, energetic, working with the congregation to make the connection between scripture and poverty: addressing poor education, lack of affordable housing, voter suppression and seemingly simple things like access to good food (it's a thirty-minute walk along a busy road from my hotel to reach any fresh fruit and even longer distances in the food deserts of the suburbs).

Tinkering around the edges of America's social and physical infrastructure is not enough. Nor is it enough to just pray in a one-to-one relationship with God. FWBC engages in the public square with acts of charity and demands for justice for their primarily Black community. Connecting the political and the structural to the personal practice of faith and their interpretation of Christian justice, the church aims to be deeply engaged in how laws and policies are constructed before they are implemented. For Reverend Danielle, this work is necessary because those laws and institutions have created a social hierarchy in terms of who is more deserving and entitled to resources, including freedom.

Freedom is not a term Reverend Danielle uses or feels affinity with. It's loaded, abused. Life, liberty and the pursuit of happiness 'depends on who you're talking to [...]. It may be freedom for some, but not freedom for all.' Instead, a key action is dealing with 'the sin of racism', and the crucial term is justice. She invokes 'just relationships with self, others and our social structures', quoting the book of Micah, verses 6 and 8.

In this Christian tradition, to have a sense of liberation is to live where the Black community can flourish, where they can build lives in homes with equal mortgage rates, vacationing with children who attend good schools, sending them to college, not worrying about whether a son, husband, brother will get home safely. Liberation is in advocating for sidewalks, lighting, code enforcement, infrastructure that works and voting safely (why the need for an armed security officer at a polling station, you may have asked, if you are lucky enough to live in a country where this isn't necessary). This is a theology in which God cares about what happens to lives between Sunday mornings, providing fellowship and belonging in an atomised city as a model for that 'beloved community' Dr Martin Luther King Jr, also a Baptist minister, talked about. This is a vision for America 'where your

systems and institutions are structured in such a way that breathes life and that don't harm. They heal.'

Pastor Jessie also expresses criticism of an economic and social system that 'only value bodies and doesn't value people, that strips people of their humanity'. But she also recognises that she participates in that same system. 'I think it's hard when your entire country functions with one system to break out of that.' Again, you have to be a strong swimmer to go against a cultural current. As centres of immense wealth and influence in a country with minimal levels of social welfare, churches can provide aid where the state does not. But even within institutions with a social justice tradition, there are schisms over the politics of change. It is not only Christian nationalism that has harmed communities; traditional or more conservative strands of mainline churches have played a part as well. Wielding cultural power, the preservation of collective purity in institutions of the church takes precedence at times over individual compassion.

The most ubiquitous targets of the desire for moral absolutism are, not surprisingly, related to that messiest of boundary incursions ... sex and sexuality. So much time and money goes into policing sex and sexuality. If only religious institutions worried as much about violence against women as they do about our sex lives. For some churches, anything except abstinence, or sex within heterosexual marriage, is outside the bounds of purity and threatening to the entire edifice of civilisation, as seen in the commentary in Chapter 5. Therefore, those who transgress these boundaries can be condemned, shamed, told they're sinful and further subjugated.

To reinforce these moral boundaries, churches can also wield financial power and property ownership. Some religious centres have threatened legal action against other institutions such as universities, to force restrictive policies, particularly around sex and sexuality. For example, on the basis that they are moral role models, some campus ministries and teaching orders have required staff and teachers to sign covenants promising not to engage in or condone LGBTQI+ lifestyles.

This binding of faith with the desire for moral order raises a cultural inconsistency in America's conservative Christianity, particularly Christian nationalism. It asserts a religious orthodoxy in public life to which all must conform, while simultaneously proffering the ideal of freedom centred on individualism. The latter would not include the personal choice of whom to love, whom to sleep with in the privacy of my home, whether to marry, when to have children or not to have any.

Restrictions on freedom of choice, or the freedom to use our bodies in ways of our own choosing, impel us to live within limits. Yet while honoured by God in some interpretations of biblical texts, such purity raises the question of what people are trying to preserve, and it's not a great leap of faith for that language to be co-opted into white supremacy and replacement theory. Like laws once forbidding inter-racial marriage, restrictions on sex and gender are designed to keep people in place.

At its best, a community of worship can temper selfishness, holding in check the tenets of individualism, while rituals of caring for others moderate desire for instant gratification. Faith can undergird incredible resilience, such as surviving incarceration. However, such fellowship is held in tension with the impulse to separate out those who do not accept the word of God, or practice it differently, reserving God's love for his chosen people, as Steph believes:

> God has a plan for our country. I want to believe that. Sometimes I'm not so sure whether or not we're in the end times, I don't know. But I know that God is in control and that he is working out his plan. [...] He says that he will take care of us and he will not allow evil to be false. That's for believers, though. That's not for just anybody.

It is unfair to assume that all evangelical Christians 'are so wrapped up in the one book that they can't get any information or thoughts of their own', as one of the Free Thinkers suggests. Steph, with her desire for moral absolutes, is also compassionate, kind and reflexive, noting the limits of her knowledge on some issues. Yet still there is little sign of a middle ground in which theological positions can converge.

Reverend Amos's understanding of the drivers of moral absolutism resolves into existential concern. 'I think the fear is that they'll be forgotten. [...] Not really them as much as their way of being in the world.' To be forgotten is not just to lose privileges; it is to no longer be recognised as having worth, magnifying the question of 'why am I here', 'what is the point of me'. Like other conversations,

Amos dates this fear to the 1960s and 1970s, the Civil Rights Movement, with racial and social boundaries shifting 'at a pace that wasn't comfortable to everybody, especially I think white Americans. The ground beneath their feet ... many of them felt as if the shifts were so sudden.'

The speed and depth of change feels like it's only increasing, ratchetting up tensions between the secular and the religious, and making the evaluation of our moral choices ever more difficult. What is moral in a world of artificial intelligence or environmental collapse? Without a solid master narrative incorporating components of justice and equality, ideas about what it means to be good and what a good future looks like start to blur. Reflections on fellowship and theology also raise the fundamental interrogation of what we are supposed to do with our freedom, segueing into the eternal question of why religion exists in the first place: why am I here, why do we suffer, what's the point of life and what happens when we die? As long as we are asking those questions, people are going to gather and talk about it, whether in church (or a religious institution of your choice), or in a library as part of a group of Free Thinkers.

What Jordan Peterson, cited earlier, was unintentionally emphasising is not that a Judeo-Christian framework is necessary as a source of freedom but that freedom is found in relationship with others. In Peterson's own words: 'wife', 'friends', 'children', 'parents' (in my words, insert relationships of your choice, it's the affection that matters, not the label). Families of all sorts, communities of all descriptions, underpinned by different philosophies and books, are also a source of freedom. The truth that takes away the sins of the world seems an impossible project to agree on, but by the grace of whichever God you choose to believe in or not, collectively we carry on.

As I pack up to leave Steph's house, she offers me a copy of the *Patriot's handbook* and the Declaration of Independence. She has spares. I add them to my collection. Later that evening, I'm invited back for drinks with the neighbours, and so we end in front of Steph's A-frame: a couple of atheists, a couple of evangelical Christians and a socially liberal one, having sundowners around another fire pit as the sun sets over the mountains. We avoid talk of religion and politics. Scaling up from cake and tea and fire pits is necessary, but in this moment we who are inherently fallible are also divine. Recalling the words Reverend Amos used to finish his service back in Dallas, in this place, at this time, 'you have been set free'.

8

How to become a libertarian: 'Don't hit other people, don't take their stuff and keep your promises'

In the autumn of 2022, Britain became the site of a libertarian experiment. Prime Minister Liz Truss and Chancellor Kwasi Kwarteng announced a 'mini' budget that would 'unchain Britannia' though uncosted tax cuts. The free market wasn't impressed. Interest rates skyrocketed, and Truss was gone in forty-five days. The country was left with an economic mess: a fall in the value of sterling and increased costs of government borrowing and mortgages for millions. Intervention from the Bank of England was required to stabilise the economy. Embedded in the trans-Atlantic cultural switchboard, Truss blamed the 'Deep State' for preventing her project, and accountability disappeared into a maw of excuses. She has since continued to hawk her account of her time in office at conservative and America First events in the USA and publicly supported Trump's return to office.

This is not the first libertarian experiment to have gone awry. In New Hampshire, a state with the official motto 'live free or die', in the mid-2000s libertarians took over the government of a small town (Grafton, population 1,000-ish), reducing public services such as libraries and road maintenance.[1] The result was not a state of utopian freedom but rather, as journalist Matthew Hongoltz-Hetling has reported, the decline of civic behaviours such as recycling and an increase in uncivic behaviours such as crime.[2] As members of the community liberated their waste management practices, bears found ready sources of food, with inevitable consequences.

In Texas, another state famous for its sense of independence and libertarian-leaning governance, a severe winter storm in 2021 caused misery for millions. A disjointed, deregulated power grid was unable to cope with the excess demand created by freezing conditions that lasted over eight days. At its worst, some ten million were without power, resulting in over 200 deaths. Poorer areas were the most severely affected.[3] Despite such setbacks, which might suggest that government regulation can be useful, libertarian philosophy continues to influence political, economic and social infrastructure in the USA. It is often expressed as a culture of individualism, although as we will see in the conversations to come, it's more complicated than people simply choosing to live 'off grid'.

To abridge the canon,[4] we are each free to define our own life and what's important to us. Libertarianism regards individuals as sovereign, created equal with 'natural' rights to life, liberty and property that are best operationalised in free markets, with as little government regulation as possible. The Declaration of Independence's 'pursuit of happiness' is replaced with property as the natural right taking precedence over ephemeral emotions. Property is the result of an individual's investment of part of their life (time and energy) and is therefore an extension of that life and must be protected in the same way. For libertarian theorist David Friedman (son of Milton Friedman), 'the institutions of private property are the machinery of freedom'.[5] Public goods or property, like education or a national health service, impose majority values on individuals and can be squandered if used in ways other individuals may disapprove of. With private property, on the other hand, we can each seek out our own needs, as long as we can bear the cost.

Libertarianism fuses with narratives of the American Dream. Anyone can make it in the USA: it just requires hard work and the government to get out of the way. Politically, we can vote for a government to safeguard our freedoms, but those freedoms are natural and therefore supersede any government. For David Boaz, author of *The libertarian mind: A manifesto for freedom*, 'the most important political value is liberty, not democracy'.[6] Any attempt by governments to take away individual decision making also takes away the freedom and dignity of the individual. Therefore, it is the exercise of power by governments that requires justification and never the exercise of individual freedom.

However, freedom within the purview of libertarianism is not just an economic or political concept. It is also a state of moral autonomy containing a commentary on the 'character' and 'quality' of people: how to be virtuous. As the libertarian activists Linda and Morris Tannehill argue, 'without free choice, morality is impossible'.[7] The good citizen is one who engages in the virtuous choices of being productive and self-sufficient, taking responsibility for actions, being entrepreneurial, making rational decisions. Principles of justice are necessary in order to ensure free and fair rules-based exchange: don't hit people, don't take their stuff, keep your promises. For some libertarians, being virtuous is a moral obligation to work towards preserving and expanding freedom for everyone.

Libertarians believe it is not an excess of individualism or private property that has eroded virtue but rather government infringing on individual rights. Expansive government undermines the moral character necessary for both civil society and freedom. Taking anything from the government, including welfare or a Universal Basic Income, creates less virtuous citizens, as people forgo developing good habits such as fiscal prudence and self-reliance.

Morally, libertarianism opposes any form of coercion and has confidence that people can make rational decisions about their own lives, respecting the equal rights of others. Cue the oft-repeated Golden Rule: 'My rights end where your nose begins.' This position is bolstered by perhaps one of the most well known of libertarians, Ayn Rand. Author of *Atlas shrugged* and *The virtue of selfishness*, among other works, the Russian-born Rand challenged all forms of 'irrationalism, self-sacrifice, brute force, and [Soviet-style] collectivism that have brought centuries of chaos and misery into the lives of millions of individuals'.[8]

While Soviet authoritarianism may be an extreme example, the possibility that I can't live the life I want without shifting someone's nose out of the way does require a limited role for government, for example to uphold the rule of law. As noted in previous conversations, freedom has its boundaries. But having set out the rules that allow people to pursue their version of good, government intervention should only be necessary to ensure that one person's freedom doesn't infringe on another's. As long as someone is capable of self-governance and making rational decisions then they should be able to determine their own life without the use of force or fraud.

Libertarians favour a non-aggression pact, and violence only used in self-defence, as conflict disrupts peaceful productivity. There may be a military but only for defence against external threats. John Stuart Mill elaborated on the idea of 'the harm principle' in his 1859 work *On liberty* as core to governing a free society. No authority has the right to interfere with an individual's beliefs or actions, no matter how stupid, unless that person is causing harm to others.

Where there is conflict over competing rights, it's because of a distinction between those that are 'phoney' and 'natural'. There should be no conflict over the genuine rights of life, liberty and property in a free society; however, there are conflicts over 'phoney rights', or 'interests and preferences' as Boaz describes them.[9] These include demands for education, health care and social security. We have no natural right to these things. To avoid conflict, they are best obtained on the free market rather than provided by a government, as argued in the libertarian case against public education (Chapter 6).

There is a vision in libertarian thought of 'peaceful, evolutionary progress' that 'naturally results from free men trading in an open market'.[10] Where there is conflict, markets will provide corrections. Where there is inequality, markets will allow for the redistribution of wealth to even things out. As the nineteenth-century anarchist Pierre-Joseph Proudhon declared, in a line often quoted by libertarians: '[L]iberty is not the daughter but the mother of order.' As people are allowed to interact freely, and their rights to liberty and property are protected, then order will emerge not only in economic markets but in civil society as well. Free markets are 'morally superior', their virtue found in productive labour, respect for the dignity of work and the elimination of poverty.[11]

In terms of social functions, libertarians generally argue that collective agreement on values is not possible. There is a degree of honesty in their assessments of human nature in that utilitarian approaches to organising society have a tendency to not work so well for minorities, who are more likely to lose out to the majority. Inequalities, when they exist, are best dealt with through models of mutual association, decentralised and most effective at the local scale. The libertarian-leaning Freedom Conservatism movement, for example, recognises that 'families, religious congregations, commercial and civic associations, local communities are the social institutions that matter most'.[12]

Most importantly, it is the ability to freely associate, rather than be subject to coercion, that reduces social conflict. A free society is a community-of-communities, by-passing the state as much as possible, with cooperation between individuals and associations backed by contracts and the rule of law. Less government leads to fewer conflicts as protagonists with different values are not forced to cooperate or compromise in order to access political power.

In summary, the answer to contemporary problems such as crime, climate change, racism, defence, welfare, health care, environment and social division is always: less government, free markets, private property, giving people choice and allowing them the freedom to take responsibility for their actions. Regulations, according to libertarians, lead to waste, weigh down economic growth and create conflict. Free markets will move towards stability and equilibrium through a 'natural' harmony of interests among peaceful people in a 'just' society. Supported by property rights and the rule of law, free markets should lead to greater prosperity and consumer satisfaction as individuals freely exchange goods and services with other actors, and prices are guided by an 'invisible hand'.[13] As a result, the efficient functioning of society should emerge 'spontaneously', according to Boaz, out of the coordinated actions of thousands or millions of individuals ... in theory.

But the smooth ordering of economic and social functions is not real life. Culture eats theory and ideology for breakfast when it comes to power and who gets to decide the rules. When Adam Smith was writing *The wealth of nations* in the 1770s, women had no vote, no property rights and were not considered equal. Spontaneous order only emerged among men, apparently, and the idea that freedom as a principle of economic and social order came first from Europe might come as a surprise to other societies.[14] While Boaz believes that the free market is 'morally superior' and a timeless principle of the American Revolution, it could be argued that the economy pre- and post-Revolution was extensively reliant on enslaved labour.[15] The women of the maquiladoras in El Paso may also disagree. An alternative view is that free market capitalism now lives off the productive labour of people and the planet.[16]

Society operates on the principle of a palimpsest: there is no tabula rasa or blank slate on which we all start from an equal footing. Economic systems don't emerge like spontaneous combustion but over the time it takes to forge everyday practices and relationship networks underpinned by a set of beliefs whose reason for existence we have generally long forgotten. Always existing vested interests with the power to direct change highlight the impossibility of spontaneous order.

An individual is embedded in a social network that requires negotiation with many other individuals, and we don't all have equal access to assets that level the playing field, such as health care and education. Back to the discussion in Chapter 1, some have more freedom than others. Always have, and probably always will. As economist Joseph Stiglitz argues in *The road to freedom* (a take on free market advocate Friedrich Hayek's *The road to serfdom*), freedom for those with power does not necessarily translate into freedom for anyone else. The central tenets of libertarian freedom such as 'rights' and 'choice' can only ever be understood within the context of unequal negotiations. To be free is to already be in a position of power, which complicates decisions about where my rights end and your nose begins.

In other words, there's nothing 'natural' about individual freedom, and 'rights' are not an immutable truth. Rather than 'natural', rights and choices can be the product of an array of human biases, frailties, general anxieties, baked-in privileges and prejudices – qualities that begin to impact on how our economic and social theories are operationalised in practice. The faith that libertarians have in our ability to be rational decision makers, for example, can be countered by the work of psychologist and behavioural economist Daniel Kahneman, who has pointed out that humans are not always very good at being rational.[17] Psychological and environmental factors, cultural frames of reference, all influence our daily interactions with each other. There is no escaping emotions such as love and hate, nor the tensions between the need for self-actualisation and the need to cooperate with others.

Libertarianism in theory, therefore, must work within the reality of our messy lives, which is what members of the Libertarian Party attempt to do on a daily basis. And what better place to cross-examine their efforts than in that bastion of libertarianism, Dallas, Texas: a city steeped in my 1980s televised imagination as a place of big hair and shoulder pads. In reality, there are fewer Stetsons but plenty of SUVs and urban sprawl.

Alex was a local organiser and member of the Libertarian Party for over twenty years. We arrange to meet in a suburban café to the north of Downtown. The conversation carries over into a second evening a few days later in a barbecue joint in east Dallas, requiring the navigation of expressways, flyovers, spaghetti junctions and strip malls. My Lyft driver is an Iranian man in his early thirties who dropped out of his PhD programme in Florida, worked in South Carolina to get his green card and is now trying to find a job in Dallas because his friends are here. He asks if I like the city. 'Not really, too many cars,' I say, 'but everyone is friendly.' Random strangers really do say 'hello' and ask how I'm doing. He laughs, and I know what comes next. 'That's because you're white.' Fair enough.

The libertarians I am meeting are mostly men, twenty to seventy years old, and we spread out over several tables. Some are heavily engaged in the party, standing at state and federal elections knowing they have no chance of winning. They could though, in a two-party system with an electoral college, generate enough votes to impact the prospects of Democrat or Republican candidates.[18]

Adherents to libertarianism are as factionalised as those of any other political ideology. Some are 'Republicans with libertarian tendencies.' Some voted for Trump and may do so again in 2024, arguing that he has policies that reflect libertarian values such as getting out of overseas wars. Some prefer the label 'anarchist'. They are scientists, professors, managers, financial advisors, sex industry workers, musicians, IT consultants and retirees.

Their pathways to libertarianism are as diverse as their occupations: cryptocurrency, personal introspection and reading the canon, finding the party 'that thinks the way I do' after a random internet search. One joined in 1973, after his first Young Americans for Freedom convention in Washington, DC. Another was inspired as a young man by Han Solo from *Star wars*, the quintessential anti-authority renegade. They don't always agree. They talk across each other and, occasionally, sweetly, finish each other's sentences. They are 'practical libertarians' with a couple of 'pragmatic anarchists' thrown in, working through the theoretical limitations, although there is agreement on the essentials. There are inherent 'natural' rights, individual choice is paramount, the state should have a minimal role and free markets are the solution.

Alex, an engineer, introduces libertarianism as 'fiscally conservative, socially liberal' but recognises this is simplistic. At its heart for all of them is the individual, who should decide their own path 'in as many contexts as possible': financial, social, personal, sexual. 'I run my own life, I do things myself, I am the champion of my own direction.' And who among us has not at some point articulated this idea when being told what to do by an over-bearing government, family, partner. There is something ineffable about the desire to say: 'Don't tell me what to do.'

Barry takes a more abstract, philosophical view of freedom, viewing it as fundamentally 'an essential component' of the individual, 'part of a boundary that defines identity'. To be free is not simply something that's 'nice'. Barry's pragmatism is the realisation that while they aim to find workable ways to reduce government, he recognises that 'if we try to do it all at once we're gonna fall off the cliff'. Advice Truss and Trump could have taken in their attempts to reorient a national economy.

Gary takes this further in making the less popular claim that 'nobody believes in absolute freedom'. He has 'life, liberty and property' tattooed on his leg. The Statue of Liberty is tattooed on his back. 'Property' for him refers not just to goods and services but self-ownership as well. 'Your body is something that is sovereign ... you are your own property.' Life, liberty and property can come into conflict with each other, but Gary keeps them in that order of priority.

For some, these inalienable rights are part of a secular morality, including a duty to work towards a society where there are no unjust hindrances to achieving freedom. Others feel freedoms are bestowed by God, if then rationalised by economists and philosophers. Rand was an atheist. Bob is Pentecostal – 'I'm about as extreme as you get as a Christian and I see no conflict' – although he was an atheist for a time. Kevin also believes that natural rights are 'given by God':

> God picked Adam and Eve out of the garden and said, 'You're gonna suffer and you're gonna work hard', and he didn't give him any extra rules. He just kicked them out there. They went on about their business and built cities and made decisions and discussed what was right and wrong and made good medicines and hurt each other and built things and created the civilisation that we have.

The depiction of life as something centred on 'suffering', 'hard work' and self-reliance is part of a stereotype that they are well aware of. They are criticised as 'selfish' for not wanting welfare; they are criticised as unpatriotic for calling for an end to overseas wars. The stereotype is perpetuated by the argument that 'an important part of freedom is not having to make sacrifices for people who don't have to make sacrifices for you'.[19] Sacrifice, according to the Tannehills, 'is always wrong', because it is destructive of the life and well-being of the individual who sacrifices.[20] This sits in contradiction to the talk of 'sacrifice' that permeates America's media and political landscape. Past military sacrifice made in the name of freedom is lionised; America First/MAGA call for present and future sacrifice in order to achieve American greatness again. The debate centres on the idea of 'a morality of self-interest', but the image of staunch, uncaring individualism conjured up by this argument is unfairly applied, according to Joe:

> We do believe in individual rights being paramount and not being infringed upon. We also see the advantage of working cooperatively together. The whole idea of a free market is the idea that most people aren't living off the grid on a farm with their chickens, sustaining themselves. They need to take the limited amount of things they can do, turn that into something, and exchange that with somebody else to get the things that they want.

The founding principle of Protestant self-sufficiency has always had to be balanced with the need for exchange. There is an acknowledgement that we live in complicated, interdependent societies, with some libertarians advocating for a form of 'social power', protecting the desire to volunteer, for charity or profit, without state interference. There is even talk of love in David Friedman's work, as a means to get what we want at the end of the day.[21] As Alex notes, 'libertarians are very big on volunteerism'. Voluntary, mutual aid societies, as described by Alexis de Tocqueville, were a feature of nineteenth-century America.[22] The community, the collective, therefore, is a moral component of libertarianism. Kevin is standing for election in an area of urban sprawl and poverty, but what he sees are people 'helping each other, they work together, they build up communities, they keep their money in the community, they buy local there. That's great. That's freedom of choice. That's freedom of association, that's freedom of commerce, and they're collectively, corporately making their lives better.' Such mutual association could be framed as an economy of affection, an idea I'll return to when exploring the Midwest.

The problem with love, however, as part of an economic principle, is that its range is limited. All the components and processes in the production chain of Adam Smith's pin factory, for example, can't happen just in the name of altruism or love for another person.[23] So there must be trade in order to achieve our ends, framed as rational rather than affectionate, centred on the question of 'what benefit do I get out of this exchange?' Boaz is blunt: society and cooperation should be driven by markets, contracts and rule of law, rather than emotion.[24] While Joe, for example, may be 'very much concerned about the welfare of other people. [...] Obviously, if I can do something, forgive me, and make a buck doing it, there's no sin, there's no moral deficiency.' Ultimately, for Joe, it's no one else's business. 'If I would work for Gary for a dollar an hour, and I was satisfied with that, if that was the best option for me, then it's nobody else's business. He's happy, I'm happy.'

Again, in the reality of messy lives, the question of mutual advantage in these exchanges is problematic. Not everyone has the choice to walk away if they are unhappy. Conversely, if Joe was to gather others being paid a dollar and form a union, in solidarity they could perhaps increase that dollar to a living wage. Choice, stick or twist, can be determined by looming starvation, moral trade-offs and/or avoiding shame. It's never so simple as 'he's happy, I'm happy'.

For others, like Richard, cooperation should be more muscular. 'I completely agree in cooperation, but it's like the Gadsden flag, "don't tread on me". [...] You don't kowtow to somebody, you stand up.' Rick repeats a trope I hear multiple times, particularly at America First/ MAGA events: '[H]ard times make good men, and good men make good times, and good times make bad men, and on the story goes, and I think we're all just kind of soft.'[25] This is a useful overview of the continuous dynamics of release and restraint in societies, but it's also a view of contemporary America as a place now pampered by welfare and public services, losing its frontiersmen, its Han Solos, its brave and free.

While the argument for reducing social benefits rests on a sense of care, the idea that welfare recipients are hurt in the long run, there is also judgement. Welfare is 'nicing people to death'; those that depend on the state are 'unimaginative' and 'neutered'. Among libertarian writers, there is a tendency to over-generalise the ineffectiveness of the public sector and project opinions such as Boaz's observation that 'people who don't own property don't take care of it as well as owners'.[26]

Rudy grew up in what he describes as Section 8 housing, in a low-income family, in an area 'riddled with drugs and gun violence'.[27] He was surrounded by welfare:

> Rudy: Most people are there because they've accepted that the government is gonna help, it's gonna help them become dependent and essentially become neutered as people. [...] [It's] all they know because their parents did it, they've done it and that's just the way it is. When you see people like literally stuck in this limbo they become like crabs in a bucket [...] anybody trying to get out gets pulled back in and they've accepted that that's existence. [...] [T]he few that get out of it is usually ... there's commerce through drugs, and things like that.
> MB: But you got out.
> Rudy: Yeah. Well, for me, I got lucky. I was lucky in the sense that ... I got out because I found something different.

He started playing music, started travelling, had a child. 'Seeing my friends and family and being like, "Okay, I'm gonna be exactly like them, and I don't like them," or I'm going to leave them. And so I actively made the choice to leave them.' There was luck and there was agency. Now, he argues that if the government is removed as a safety net, then those communities would be better off as they learn to support themselves with help from associations that can provide food and financial subsidies.

Joe pushes back against the idea that they possess a solipsistic view of human nature, stressing instead that libertarians want freedom for everyone, and for everyone to enjoy the 'natural consequences' of those freedoms, good and bad. All should be free to say and do what they want, but with that comes the virtue of responsibility and acceptance of the consequences. Libertarians advocate for the decriminalisation of drugs, for example. While Joe recognises that drug choice is not a benign decision, 'those decisions are not mine to enforce [on] somebody else'. Make bad decisions and reap the consequences. 'It's liberty to the max, right!' You can have as much freedom of choice as you want, but you're also going to have the consequences of those actions.

Some mental gymnastics are required to balance 'liberty to the max' with 'self-regulation', that is, the recognition that people should follow some rules, just not ones enforced by a government. According to Barry, 'to the extent [people] don't control themselves they lose identity and integrity and wholeness as people, and they take on the nature of puppets. Their humanity is diminished.' For me, this is a bleak view of humanity, tying in with the idea that the government, particularly social security programmes, 'neuter' people. But the philosophy underpins why Barry argues 'we are morally obligated to work toward preserving and expanding freedom', so that as many people as possible can utilise freedom to the max without negative consequences.

In their own analysis, the group picks up on some of the inconsistencies and shortcomings of libertarianism in theory and in practice. There is recognition of inequalities. Everyone agrees that some have more freedom than others, related to money, race and gender. Rand called it the 'aristocracy of pull' – the unwillingness of elites to let go of privileges while restricting others' freedoms.[28] Otherwise known as structural inequality. In recognising the need for social capital as well as money, Rick knows that 'not everyone is gonna start from the same starting point. We just think the government is a really lousy venue or a medium for that to take place.' There has to be negotiation about where rights end and other people's noses begin, but government gets in the way.

History in the USA and elsewhere is replete with examples where government has made things worse for some in the name of utilitarianism; people voting for segregation in the Southern states would be one. For Rudy, it is 'immoral' and 'ridiculous' that his personal rights should be up for discussion by anyone else, 'just because the majority will deem it as better or as right doesn't mean it's right'. Cronyism, new authorities with legal oversight such as the Occupational Safety and Health Administration, and over-incarceration are all given as evidence of government overstepping its bounds with negative consequences.

'Just governments' should instead focus on preserving the rights set out in the Constitution: life, liberty and the pursuit of happiness/property. For Barry, a solution is found in explicitly accounting for freedom in a cost–benefit analysis whenever we are collectively deciding what to do (preferably to be written into law as a principle for making government decisions, if Barry had his way).

I find it hard to disagree with some of their arguments, particularly in relation to issues of drugs and incarceration. But shifting to hypotheticals, I pose the question that if a member of the Libertarian Party had been President in 2020, what decisions in response to COVID-19 would they have made. For some, it was kicked to the states to decide. For others, like Alex, handing decisions to the states just passed the ball to another government jurisdiction. 'There's no basis for the government to be restricting businesses or forcing people to wear masks if they don't want to.' The government's role should be to inform and then leave it up to the individual to decide. Some were vaccinated, some were not and some think COVID-19 created 'two years of tyranny'.

It becomes a question of trust. For Gary, 'basically, every major actor here has given us reason not to trust them'. There is a genuine question to be asked about why people should trust a government that in the past carried out the Tuskegee experiment,[29] for example, or that lied about weapons of mass destruction, leading to a war in the Middle East that cost hundreds of thousands of lives. 'We have a lot of good reasons not to [trust governments], which really sucks for the people that think most adults could benefit from having this vaccine.'

The lack of trust is such that the state is widely regarded as a threat to freedom. When I joke that 'the government thinks libertarians are covert terrorists and have to be taken down', there is animated discussion and 'yes!' I tug on a raw nerve. Kevin reminds the group that 'they have called us terrorists before!' Memories are invoked of Waco, an hour-and-a-half's drive south of Dallas, where an FBI siege in 1993 left seventy-six members of the Branch Davidian sect dead.[30] For Rudy, 'there's no law that the government won't enforce up until death'. Canadian Prime Minister Justin Trudeau's decision to invoke emergency powers to disband the Truckers' Convoy in Canada in 2022 is viewed with disgust.

Other examples follow, including civil forfeiture, where police are allowed to take assets if they suspect criminal activity without due process, that is, no one needs to have been charged with a crime. Those who have had property or money forfeited often have to sue law enforcement agencies to get it back.[31] 'Most of the things that are hindrances on our ability to choose and practice our liberty come from the state, in fact, I'd say is almost exclusively the case.' The feeling and the evidence they present is that there are too many regulations, restrictions and lifestyle choices forced upon them.

There is a special ire saved for the discussion of tax, tantamount to theft for many libertarians. For Alex, '[government] openly tell us, they know what's best for us while pointing a gun at us and stealing from us'. The argument goes that that money could be better directed to 'things that we want'. There is no state tax in Texas, although several complain about the high level of property tax they pay city authorities. The world's richest man at the time of writing, Elon Musk, moved his companies to Texas from California to avoid that state's higher tax rates.

The state's monopoly on the use of force also goes against the libertarian Non-Aggression Principle and is considered dangerous to personal freedom. That America regards itself as the leader of the free world, defending freedom globally, is met with eye rolls, although Phil, an older, quieter voice, makes the case that overseas troops can act as a 'tripwire' and are needed to ensure peace and economic trade. He is pragmatic about the interconnections that globalisation has created. 'We can't back away from the world because the world owns our homes, our paper [bonds]. We rely on the world to buy our bonds.' Splendid isolation is not always possible. For others, it is too costly to 'police the world' and has resulted in an expensive military industrial complex.

It feels unusual at this febrile time to be in a political space where U-S-A isn't chanted at the mention of foreign policy. Instead, we sit in a BBQ joint in suburban Dallas and make abstract pronouncements about the fates of other countries over cuts of meat and various sauces. How far should Russia be allowed to encroach on a buffer zone in the Baltics? Why should US foreign policy dictate how other countries enact 'freedom'? The USA is viewed by some as 'hypocritical' in its foreign affairs. For Mary, 'it's kind of foolish to go all around, trying to say that you want to be free, but then only your version of free is supposed to be everybody's version of free'. 'Bad actors' complicate geopolitics and national security concerns, fomenting mistrust, but at a minimum, if there has to be a standing army, then it should remain in America and be used for defence only. In this instance, nationalism makes an appearance. 'Nobody could come and project their power over here and take us over. They could never do it, the Chinese couldn't do that.' For others, better to take Switzerland's approach and be non-interventionist.

There is only one set of institutions this group seems to trust, and that's 'the free market', or at least, 'trust but verify'. 'We trust [it] more than the government. It's not perfect either. There's no perfect system', but never let the perfect be the enemy of freedom. In this view, the free market enables choice, while government is just sand in the gears. In a country that is the most unequal of the OECD, there is collective agreement in this group that free markets are 'more efficient' and 'better than government'.[32] Multiple nodes can compete with each other, giving and gaining information on what works and what doesn't, what people want and what they don't. Governments, on the other hand, are bloated, monopolistic and can't process information efficiently. Charts are produced to show how social security and the military 'eat up' the federal budget.

In the free market, 'you get rewarded by serving other people', working towards 'mutual benefit', 'incentivising people' and 'maximising resource distribution'. Innovation is stimulated and resources go to the people that can best provide what's needed. There is space in the marketplace for choice: electric or petrol cars, vinyl or digital music.

Collective harms, like environmental destruction, can be dealt with by the market and the rule of law. If a polluter upstream harms someone's property downstream, the latter can sue. Legalising drugs and making police carry liability insurance are libertarian solutions to crime and police brutality. If bad police continue to violate rights, they will eventually be unable to afford insurance premiums. It will become too expensive to hurt people. There is an assumption in this reasoning that 'the natural state of people is peaceful', which is a nice thought, although I wonder if this is the kind of rational decision making least likely when we are in a rage with a weapon in hand.

Even migration can, contentiously, be managed by market forces. Kevin emphasises the point that 'all peaceful people should be able to live wherever they need to, [...] the border is only a place where one country's laws end, and the other country's laws begin'. In other words, a border has a legal definition but not a moral one, which might find some agreement with those living in El Paso. Phil, in a Texan drawl that could convince me of anything, suggests that immigrants pay the government, rather than human traffickers, a fee to come to the USA. The money collected can then be used to pay down the national debt. Reducing debt is also a central platform for the Libertarian Party. For Phil, 'we can't be free if we're in debt. We owe the world $30 trillion', and 'it's enslaving future generations'.[33] On this, they would find common cause with many of the students I spoke to who feel the heavy weight of debt on their futures.[34]

Phil's solution, however, doesn't address the anxiety that once in the country immigrants will 'help vote away the resources of everybody that was already in the country', which he notes wouldn't be very libertarian. This troubles Rudy, even though, as an anarchist, he acknowledges he doesn't respect 'plenty of laws' including the 'artificial' creation of state borders and the illegitimacy of the state itself. 'It's freedom of these people to migrate to try to [find] prosperity for their families. Where they're born is irrelevant. [...] So I can't say that these people should obey these laws when I won't respect certain laws.' But a gnawing discomfort persists.

There are other trade-offs and triages, particularly centred on 'safety and security versus liberty'. Bob was 'nauseated and saddened' to see how Australia 'gave up their guns' and capitulated to COVID-19 mandates. I explain our need for biosecurity and how most of us don't really miss people having high-powered weapons. Joe questions how much Americans sincerely value freedom, referencing the difference between theory and the reality of feeling safe:

> We've seen far too many people would be willing, if they had to choose security and safety, or at least the illusion of it, over the right to determine the course of our own lives. So I would say that freedom is important in theory, but when it comes into practice, far too many people are willing to put that aside.

The choice is reduced to safety versus 'the ability to live my life', and for Joe, 'libertarians usually keep that right up top, even if it's riskier, because we know what comes with authoritarianism'. Stalin and Pol Pot are given as examples. It is a zero-sum equation: the promise of 'safety' and being 'taken care of' by a government leads to the loss of freedom. There is criticism of Scandinavian countries for providing safety at the cost of high taxes but no recognition that Norway's sovereign wealth fund, for example, allows for up to 3 per cent of it to be spent on public services each year, and the country has a consistently high rating in the Global Happiness Index.

There is discussion and disagreement on all these ideas, particularly on who holds the burden: taxpayers, businesses, individuals or associations. When I point out failures, the response is generally that it is because the current system in reality is not a 'free market'. Government interferes through subsidies, tax loopholes, bailouts and tariffs. Libertarians are generally not happy with Trump's current approach to the latter.[35]

Finding a strategy to maintain freedom 'to the max', to find a place with minimal government interference, returns us to the discussion on education and the question of why should people try to find a way of navigating differences just because they happen to live together. Is there something to the idea that the world would be a more peaceful place if we all lived in separate spheres with our own values, interacting on a voluntary basis to non-violently exchange goods and services when necessary? For me, it still feels too much like segregation ... and possibly very boring. For these libertarians, if feels like choice, as Rudy argues:

> If I want to be in the socialist area, it should be my freedom to be in a socialist [area]. [...] I do what I want ... that's the point. It's a choice! You might not agree with my lifestyle but to me I'm happy with it [...]. As long as we're peaceful to each other. [...] just because they're our countrymen and we're born in the same geographic area doesn't mean that we need to get along.

The movement of people in a post-pandemic America has shown that many are willing to make this decision to relocate to areas where they feel a greater alignment of values – moving to states that didn't introduce mandates, for example, like Florida, Texas and South Dakota.[36] Americans can weigh up state-based differences: do you want to live where there is the death penalty or abortion access, lower taxes or more public services? There are fifty states with diverging regulatory regimes. Make your own choice.

This 'freedom of association', as they would call it, is bolstered by the non-aggression pact and just the 'bare minimum of laws' governing fraud and protecting property in order to keep the peace. For Rick, it can be done if 'we all agree not to hurt other people, and not to take their stuff, if we all live by that principle [...]. There are mechanisms to have peace without everybody being on the same page on everything.'

This approach discounts the fact that not all can move when the rules and the neighbours change around them, as later conversations in rural communities in Indiana and Colorado will explore. There is also a downside to this movement for those already in places that have seen an influx of new residents. Parts of Texas are turning 'blue' (Democrat) as people move from a 'liberal', high-tax state like California. Some of the libertarians express less enthusiasm for this movement, as it has increased property prices and taxes. Revenge perhaps for the residents of Grafton, New Hampshire, who didn't have much choice about libertarians moving into their neighbourhood and changing their way of life. It may have been without force, but the impositions of ideas can still have detrimental impacts.

For Alex, if the government just respected the rights of every individual, it wouldn't matter where we lived. 'You could re-form yourself, live the way you want to, different [from how] the guy 10 feet away from you lives.' In other words, distance shouldn't matter if everyone is, truly, treated equally. Alex returns to his belief that it all centres on individual rights. 'It doesn't really matter so much where you are geographically in the world, if everyone's individual rights are respected that's the ultimate goal.'

In fairness, libertarianism in practice doesn't hold out for a perfect society but a 'freer' one, in which more of the decisions that impact our lives are made by individuals. There is recognition of 'moral pluralism', of different ways to pursue happiness or conceptualise the meaning of life. Even Boaz recognises that libertarians need to be 'humble', as their philosophy might be wrong, and therefore they should oppose the imposition of any moral code.[37] As Gary puts it: '[W]e realise the limits that human nature imposes on things and we don't set our sights high enough to think we can hit the perfect society even if we want to improve [it].'

Bob is ever the optimist. 'I just think it's in the human spirit to want [freedom], and it's just going to get better all the time.' Kevin, who was standing for a Texas congressional district in 2024, is also hopeful that the electorate are ready for a change:

> People in general [are] starting to say 'this is all ridiculous and I'm tired of all whatever this clown world is, I'm just ready to have a regular life'. And if that faction of sane America in the world is successful then maybe we'll have a renaissance in classical liberal thought and behaviour and maybe a reduction in government.

Unfortunately for the Libertarian Party, that renaissance may have some way to go. While the party has seen its membership grow in recent years, its vote fell in the 2024 presidential election to just 0.4 per cent, down from 1.2 per cent in 2020.[38] The seat Kevin was standing for was won by the Democrats.

Despite these setbacks, and, contrary to its reputation for self-interest, there is a degree of hope in the theoretical underpinnings of libertarianism, especially in its belief in the possibilities of being human: that we can be trusted to govern ourselves, that we shouldn't coerce or harm others to get what we want, that we can behave with honesty, that we can be good even when motivated by self-interest. These would seem virtuous characteristics, but evidence, including power outages in Texas, bears in New Hampshire and Truss in the UK, would suggest that reality is always ready to overwhelm the theory. In the name of freedom and the creation of virtuous citizens, decent people can lobby for policies that may hurt others and themselves because they believe in placing a premium value on a life of maximum freedom. There are no institutions as yet arising 'naturally' out of markets to smooth out inequalities and keep us safe in an unpredictable world made even more precarious by unregulated capitalism and a President on a mission to change the fabric of American society and global order.

At the end of Boaz's *Manifesto* is a quiz to find out how much the reader tilts towards the libertarian version of freedom. I'm definitely a 'liberal', quite a way from 'libertarian' and 'conservative' and a little too close to 'authoritarian' for comfort. But the questions, as always, are too binary. Who should decide if I have uncensored access to the internet? Me, but … and there's always a but … there's content on it that needs to be regulated (e.g. disinformation, violence and abuse), so the government I delegate authority to needs to be in there.

Personally, I am happy to trade off some of my freedoms for a collective safety net and to make the occasional sacrifice for someone who doesn't have to sacrifice for me in return, who may never even know that a sacrifice has been made. I cannot conceive of freedom, in theory or in the messy sand pit of life, without some bonds of affection to stop us all spinning out of life's centrifugal orbit. New movements for freedom that emerged during the COVID-19 pandemic pick up these tensions: on the one hand demanding less government regulation but on the other calling for new forms of collective belonging in a country that feels increasingly dispersed and polarised.

9

The enchantments of medical freedom and future dystopias

> You're either voting for our freedoms or you're voting for those freedoms to be taken away and our country destroyed. [...] Constitution up and down the board, I came out to save it today.[1]
>
> Joan, voting for Donald Trump, November 2024

Over the past decade, the USA has been roiled by change on many fronts: demography, social expectations, technology, geopolitics and a chaotic presidency. Throw in a global pandemic for maximum uncertainty. More than four years after the worst of it, COVID-19 is still impacting American life and politics, for example influencing voting choices like Joan's in November 2024.

During COVID, tensions quickly surfaced between individual and collective freedoms as the ability to gather was taken away. Lockdowns generated narratives of loss and heightened fears of tyranny against which freedom had to be protected. For some, it was a deliberate alteration of everything that holds community together. Mandates became a metaphor for powerlessness and evidence of an invisible, global elite that threatened freedom, employing ridicule and shame in order to effect control, or, as Tucker Carlson put it, to 'humiliate you and get you to obey'.[2]

Against COVID-19, some put their faith in God, Vitamin D and Ivermectin. Others got active, involved and politicised, 'waking up', finding other like-minded people who shared their truth. New movements for 'medical freedom' gathered disparate supporters from across political, racial and class lines, hauling together strange bedfellows: a version of 'the left', libertarians, MAGA, the religious and secular.

As activists argued that distancing mandates and vaccinations were an incursion on their inalienable freedoms, they were depicted as being radically selfish, ignorant, conspiratorial, sometimes threatening. But it is a more complicated picture. Parts of the movement began to articulate a vision of the future rooted in love, community and care – a return to collective living in the face of an atomised society and the economic and social dislocations of capitalism. There is more to life apparently than how many toppings are available for pancakes. These ideas signalled a rejuvenation of the 1960s counter-culture movement that advocated new ways of thinking about work, leisure and art, in order to free humans from economic drudgery.

I stumble across the New York Freedom Rally (NYFR) on the way to the Saturday morning Brooklyn farmers' market, yet another sign of change in this once poor neighbourhood. There are forty to fifty people, and, as activists like to point out, they are very diverse in terms of age, ethnicity, race and class. Vegans chant alongside the Sons and Daughters of Liberty. Trump supporters and BLM activists, farmers and city dwellers march together.

Their revolution will be photographed and re-tweeted, Insta'd and TikTok'd. They speak of having nothing to hide and standing by everything they say. John, part of Sons and Daughters of Liberty, wears a GoPro in case he's arrested, draped in the red and white striped flag of the Sons of Liberty but incorporating the Gadsden 'don't tread on me' rattle snake. The standard USA flag is also worn and waved, along with the Whisky Rebellion flag, Fuck You Biden, and the Statue of Liberty. There are references to the Matrix films (red pill/blue pill) and constant reminders that 'coercion is not consent'. T-shirts and posters proclaim they are 'living without fear'. Their revolution will also be accompanied by merchandise and a soundtrack that includes music of the Civil Rights movement (Nina Simone's 'Backlash blues' is popular), posters quoting Dr Martin Luther King Jr and his call to defy unjust laws and images of Rosa Parks accompanying a sit-in campaign in restaurants.[3] The abortion slogan 'my body, my choice' is reappropriated.

There is a heroic, messianic narrative embedded in this activism, stressing that 'the universal law of liberty says that I can go wherever the hell I want to go'. They are 'warriors', 'holding the line'; only they know the 'truth' that COVID-19 had nothing to do with health and everything to do with control; only they will be saved. The anthem, 'This is a war', is played over a mobile sound system and captures the mood: 'This is a war on religion. This is a war on the children. They give you the cure with the sickness. This is a war on tradition. [The vaccine] is a lethal injection [...] built by the elite.' 'Slave' is juxtaposed to the question of 'where's the bold and the brave'.[4]

This rhetoric of 'war' sits alongside a message of 'love'. A rapper from Illinois reminds the crowd that he 'loves' them. I speak to a young woman with a 'freedom from fear' sweatshirt and 'save the children' poster. She loves everyone, vaccinated or unvaccinated. There is call and response from speakers who all emphasise non-violence, although one man has brought a baseball bat. Derrick Gibson, who's running for New York state Governor (he'll lose), begins with: 'Do you love your freedom?' 'Yes!', is the reply. He calls the mayor a 'tyrant'. Another speaker shouts out: 'I'm out here with you guys for what?' 'Freedom', is the reply. A young Black woman takes the microphone on the steps that are now a makeshift dais. She describes herself as a Christian, a 'momma bear' (a fierce mother), and makes a point of telling us that while she only has twelve college credits, she knows 'the truth'. Knowledge is part of the injuries of class. The year 2030 is named as the date of the Great Reset, and she speaks of *their* plans to 'exterminate' children. Her words. And now it starts to unravel. A passer-by begins to shout at her. She shouts back. Others in the crowd move towards the man to argue. Community police officers intervene. The speeches finish, and the young Black woman leads the chants of 'no more mandates' as they head off to protest in front of the mayor's house.

A few weeks later, Telegram channels announce a coordinated Global Day of Action for Medical Freedom, and these will continue into 2025, although on a much smaller scale. NYFR planned to gather at Times Square, but when I arrive (on time) it's just me and the tourists. It takes another forty minutes or so for a handful of activists to appear. They distribute leaflets, including a mock petition satirising Centers for Disease Control shielding guidance. Liam, a tall, thin young man tries to get people to sign it, while two other activists film the interactions. Liam picks up on my accent and mentions how indigenous communities in Australia have been affected by COVID-19 mandates. Circulated on Telegram, there are stories of 'concentration' or 'internment' camps for those who will not comply. 'I think Australia is a canary in the coal mine of where *they're* taking us.' This and gun control are the two things that make Australia famous in America, both contexts misunderstood.

Times Square carries on around them: the Black Friday shoppers, the touts, the Broadway ticket lines, the ill, the homeless, the shoeless, Batman and Mini Mouse hawking photographs. The high-definition LEDs of consumerism above us take turns occupying the sides of buildings: Coca-Cola, Samsung, Swarovski. The naked cowboy is a constant, with his guitar and star-spangled underpants. The smell of marijuana mixes with the pretzels and candied nuts.

Liam directs me to Cat Maguire, a dynamic woman in her late sixties. Cat seems to know everyone. Giving rapid-fire responses, barely pausing for breath, she tells me there is so much to do, to argue for and against. Today's event was thrown together quickly, but they have had larger demonstrations of 'thousands' in Manhattan, Albany (the New York state capital) and, joining forces with other groups, Washington, DC.

For Cat and other campaigners, the medical freedom movement is ostensibly about bodily autonomy. The body is seen as the gateway to other systems of control and the final frontier yet to be fully co-opted by governments. 'Under the guise of safety', COVID-19 mandates asked us to surrender our bodies 'in return for the freedom to eat in restaurants and to go to school'. For Cat, it was a price not worth paying. Also troubling her is the loss of other freedoms, such as being 'able to speak your mind', to dissent from medical orthodoxy. In her view, COVID-19, its mandates and vaccines, was the crux of a strategy of 'control' – a word representing the antithesis of freedom that is mentioned thirty-two times in our conversation. 'We're at a very crucial point where we might not be able to control our own lives once they get that vaccine in us, in people. It's DNA altering.' Describing the vaccine in this way also articulates a discomfort that the very essence of who we are as humans is changing. The 'chip', the 'programming', the 'bots' that take away our autonomy have become an explanation for how we could possibly acquiesce to a world in which there is so much inequality, injustice, pain and suffering.

Cat and I meet later in her West Side railroad apartment. Her sister sits on the floor of the small living room making posters for a demonstration they are attending later outside the mayor's house. Cat is animated, articulate, well educated, well travelled – a white collar professional and a campaigner and community organiser for a large part of her life for feminist, animal rights, anti-racism and anti-war causes. She values education and considers herself an intellectual first and foremost, reading 'libertarian', 'progressive', 'conservative' material across 'the whole spectrum', political, philosophical and spiritual. Despite her dystopian view of our relationship with technology, she worked as a computer programmer before becoming what she describes as a 'truth activist' and 'freedom organiser'. For her, the post-pandemic moment is catastrophic: 'What they're doing right now is probably in the history of our species, the biggest strike against freedom that ever happened, [...] this is the entire planet now that they're going for. They're going for broke and they're using everything they can to break the human spirit.'

It was 9/11 that began Cat's process of investigating 'alternative scenarios'. Influenced by her sister, a lawyer, she 'started just opening up that door', then kept opening more and more. She is aware there is disinformation and 'it takes a lot of vetting' and 'an extremely open mind':

> I really started just throwing away the shackles of orthodoxy and just letting facts lead me wherever they may. I'd like to think that I'm completely objective and open minded. That's hard to say for most people, we probably all have our prejudices. But I feel like I've really gone way beyond where I ever thought I would be.

Mandates and vaccinations may be the immediate issue, but for Cat, medical freedom is part of a wider 'truth movement'. COVID-19 restrictions were simply 'distractions' from a 'global coup d'état' stealing 'literally trillions from us and completely upending our entire world'. It was a deliberate strategy, a 'fake pandemic', just one in a long line of attempts to encroach on freedom (9/11, 'false flag' operations and 'other crimes against democracy'). But while past events, such as the War on Drugs, only affected freedom for some communities (e.g. increased surveillance of Black and minority ethnic communities), COVID-19 was a 'brilliant' strategy, as now everybody was involved.

Some activists genuinely believe that vaccines are a way of 'chipping' humans, for surveillance, eradication or to 'geofence' us, restricting our movements.[5] Cat adds to this with the belief that 'there's some form of massive mind control going on', to return us to a state of 'neo-feudalism'. Referencing studies into solitary confinement, she argues that lockdown was 'giving everybody micro doses of torture, so people's minds have been messed up. It's an invasion of freedom that is almost ineffable.'

They, the ones responsible for all this, are the 'ruling class', 'the elites', 'the powers that be', 'plutocrats', 'anyone at the World Economic Forum', the controllers of finance, 'perception management' (media) and technology. *They* are 'psychopaths', and 'they've' been planning this for a while. Presidents, governments, bureaucrats, even WEF founder and chair Klaus Schwab, are merely factotums, servants of the real power that lies behind the WEF. 'It is the 1 per cent of the 1 per cent.'

According to some activists, there are about 5,000 or 6,000 elites controlling the global economy and, through it, us. But as there are over eight billion of us, *they* need to cull us to a manageable number: 500 million to a billion. This is 'the Great Reset', the WEF's plan for a New World Order that will radically transform society. 'And *they* keep saying, "Oh, it's going to be wonderful." No, *they* have a dystopian mind. [...] *They* want to keep us weak and oppressed so that then *they* can monetise our behaviour and our labour.'

Many social scientists and political theorists have argued that the monetisation of our behaviour and labour is already well established without the necessity for a Great Reset.[6] Capitalism, particularly in its neo-liberal form post-1980s, has swallowed all before it. There is nothing that cannot now be commodified, including our bodies. But the rhetoric of the '1 per cent' and the focus on transnational economic power places the medical freedom movement as the legacy of Occupy – that sliver of hope in the late 2000s, post-Global Financial

Crisis (GFC), that might have led to some change in societies now wedded to unregulated capitalism. The GFC still lingers in political and media shadows, almost two decades later. The Heritage Foundation lists it as one of a handful of crises that have destabilised the USA, and from which Western democracies have never really recovered their bearings.[7] But what was once a creative movement for change has become deluged by conspiracy, including the intentional culling of much of the world's population.

The belief in a shadowy global elite controlling economic and social life is held by a key constituency of the medical freedom movement: the 'left who left the left'. Cat is politically orphaned. She identified as left ('real left and not liberal. Liberal to me was a bad word') but feels that the Democrats have now become too focused on identity politics and being 'woke'. Yet she is not a Trump supporter. The recurrent theme of political failure in the USA creeps in. Cat now takes an 'issues-based' approach to her politics, and 'truth' is the preeminent issue.

Part of her 'truth' is that society is being rendered into 'disparate broken-down peoples'. It is not only mandates that separate us; identity politics is seen as a deliberate strategy to 'divide and conquer', destroying forms of solidarity including family and neighbourhood, robbing us of the sense that we are in community with others, 'not just your own neighbours but with other races, with other countries'. It's a recurrent theme of an 'old' left that sees identity politics as a distraction from class struggle. The education system is also blamed for corrupting innate, inalienable freedoms through 'brainwashing kids [in] these re-education camps', namely universities.

The philosophy of postmodernism, and the idea that 'there's no one single truth', is blamed again. There must be certainty. There must be a master narrative. There must be solidity to hang on to with grappling hooks. Without the central thread of freedom that binds us together, society, according to Cat, is destined to become governed by one centralised, global organisation. *They* will control us via English philosopher Jeremy Bentham's eighteenth-century vision of a panopticon prison, where the prisoners can be viewed at all times by an unseen guard.

Cat is well aware that her ideas may 'sound like this big conspiracy theory'. She is aware that people will ridicule her for her beliefs. She has lost friendships over this stance. There were many other conversations for this book where people excoriated the medical freedom movement. As we talked over several hours, I oscillated between 'plausible' to 'not at all'. There is exaggeration, but there is also cogent analysis at times of how centres of power like governments can use fear, propaganda and behavioural psychology (e.g. nudge theory) to get us to go along with things that we may not necessarily think are good or that we feel we have no power to resist.

There is 'truth' in that Big Pharma has profited enormously from COVID-19 and other health crises, including AIDS.[8] Tech companies have inordinate power, and debate continues as to whether they should be treated as utilities and broken up.[9] Security threats generate fear and boost military spending, increasing wealth for the military industrial complex. Borders divide and conquer 'with the same tiers at the top controlling it', although Cat is not arguing for open borders. Rather she opposes their removal as part of paving the way for a single global society in which we are 'serfs to a sort of global Godhead figure and that ultimately will undermine our freedoms'.

I might agree with Cat that we have, in reality, little control over our lives, particularly if we sit at the intersection of several inequalities. Powerful countries such as the USA, and agencies such as the WEF, the International Monetary Fund (IMF) and the World Bank, can destabilise local and national self-determination. The wave of IMF-induced structural adjustment programmes in the Global South in the 1990s, for which countries are still paying economically and socially, is testament to this, and it continues. I would also agree with Cat that 'the biggest division that we have is one of economics. And that's the 99 per cent versus the 1 per cent.' Where Cat and I diverge is that after diagnosing the problem as economic inequality, the explanation for its existence veers away from capitalism and into a realm of conspiracy.

Fragmented information is filtered and re-sorted through social media echo chambers. There are myriad 'alternative' sources, podcasts and websites to support a belief or theory, to create new patterns no matter how improbable. No one is alone; no matter how unlikely it sounds, there is someone else out there who might share your belief and help you make sense of the amorphous feelings of discomfort created when cultural infrastructure shifts.

This feeling that something is wrong, something that people cannot quite put their finger on or articulate, is repeated throughout conversations, rallies and media ecosystems. People *feel* that something is not right. As Santa, one of the organisers of the USA People's Convoy put it, 'I think a large portion of the American population right now knows there is something wrong. They just aren't as in tune with political happenings as some of us are, but they know in their hearts they feel something is not right in their nation.'[10]

With so much unseen, at the distance of nation-states and transnational connections, change must be substantiated, shifts in privilege must be explained and the fearful, seemingly harsh responses of good people rationalised (including the idea that hundreds of millions of us will be 'exterminated' in the Great Reset). There must be an explanation for our general compliance in the face of economic loss and social upheaval, for the way we act like frogs in a slowly heating pot. There must be something else happening, for example 'mass crowd control using 5G and who knows what weaponry'. Otherwise, why would we go along with a world so obviously self-harming?

The expert is of no use in soothing this cognitive dissonance. 'For those who can connect the dots', who have their 'organic integrity', the right knowledge, they can see the truth of what is happening. 'They may not have studied history', but they know this is 'evil and wrong'. There are those 'who understand what it means to be truly free from their technology, from their invasiveness, and their control over how we live our lives'. The rest of us without this truth are 'sleepwalking into dystopia', distracted by our screens and ongoing economic and political malaise.

In reality, we are already well socialised. Cultural reproduction doesn't need 5G. We are doing it every day, reiterating the grooves laid down by years of habit. Conversely, it could be argued that COVID-19 reminded us that alternatives are possible. We didn't have to go to an office every day, the sky didn't fall down when we worked from home, when we did things differently. There is freedom in this as well, something that a burgeoning 'well-being' and 'natural healing' movement has picked up on, in tandem with medical freedom.

I meet Elizabeth in her condominium, facing the East River in New York. Like Cat, she is articulate, well travelled, well educated and passionate, often hitting the table with her hand while making a point, for which she apologises. She hesitates to clip on the lapel mic. Thinking this was related to germs, I reassure her the equipment is cleaned after each interview, but Elizabeth is more concerned about radio waves. We use the table mic instead.

Elizabeth 'cares a lot about freedom', aligning with the libertarians in that it is very 'un-American to not be concerned with your freedom'. Freedom is inalienable, 'natural', not granted by governments. 'You never find yourself in a situation where you have to ask yourself whether you can be free; you are free as a start.' She was born in a small working-class town, left home to go to boarding school and from there to a local college. She moved to New York City to finish her degree, staying in the city for over twenty years interspersed with travel. She has a long-standing interest in alternative education practice, running a forest school for a time. Her substantial reading list includes the *New York Times*, the *New Yorker*, the *Atlantic*, blogs and Substack writers, while her podcasts of choice include a roster of 'independent' voices such as Whitney Webb, Robert Kennedy Jr, Joe Rogan and Jordan Peterson. Elizabeth's relationship with Rogan's podcast is indicative of her political shift, catalysed by the pandemic. 'I couldn't see myself hanging out with him five years ago, but I could see myself hanging out with him now.' She never listens to National Public Radio (NPR) anymore.

Elizabeth has no lack of exposure to perspectives she disagrees with, being 'inundated with that' in her personal life, from family and schools that all have to be navigated. Like Cat, she has lost friends over this. Those she went to classes with, whom she campaigned with years ago, can't believe that maybe she 'sees something they don't'. And what she sees is people

> just walking into their enslavement in the metaverse, in the internet of bodies and things, and that everything is going to be trapped and that

they're going to have to continue to show papers for everything, and papers are not going to be papers. Papers are going to be medical screenings. So are you clean? Are you safe?

Bio-political to its core, this belief equates safety with being compliant, obedient and free of contagion. It's a fearful future where all our bodies and transactions are tracked, moderated and controlled.

From the depths of this despair comes a hint that for Elizabeth and Cat what is most disturbing is the idea that God will be replaced. This is not necessarily referencing the God of Christian nationalism but rather a more encompassing idea of 'the divine'. The after-effects of the long march of secularisation and industrialisation have removed the idea of the sacred from everyday lives. Conservative political theorist Patrick Deneen, author of *Why liberalism failed*, suggests there has been a material and spiritual degradation of American society.[11] The awe and wonder of what it is to be human, and the idea of transcendence, has been lost in economic drudgery, precarity and techno-supremacy. This is perhaps why there are references throughout the conservative and medical freedom movements to 'a spiritual war' or 'a battle for the soul of humanity'. Visions of a techno-dystopian future are accelerating the dissolution of a relationship with something other than ourselves. Life and imagined futures are filtered through digital anxieties 'where we become cyborgs', and freedom is diminished as a result. As Cat puts it, in this 'hyper-technological alienated nihilistic kind of Blade Runner world', our reason to exist has been removed: if AI can do us better, what's the point of our existence?

Both Cat and Elizabeth feel this evisceration of the connection to a higher authority, 'a greater divine', that for Cat 'is something integral to humankind'. *They* want to destroy 'even our connection to God, our spirituality'. In what anthropologists have referred to as 'conspirituality' (conspiracy + spirituality), weighty concepts such as postmodernism, secular humanism and empirical materialism are nominated by Cat as steppingstones to a world where the new gods wear 'white lab coats' and 'want us to believe in them as the greater authority'.

Elizabeth's antidote to this disenchantment of modern life is to be found in the familiarity of local communities, and in an idea of 'wellness' that centres trust in the body, in intuition and in feelings. Medical freedom is at the core of this belief system, defined by Elizabeth as the freedom to be sick when we need to be and to seek forms of care not determined by Big Pharma or the medical industry. She trusts the messages she receives from her body via a 'direct relationship with spirit and god and goddess and life'. 'Without doubt, without denial', Elizabeth will make decisions based on the way she feels. 'You can't be free without trusting yourself.'

This faith in the body and our ability to heal ourselves stems from mistrust of political and civil institutions, but it is also facilitated by the increased possibilities for self-reflexivity and DIY identity enabled by consumerism. In the narratives of the wellness industry, people are rendered ill, spiritually and mentally as much as physically, by technology, social anomie, unrepresentative government and the education system. For Cat, 'our species is really hurting right now'. All these factors suppress people's innate curiosity and goodness. In this world view, if we can just peel back the pollution of modernity and secularism, then the true, authentic self will appear to provide meaningful responses to ill-health and the dilemmas of the world around us.[12] The ability to heal ourselves is then a sign of the divine within us, as well as a sign of resistance to external authorities' attempts to control us.

A pillar of this argument, a nugget of truth, is that Big Pharma and the medical industry has too much power and money from the commodification of our bodies. 'It's snake oil,' according to Elizabeth. What America has is 'a healing crisis', and the prescription for that is the right to 'good food and rest', not only access to pharmaceuticals. Elizabeth is not suggesting that emergency medical care isn't necessary at times but that the medical industry is exploitative. It's hard to argue against this position in a country where over 60 per cent of bankruptcies are due to medical costs.[13] The widespread pain caused by privatised health care in the USA contributed to the making of a violent folk hero in December 2024, when Luigi Mangione murdered United Healthcare CEO Brian Thompson.

For Elizabeth, what people need is 'to divest entirely from the system of care that has kept them sick'. She had home births for her children and has no health insurance. Given the cost of health care in the USA, this is a very brave decision. Elizabeth has the resources to be able to seek care from practitioners if needed, but she's also a lay herbalist.

Given these views, I was surprised when Elizabeth said she was 'fine with capitalism'. When I suggest that Big Pharma is part of capitalism, for Elizabeth, 'it's also part of socialism'. I feel my regular defence of the UK's National Health Service coming on, but Elizabeth's argument is that the model of economic production in the USA today is not really a free market (something the libertarians might agree with). Farmers' markets are as close as Elizabeth gets to her idea of a free market, because she can build a relationship with a supplier while engaging in transactions underpinned by supply and demand. This is not an outlandish perspective. The economic historian Fernand Braudel argued that capitalism is 'anti-market', based on exploitation, concentrating power and wealth through control of the 'rules'. In a move reminiscent of libertarian thinking, he argued that markets, on the other hand, are part of economic life; points of exchange in which we should encounter one another as equals in order to trade goods in a process marked by transparency.[14]

Elizabeth's also okay with nationalism. This doesn't mean she is supportive of all of America's foreign policies, 'wars and things', but she's 'okay with wanting America to be a good place'. The Second Amendment gets her support as well. 'I'm not pro-guns in urban environments and gun violence and things like that. But I am very pro-Second Amendment for sure. [...] I believe that people should have the right to defend their freedoms.' Her children have been spending time recently with their grandfather, learning to shoot with a small-gauge .22.

We all manage to house our inconsistencies and simultaneously juxtaposing views, making trade-offs where necessary. Cat, for example, is opposed to someone smoking cigarettes in her space because it invades her lungs, but as COVID-19 was no worse than any other flu in her view, mandated lockdowns and vaccinations were untenable incursions on freedom. In other words, the medical freedom movement was never just about opposing mandates or vaccinations. It was about combatting an overreaching government and regaining a feeling of control while the world shut down around them.

As a parent during lockdown, Elizabeth felt isolated in her concerns, without a space to come together with other parents to discuss their fears, especially those who felt there was insufficient proof of harm when weighed against the disruption to their lives and livelihoods. Friends who moved or 'dropped out', away from city mandates, are described as 'medical freedom refugees', but Elizabeth didn't want to go to Texas or live off-grid in a yurt, as other friends have done.

Instead, she did what she has done for many years: she began organising. Another politically homeless 'lefty who left the left', and former campaigner for the Democrat party, Elizabeth feels there has been a decline in community organising since the late 1990s. Recent efforts are too centred on 'woke things', lacking coherence and sustainability, criticising rather than creating a new society. She is, like Cat, somewhat dismissive of the civil disobedience strategy of other medical freedom activists. While noting acts of civil disobedience can be 'remarkably beautiful', they are also theatrical performances. 'I'm not going to go out and fucking protest to get into Burger King.' Legislative change also has limits in her view. 'If you lose [a vote] you lose everything.' Instead, Elizabeth began articulating a vision for an alternative society. 'We're going to build the thing that we need and we are not doing it with permission asked.'

As an artist, this is part of her creative practice, influenced by the nineteenth-century literary movement of American Romanticism: Emily Dickinson, Ralph Waldo Emerson, Henry David Thoreau and Walt Whitman. These writers celebrated nature and the possibilities of the unknown as the USA expanded westward, opening new frontiers and allowing ordinary people to become explorers and adventurers. For Elizabeth, this was 'just a very bright period of American history', and she believes that people are ready to return to that way of living, before 'real' freedom was ceded to convenience and consumption:

> People are seeing that there's something better in life than being part of these oppressive systems which are really *not* [her emphasis] bringing people happiness. [...] I'd rather live in a shack that's crumbling and falling down and have a relationship with my farmer and do some gleaning or trade skills, and go to the Community Church and have potluck

dinners and like, help one another out stone soup style, and be okay with like having less crap that never brought me happiness in the first place.

There is a joining up here with nationalist populist commentators like Tucker Carlson who waxed lyrically at AmFest about rural idylls as an antidote to modern life. But the 'broad church' approach creates a dilemma for this vision. While, on the one hand, Elizabeth feels that 'everyone needs to be in', she is also clear that people are free to explore their own ideas of freedom in the way they feel most connected to. She is 'not looking to change other people's ways of doing things', nor does she want to negotiate. 'I'm not responsible for your happiness, you are, trusting yourself.'

In Elizabeth's twenty-first-century version of American Romanticism, she hopes to move to upstate New York, where a medical freedom community and anthroposophical movement is already gathering the like-minded. Her call to others is simple: if you see beauty in what they are doing, join in. If not, go form your own community somewhere else. 'You can fight these institutions for your entire life or your children's entire lives. Why waste time on that? We're not going to win that.' They are building an intentional community instead.

These ideas of rebuilding society outside capitalism are not new. The visionary architect Buckminster Fuller was there in the 1960s. The author and activist Wendell Berry is attempting it in twenty-first-century Kentucky, as we'll see in the next chapter. There is a yearning for a time when we had closer concentric circles of connection. The 'local' is the ideal, decentralised, community for Cat, made up of 'people who you know and interact with', a space that removes the complexity of the unfamiliar and caters to 'our natural inclinations to take care of each other'. She argues that legislation, such as anti-discrimination laws, are only necessary when we make people strangers of each other. The more distant our connections, the more others are strangers, and the more the need to be governed by rules set by others – anathema to those in this movement.

Echoing libertarian thought, people are better off if they stay in their own countries or communities without 'forc[ing] one to assimilate or not assimilate. It's not good for anybody.' Stopping immigration is necessary to prevent social breakdown, but for Cat, it's not about punishing individual people (I refer you back to 'I don't mean you' in Chapter 1). Rather it is *they* (politicians, the elites) who know how to weaponise differences and create conflict. 'So I think it helps if we stay local, because then people aren't strangers and we can work it out together.' Throughout the conversation, Cat and her sister debate what to write on their protest signs; they're going to a demonstration outside the mayor's house to protest against new legislation that would give voting rights to 800,000 'non-citizens' in New York City.[15]

As appealing as American Romanticism and localism might be for some, the possibilities of obtaining that good life were as unequally shared in the nineteenth and twentieth centuries as they are in the twenty-first. There is an over-romanticisation of a 'simpler time', 'the working man', 'labourers', 'rural folk', 'the muscular class', as white-collared Tucker Carlson and Charlie Kirk refer to them. Those who are screwed by 'the system', as Cat would argue. There is recognition that economic necessity, or even 'to experience certain comforts in life', is a reason why people may not 'have a sense of their own freedom that's deeply committed and or sophisticated'. There are limits.

Elizabeth knows we cannot go back to an agrarian society. Instead, she aims for 'parallel communities, where they can do what they want and create the kind of world that they want' – a more 'natural' life where there is greater self-determination, greater autonomy and control. With a preference for the local and the like-minded, a utopian future can be made real in small-scale gatherings. For Elizabeth, 'there's nothing more powerful than getting together and talking about what you care about, even if it's about what you fear'.

Both Cat and Elizabeth see the essence of freedom in the power and success of community. To separate people is to decrease their ability to contest power (something state authorities practise today in the increased privatisation of public space that restricts the right to gather and protest). Elizabeth organises gatherings around the solstice as a way to build 'new realities', in communion with others:

> I think that this is a way to say to people, it's not about 'do you believe in freedom? Do you not believe in freedom.' It's to say, 'I believe in freedom

and I believe in your freedom too and I want this gathering to connect us again in a way that is about our shared humanity.' [...] [C]ome as you are, and leave feeling really good.

Cat also practises gathering, in demonstrations out in the streets but also in small groups of people coming together in manifestation circles as a 'practical system for reality creation'. Manifesting for world peace, for your vegetable garden to grow well, to heal people who are sick. Cat knows that 'it sounds really new-agey', although my community of Buddhists might well argue that we have used similar practices for centuries as a means to shift our perception of what's possible.

Cat recognises that returning to a more 'simple life' is difficult, given how tightly knitted in we are to our system of capitalism, a form of 'economic extortion' almost too complex to work with and heal in her view. Barbara Ehrenreich's *Nickel and dimed*, Jessica Bruder's *Nomadland*, and Eyal Press's *Dirty work* highlight the toll of America's hyper-capitalism in creating inequality. Yet she also holds opposition to initiatives that might relieve economic distress in the USA, such as universal health care or a Basic Income. The argument rests on a belief that the more dependent populations are on the government, the more *they* can pull the strings. It is the libertarian position: every time the government gives you something, it's taking control of that part of your life.

The solution for Cat is to start again. 'Let it fall', and then rise anew, where each would become their own leader, without 'these overlords'. The sentiment finds common ground with social justice activists and Gen Z voices. There is no hope in tinkering with the edges of the current system. It is too moribund. Too corrupt. Hope lies in its complete rupture and rebuilding. The time frame for this revolution shifts throughout our conversation, 'it might take fifty years or more'. I admire her faith but also worry at the thought of how much suffering there would be in that fall and who would be in charge of the rebuild. If it were Elon Musk, I would be worried.

For Elizabeth, the loss of freedom, from mandates or all-encompassing economic systems, wouldn't happen if people had a sense 'of how they navigate the world'. We acquiesce because we have become a little lost. Metaphors of map-reading and way-finding work their way into many conversations in this book and fill me with joy as a geographer. Human bonds need compass bearings, demarcating what it is to be good or to do good.

For those who are 'freedom fighters', according to Elizabeth, they have developed their own compass, 'their own way of navigating truths' in order to explore ideas of freedom within a new terrain. Part of the conversation with Elizabeth becomes a reminiscence about the time before smart phones, when we used different navigational tools to connect with people, when it felt okay to be a little lost geographically and socially:

> I remember a time of organising and meeting friends and having poetic exchanges and stopping by people's studios without one of these [smart phones] and finding one another in a city of ten million people. You could easily at the time write a letter and stick it up at a café where you knew your friend was going to be. Or you could say 'hey, let's meet on Tuesdays here or you know where to find me', because this is a community that I'm committed to, that I live in. And you know you're going to find me at [a café] having coffee. Why? Because you and I have a map of one another's movements, and we're connected that way. [...] [W]e've lost our ability to communicate the math in our communities, and each of the markers of community that used to be parts of the compass have also been decimated. So now we have a complete reliance on an intermediary which also sends us information. And this is really tragic.

Elizabeth's nostalgia, and mine as well, is not just about arranging a cup of coffee with friends, it is an act of resistance against the monotony of contemporary life by creating a vision of a future where it is magical to trust that we will find others.

The analogy of navigation and way-finding resonates with much of the anxiety highlighted in other conversations, in both 'liberal' and 'conservative' circles. In this current era of rapid change and dislocation, not only in the USA but in liberal democracies globally, bearings have shifted or disappeared altogether. Our internal navigation systems, our homing devices are broken, or at the very least, 'not properly tended', according to Elizabeth. Godless, whichever God or none you choose to believe in, we have lost points of authority. We are wandering about in the cultural wilderness, to use a Jordan Peterson metaphor noted back in the chapter on religion.[16]

Despite the dystopian visions, Elizabeth believes in people's good-ness, engaging with the search for a deeper connection with life, with 'love and people' who are motivated to be good. Most people want to do the right thing, and both Cat and Elizabeth care about others. In this collective movement, they feel they are not just fighting for their own sakes but for all our sakes. Merging with other conversations, libertar-ian, conservative and progressive, freedom is sacrosanct and never just about the individual.

Cat's understanding culminates with hope. While it's going to be difficult to walk back from the current situation, there are still those 'who get it, what it means to be human, and to work hard and be resourceful'. 'I'm hoping humanity, those who wake up, will change so that we can really truly have the kind of flowering freedoms that we deserve.'

There are still difficult conversations to be had over how different understandings of freedom are enacted, particularly if they impact on others' ideas about what freedom entails. There is a solution of sorts proposed in re-sorting America, with people moving around the coun-try to seek out lower taxes, a better work/life balance, different educa-tion systems, reproductive rights and/or cheaper housing. There is a re-sorting of moral trade-offs in the process. But eventually the borders of everyone's ideal communities are going to run into each other, necessitating negotiations in the future with other ideas of freedom. Moving is also not an option for everyone, as conversations with rural families in the next chapter make clear. At some point, there is a bal-ance to be struck between freedom in mobility and the freedom found in staying in place.

10

'It all turns on affection': Family, freedom and the land

New York City, 5am. I'm walking to Nostrand station to catch the A Train out to the airport. Even at this hour, the city is all clash and siren. I have not had a full night's sleep for months. The subway is busy as the city's straighteners come home or head out: cleaners, security guards, all people of colour except me. Taking off with the sun behind us, NYC's geometry of gridlines and towers makes way for the flat squares and circles of the 'fly-over' states: brown fields, green patches of irrigation, the occasional impressive river cutting through.

The myth of America that still pervades popular culture and political rhetoric leans heavily on the cliche of taming a wild frontier. Yet the reality of rural life today is more often boarded-up shops and feelings of abandonment. Stereotypes have become the language of political debate, evangelical meetings and water cooler conversations, etching hard borders between urban America, leaning Democrat, imagined as places of violence and disorder, and rural America, leaning Republican, imagined as 'deplorables', 'red necks' and 'hillbillies'.

Much of the USA's power, economic and political, is found on the Atlantic and Pacific Coasts, in the noise of its major urban centres. The middle bit, the Midwest, the fly-over states, feel ignored except when electoral college votes become crucial in deciding who sits in the White House. Yet despite distance and cultural difference, I know these people. They are my folk. I grew up in rural Australia, on dairy farms mostly. I have shovelled shit for pocket money. I know the despair of dying communities as borders open to cheaper imports and in a stock exchange somewhere a trader bets on the future price of food. Supermarkets push prices so low that only agribusiness can make a profit, and family farms fold. Nature twists the knife as livestock die of thirst or crops drown.

Yet there are those who still choose this life, creating a place with deep roots to settle into while the rest of the world seemingly thrives on a constant drive for newness and movement. These people are 'stickers', in the words of writer and advocate for rural economies and communities Wendell Berry, whose work I find both inspiring and frustrating in equal measure as I wrestle with it later in this chapter. 'Stickers' are oddities for wanting to be tied to one place; the wrong kind of people in an urbanised, industrialised and increasingly mobile age.

My conversations with libertarians and members of the medical freedom movement emphasised the importance of mobility in managing change, but it is not always possible for those for whom place is part of their sense of self, their legacy to future generations, and where their community is embedded. For those who have lived on the land for generations, who feel their belonging in that dirt, freedom is here, along with faith and family and a way of being in the world. Fighting against being forgotten in the equations of politicians and bureaucrats a thousand miles away, they are not going anywhere as the world moves around them.

This is not to romanticise rural life or to suggest that those of us who live in cities have no sense of affection for place. But on the land there is no concrete or tarmac, no clash or siren, to come between self and nature. The veneer of human invincibility is thinned out when there is no neon distraction from the realisation of how much we need each other and the earth.

Back at ground level, the Midwest becomes rolling cropland and forest as I drive through. Giant silos mark the raising of grain and corn in Indiana, but in a bleak March with no sign of spring, there are only stalks cut back in barren fields. Despite a clear sunny day, the forest is grey and leafless, punctuated by towns and hamlets with a main street and not much else. There is an occasional Amish buggy, white weatherboard churches and geometric barns. A banner reminds me to 'Trust in God' when there is no-one else. USA and Trump flags fly from trucks, houses, stores and public parks. Two barns next to each other sign 'Praise God' and 'Through Jesus'. Roadside hoardings are dotted with calls to repent and stop abortion, while Christian posters adorn homes, cars and businesses. There is the occasional atheist rebel.

On the Ohio River, slow-moving barges of Kentucky coal slip by in all their dirty glory. On the road, all turnpikes and tollways lead to Travel Plazas, giant hangars with everything the driver needs: Hardee's takeaway grease and free iced tea, information desks and maps, super-clean rest rooms and games area. Strategic repetition of services, as predictable as the endless fields. In the towns, Main Street is walking khaki and beards, trucks and Christian number plates. There are repeated acknowledgements of veterans' service. The Legion collect used flags in the boxes out front, with respect and reverence.

Americana decorates local diners, mostly closed on Mondays and after 2pm the rest of the week: faux wood panelling, Formica tables, tapestry wall rugs featuring the flag and cowboys. A Christmas tree is still up with Easter egg baubles, while St Patrick's Day tinsel and green hats are heaped up on a table next to me. I have noticed Christmas decorations lingering in front yards and homes, 'Be Kind' lawn signs and notices in shops and churches as I drive through. I wonder if people need cheering up.

I am greeted warmly everywhere. I fit right in. In Shoals, Indiana, they love my accent, and the waitress asks about London; she imagines it's very pretty. Kids run in and out. There are tales of catfish that grow from breath to breath. I try my first of many, deep-fried with corn bread, pinto beans and fresh onion (there has to be onion). A side of cherry whip[1] is purchased for me as an act of hospitality (or flirting, I would guess, given how the ladies in the kitchen giggle after the man leaves). Farther north, in Kokomo, the waitress loves my accent. I love hers. The blueberry pancakes are the best. A man at the counter asks how I'm doing. Fine thanks. Across to Marietta, Ohio, there is a table laid out for the fallen soldier and a montaged Israeli/American flag hanging on the wall inside. The waiter loves my accent. I love his. I pick a long route to Point Pleasant, West Virginia, the home of Mothman, a mythical creature sighted in the 1960s and now with its own dedicated festival. A group of young people ask me to take their photograph in front of the statue. They love my accent. I love theirs.

In Maysville, Kentucky, the regulars ask about the Royal Family and hope they're okay.

Back in Indiana, it's biscuits and gravy in Rising Sun, where a fading sign on the door indicates that masks are neither needed nor wanted. It has a 'Veteran Friendly' flag outside and military paraphernalia within, along with a map of the USA on the wall where people have pinned their hometowns. The woman at the table next to me is nursing a hangover and has injured her hand. She's not sure how. She's been a dealer for more than thirty years in the rusting hulk of a paddle steamer docked nearby and converted into a low-rent casino: slot machines in the day, blackjack, poker and craps in the evening. Smoking allowed. The TV is on in the corner with the local Fox19 channel playing. An advertisement for Josh Mandel, running for Senator, calling on people to 'fight for faith and freedom': 'Pro God, Pro Gun, Pro Trump. Send in a marine.' He will ultimately lose the GOP primary nomination to J.D. Vance.

Roads become smaller, gravelly, then dirt, until a final turn into a homestead. It's a cold, wet, wind-swept day lashing this part of Indiana. A hard land to feel attached to but one that means so much to Carol that she begins to cry thinking about it:

> It's important to us that [the farm] is part of what we give to our children. And so I think freedom is like ... kind of just being left alone to do our thing with what we have. ... and come back to me, you let me get myself under control.

Land as legacy enables a future to be mapped out for generations, embedding a community of affection in place that provides a wellspring of support and hope in a fragile world.

There are three generations in the sitting room, the youngest, at seven weeks, rolls on the floor and burps. They are 'probably pretty conservative' but not aligned with a political party per se. 'We're going to vote for the person that we feel is going to leave us alone and let us make our decisions to the best of our ability.' That did mean voting for Trump in the past, but it was not an easy decision. Danni, married to Carol's son Peter, is more 'liberal', coming from suburban Cleveland, Ohio, but she can see things from her in-laws' perspective. Her Christian faith does not preclude her having a gay best friend. That's between him and God. Similarly, Monica, Carol's daughter, is 'definitely aligned more with the Republican Party, but I see so many things in a Democrat view'. Peter is trying to persuade them to swing towards the Libertarian Party (he'll become even more convinced that the current system is broken after the 2024 election campaign).

Unfailingly polite and generous, they are conscious of not wanting to 'step on other people's toes and [be] hurtful'. There is recognition of the need for 'some rules in place', but they 'don't want to impose our views on everybody'. There is an overwhelming desire for the government to 'leave us alone', encapsulated by Ben, Monica's husband:

> I'd say, to us here, [freedom] ranks probably about as high as they can, as a nine or ten for us just because where we live in the country in the way that we operate, we don't really like people to tell us much what to do. So we'd like rules and there to be things in place, but as long as people are leaving us alone in our day to day and we can do things. That's essentially what we think of as freedom here, is like, we can just live our lives and not have people telling us what to do often.

The problem is one of scale. How can a government in Washington, DC know what is happening on this small family holding in the middle of the country? How can they know what life is like here or how universal laws affect this piece of land that is not just a source of income but a legacy for future generations? This disconnect generates anger in the Midwest. It 'feels like the federal government is pushing the values of the east and west coasts on the people in the middle'. And those values are? 'More liberal ideas.' Danni defines them as 'climate change for sure', abortion, welfare, government spending.

Here there are other values preferred, other ideas of what 'good' can mean, weaving together independence and interdependence. It is what sociologist Robert Wuthnow, in *The left behind: Decline and rage in rural America*, refers to as 'moral communities': a sense of place, of being at home, where people feel mutual obligation to each another. Family takes precedence. Monica, a nurse, doesn't live on the farm now but visits most weekends, something her city colleagues 'just don't get':

> The farm is where I want to be, and I just want to be here and love on my family. And I don't know, I don't know, it's kind of hard to put into words sometimes [...] everything's about family ... if you have your family and you have your faith, then you're set, like, that's all. That's all you need in life.

'It all turns on affection,' according to Berry, and the constellation of other emotions that surround it: care, sympathy, love, respect. It is in affection that Berry finds 'the possibility of a neighbourly, kind, and conserving economy', with both producers and consumers belonging to a place, bound by their community.[2] As utopian as it sounds when up against the dominant model of agri-business, this possibility of rural life to create community resonates with the freedom narratives in the previous chapter. It is a way of being in the world that pushes back against punishing economic structures.

I figure it's worth a small detour to Berry's hometown in New Castle, Kentucky, as I make my way from Ohio to Indiana, even if the man himself is unavailable (the near misses and regrets of field work). The Berry Center is a white weatherboard building housing an archive of his writing: poetry, fiction and non-fiction, often incorporating freedom as a theme. His archivist, Michelle, gives me an informal tour (visits are normally Wednesdays, but no one else is around). I admire his work, his convictions, the vision to see another way of life that preserves rural culture. He has long advocated for rural communities as part of functioning regional economies, underpinned by sustainable land conservation. And he lives his words, working on a farm in northern Kentucky for sixty years, advocating low-tech solutions within small-scale, locally adapted, human dimensions, always with ideas of stewardship in mind.[3]

Conservationists and social scientists have long pointed out that our dominant economic theories exclude environmental inputs and human impacts from their models, which, as a result, set out an imagined economic growth without limits. With culture excluded from economic assumptions, rural economies have been discounted or maligned as 'backward', unsophisticated, unmodern, reactionary, nostalgic, anachronistic. Rural voters are pathologised for voting against their own interests, reinforcing the stereotype that urban elites 'look down' on them.[4]

This failure of mainstream economics and politics to recognise rural communities has led to a ruinous relationship with agriculture in America (and globally), decimating not only the land but also people. As Chloe Maxmin and Canyon Woodward show in their book *Dirt road revival*, agriculture in the USA is in peril. The number of farms has fallen from seven million to two million over the last 100 years, and farming income is in the bottom quartile. Research by the free market think tank American Enterprise Institute (AEI) in 2024 found that farms and land being farmed have steadily declined over four decades, even as agricultural output has steadily increased in response to technology and economies of scale.[5] While the AEI lauds this as a positive development, with 'no reason to be concerned about the declines', it is a tragedy for small-scale family farmers, who have lost their land and livelihood. To add to the pain, this loss garners little of the attention directed at the de-industrialised attrition of urban communities.

Rural communities suffer persistently higher rates of poverty and death than urban centres, as well as facing declining sources of work, levels of education and rates of marriage (three key pathways out of poverty).[6] Rural populations are getting older, and the young who leave are less likely to return. Even in one of the richest countries in the world, there is a rural tax: increased costs and poorer access to services such as health care, broadband and phone coverage. The digital economy is concentrated in cities far removed from an analogue rural life.

Agribusiness, often part of transnational conglomerates, influences the economic fate of thousands of small-scale farmers, through price and seed controls and driving demand for particular products. The American Tobacco Company, for example, forced Berry's own family into poverty two generations ago.[7] The second farm of my childhood, part of a dairy cooperative, was closed after it was no longer profitable in the face of cheaper dairy imports from New Zealand (our first farm closed after the local council decided to build a road through it). My politicisation began with economic precarity, fracturing families and communities, and having no choice but to move.

It is the memory of this childhood that fuels my frustration with the work of rural advocates like Berry: in reality, so little has been done to protect rural communities, and what is done is often small scale, piecemeal and re-packaged as farmers' markets for middle-class incomes. This of course is not the fault of Berry. There are wider structural forces that need to be addressed. As he documents, following the Depression in the 1930s, the USA did develop a support scheme for farmers to provide a guaranteed income. In Kentucky, a tobacco-producing state, if the price fell below a certain level an upfront loan was made to farmers that had to be paid back. However, 'Freedom to Farm' reforms, part of the 1996 Federal Agriculture Improvement and Reform Act, ended the practice. The loan was regarded as a 'subsidy' and therefore suspiciously socialist.[8] Bill Clinton, like many political leaders before him and since, preferred industrial policy, with its potential for grand edifices that could bear his name for posterity.[9]

Berry advocates for the return of a farmers' support scheme and is trialling beef production in a region more suited to cattle than the monoculture of soya beans and corn that now dominates Kentucky. Closing the production loop, grass-fed, locally raised and butchered cattle are served at the restaurant across the road from the Berry Center. In principle, a great idea, but one that needs to join up with campaigns to end food deserts in impoverished urban centres. In an interconnected society, rural communities cannot remain isolated in their struggles for economic security nor romanticised for popular consumption.

Back at Carol's family farm in Indiana, they exemplify what Berry means when he says 'it all turns on affection'. Maybe not to the extent it is imagined, but traces of an affective community remain. 'We take care of each other in the Midwest.' Keys are left in the car, and back doors remain unlocked. For Carol, 'we take care of the land, we take care of our cattle, we take care of things without the government telling us we have to, because that's my kids' legacy'.

In counterpoint to the care they show the land and the bond of affection they show each other, there is a feeling that mainstream politics doesn't care much for them. They are reduced to statistics, to which affection does not apply. They do not figure in the imagination of national policy. This neglect rebounds as increasing involvement in their local community, finding spaces where they can 'get your voice heard', such as on school boards. Rural activism is increasingly linked to populist politics as conservative rhetoric appropriates this community's anguish and regurgitates it in calls for a fictitious arcadia.[10] The result, as Carol's family see it, is reinforcing polarisation, creating a public sphere where 'nobody can be wrong. Everybody has to be right', and 'people just hate each other'.

As many others have done in previous chapters, Carol diagnoses the problem as a lack of trust: 'We distrust our government, we distrust politicians. We distrust the media. We don't believe what they say. We distrust what we see on social media. We distrust the fact checkers, we distrust everything. We just don't believe what people say anymore.'

What can be relied upon is family and a community bound by the familiar. Yet, as with other conversations, rural and urban, there's a sense that these ties are becoming weaker, bringing with it an unease about the future. Immigration and changes in social policy are key issues, but the impact of COVID-19 still lingers. It 'pitted neighbour against neighbour'. 'It was that fear.' They're not antivaxxers, but as Carol points out: '[T]hat the government that you don't trust is telling you to get [the vaccine], that's the kicker.'

For holding these values, they are aware that the east and west coast may think they are 'hicks', 'idiots', 'uneducated' (despite all being university graduates). Some 'liberals' in my conversations did express these stereotypes: for example, many Americans 'don't leave their little Midwest town where they grew up and marry their childhood sweetheart, and then have four kids, they never see what's outside'. Yet Carol's family are thoughtful and empathetic, thinking critically, never losing sight of the complexity of their arguments. Every time I think of a counter to something that's been said, someone else in the family is there before me. Monica, reflexively and with humility, circles back to an earlier comment she made to add nuance and capture their concerns in more depth, balancing, as we all do, the desire to stay in our 'bubbles' where it's safe with the need to engage with the wider world:

> I've been stewing on how you said it, because I think that it's selfish of us to say, 'oh, yeah, let's just stay in our own little bubble and not worry about anything else in the world'. I think it's very difficult. I think difficult is a good word, it's difficult for us to have to think about that kind of stuff to get outside of our lives. [...] I have to remember that when I get in this mindset of yes, my family is most important and yes, I want to stay in our little circle. But there are a lot of things outside of our little

circle that really matter and that are really important that if we just stay in our circle and don't worry about those things it's just gonna get worse.

It is repeated several times throughout the conversation: 'I don't know what the answer is.' 'I don't know how to fix this.' 'I don't know the answer, but it's a mess.' Grappling with right and wrong, tinged with notes of despair at the state of politics but also expressing gratitude for their 'luck' at being able to access America's freedoms, they articulate the 'fine lines', 'blurred lines', 'ambiguous lines' that we all have to navigate, especially at times of change.

With such differences in deep-seated values across the country, the discussion turns to the possibility of civil war and fears for the future, but there is also optimism. Frank, Carol's husband, comes home after tending a calving cow. All are well, although they joke about the vet's bill to come (the cow needed a c-section). We sit at the table, eating Amish cake I bought at the farmers' market in the morning. He didn't join in the conversation earlier as he thought it sounded 'political', which he avoids. So we chat about the farm and my parents, both now retired and living in town. None of us children wanted to continue farming. For Frank, it would be inconceivable to give up the land. 'I don't know how you give up something you've worked your whole life to attain.' His vision of the future is one of continuity and hope:

> It has changed so fast in my lifetime, so much in my lifetime. Used to be things were a little more simple. Now with technology things change every six months. I can't keep up. [laughs] I'm too old for this. But, you know, I have hope for our country, I hope it'll be better. I don't know that it will ... But certainly hope so because I have kids and grandkids. I would like them to have the same opportunities that I did, the same enjoyment of life that I've had. We have a farm here, a family farm that we will pass on, and hopefully they will enjoy, even if they don't farm. To have the opportunities to do what I did, you know, fish and have freedoms, all this land is ours that we can do things on. I'd like to at least have the opportunity. I think they will.

He finishes by adding that he 'doesn't like being told what to do'. There is a burst of laughter. 'Yes,' I say with cake, 'I get that none of you like being told what to do.'

As I move farther west, the plains meet the slopes of the Rocky Mountains. The seasons are in that interstitial moment, shifting from one day to the next. The air is hot, dry and hurts my eyes. A little out of Denver, the ethereal voice of Phoebe Bridgers echoes in surround sound over boulders and cliffs – a soundcheck at the Red Rock Amphitheatre. I'm thrown back to a childhood listening to parentally approved John Denver albums. Taking the long way to a meeting, there is time for breakfast in a diner where the wait staff seem to have enjoyed some 420 (legal in Colorado). The folks at the table next to me are ordering Bloody Marys and Irish Coffee at 10am. A section of Main Street, including the café, has the classic wooden frontage of the Wild West. Foregrounding foothills with snow caps in the distance, red earth is cut open by jagged bones of rock poking through the skin, forced upwards by a deep rumble an aeon ago. I sit under the trees to take a break from driving in heat that smells like another home.

Twenty-four hours later, it has dropped to 4 degrees (Celsius), with heavy snow most of the day. In the white out, rumble strips alert me when I veer too close to an edge. Passing through the town of Vail, home to one of the United States' largest ski resorts, reminds me that not all rural areas are poor, and at the Honey Butter diner I'm reassured that everything is 'awesome', at least according to the very tall server, a snowboarding, skateboarding, ice hockey kind of dude.

Once I'm over the high passes, the snow turns to rain that the Western slopes are glad of. The region has been suffering drought for several years. The land is a patchwork ordered around ditches: the water system that is the lifeline for smallholders, residents and farmers, stressed not only by drought but by a growing population. Cheaper housing, lower taxes, better weather, a beautiful view has attracted new residents and new industries to Colorado, supported by the postpandemic realisation that we don't have to be tethered to a desk all day. Smalltown Americana now contains the markers of creative gentrification: murals along Main Street, quirky boutiques in historic downtown areas, craft beer and arts centres looking for artists. These shifting demographics, coupled with a climate crisis, are transforming land use and environmental regulations, foreshadowing more change.

Off road, it is a bumpy drive, with axles deep in mud at times. A stele at a ranch gate traces a family tree across several generations. I'm travelling with a friend, Travis, to his cabin on one of Colorado's mesas, but we stop off at a neighbour's ranch, an hour or so away. Seth's family has been on this land for over a century. They arrived as 'homesteaders' in 1891, moving to the mesa in 1914. Of Scottish descent, he is stocky, gravelly, appearing from behind his truck with his son and eight-year-old granddaughter, all in camouflage. They've been hunting turkeys. Seth's son, Mike, was raised here – 'like a painting on the wall. Yeah, hanging around.' The grandchildren will be the sixth generation on this land.

Mike is quiet but jokingly sets the tone straight away. 'Well, I hope you didn't think we're a bunch of random hillbillies here.' Seth is more direct: CNN is 'the communist worst'. He enjoys reading the *Epoch Times* and considers the local government a 'bunch of liberals'. They are a Christian and National Rifle Association (NRA) household. 'That's your freedom', to own a gun or not. Seth was a supporter of Trump, though he's disillusioned with him now. They have their own border: 26 miles of high fence around their ranch, where they manage elk for hunting. The lodge is spacious, wooden, rustic on the outside but all mod cons within, including a lounge area, pool table and bar for the guests who come in the autumn to shoot. It is wall to wall taxidermy, heads and bodies: mountain lion, bears, turkeys' tail fans and beards, moose and elk. I try lifting a full set of antlers, easily a metre long, and barely manage to get it a few centimetres off the ground. If antlers lock when sparring, elk can exhaust each other to death. I take it as a metaphor for current politics.

Seth's granddaughter has been sitting on a large leather couch reading her Bible while I toured the lodge. She joins us at the kitchen table, where we drink coffee and finish some ginger muffins. I ask her if she will take over the ranch one day: 'That's what my dad says.' Seth adds: 'And the next [generation], I've preached to these guys, and it's been preached to me, and it was preached to my dad.' Like Carol's family, Seth has a love for this land that is beyond monetary value:

> Let me tell you, there's a certain satisfaction, [Mike] and I get it. Because we live here and we get to go do what we did this morning [hunting]. I mean, this is heaven, you know, it's like heaven to us. Oh, it is just so pleasurable to be there. [...] It's just something unless you have lived it you don't get it.

America's divide is marked out by the incommensurability of 'not getting it', like Monica's city friends who don't 'get' why she returns to the farm most weekends. But again there is a sense of unease as the old ways change. Former points of authority decline, like the membership numbers of the Masonic Lodge that Seth belongs to. There is the now familiar list of threats to freedom: cancelled speech, changing curricula, sex education, government interference and lack of trust in politics and civic institutions, China, DEI, Big Tech, mainstream media. Seth is strongly opposed to the 'loss of control' at the border. It means losing control of the country. When I mention the demographic shifts in the USA, Seth notes, 'it's gonna be a different world' and asks 'who's gonna take over, the Latinos?' It's unlikely there will be one dominant ethnic group, but the key point is that it will no longer be a white majority. It will look and feel different. Seth doesn't want to talk about race.

Closer to home, it is the changing demographics in the region that is a more immediate concern. An increasing human presence on the mesa, which Seth links to the increase in remote working, puts pressure on the land. It's impacting on elk numbers. They regard themselves as 'environmentalists' but acknowledge that other environmentalists would probably not agree with all they do, and vice versa. There is another 'fine line' to be navigated between different versions of stewardship, demarcating change and the intangible feeling of discomfort as control slips away. Seth worries for the viability of his home and his grandchildren's future on this land. Like Carol and Frank, he dislikes the idea that someone else has control over their lives and livelihood.

Property rights run deep, inscribed in the boundaries and the roots and the rocks. The mistake in America, according to the early twentieth-century American poet and social commentator Allen Tate in his essay 'Notes on liberty and property' (1936), was to convince ourselves that there is just one kind of property: big or small, owned by a family or owned by a conglomerate, it's all the same. Devoid of affection, in policy and economics, property is a transaction, a profit centre.

This is clearly not how Carol or Seth or Travis see their land, and Seth's overriding concern now is that their future, along with property rights, is being eroded. 'Private property rights are infringed on all the time in this country. [...] There's a lot of people in the United States that feel like those of us that are landowners ... It's unfair.' For Seth, those people doing the infringing are mostly 'liberals' who want to impose 'limitations on the Constitution' which should protect his property rights. He is a constitutional absolutist.

Those directing change are increasingly remote from the actual experience of rural communities, yet the impact of decisions made elsewhere, by governments or corporations, is felt very closely at home. From county to federal, Seth does not like nor trust the government, particularly concerning matters key to his family's continuing on this land: wildlife management and water rights. Water has particular currency, and their access to a ditch is like a title to property. 'It's yours.' So as the rivers and springs and ditches empty in a seemingly endless drought, and water is rationed or diverted for urban consumption, there is fear they will also lose those rights and eventually the land.

The diagnosis, that this discomfort is the fault of 'liberals' or an overreaching government, is mismatched to the control of economic markets by a handful of private companies.[11] Corporate behemoths, from the 'robber barons' of the nineteenth and twentieth centuries (industrialists such as Vanderbilt, Carnegie, Rockefeller) to the new Tech Bros of Silicon Valley, exalt capitalism but don't quite play by the rules of the free market in their curtailing of as much competition as possible. Seth acknowledges that some industrial sectors like meat processing are controlled by a handful of companies.[12] But the problems of monopoly are heaped at the doorstep of the government, who are simultaneously blamed for allowing the problem but also told that their interference is unwelcome. The logic doesn't hold.

An hour or so from Seth's ranch, Travis and I drive to his Mesa along narrow, rough track, crunching through fallen aspen after strong winds the previous week. His 'cabin' is actually a beautifully crafted, Scandinavian-style, curved-roof structure, with a decked yurt on the side as the master bedroom. Travis is clearly a handy man and has set up a decent water, sewerage and electrical system. He shows great pride in taking me on a tour. Religious icons mark out the perimeter: a Buddha in meditation, a Hindu god, small plaques on trees saying 'hope', 'peace' and 'love'. Travis has sourced the local arts community and family to paint murals or add pieces to the land and its buildings, including a wrought-iron sasquatch. There are several outbuildings dotted around: storage sheds and small guest huts. Through a forest of trees is mine, the original cabin. It's rougher but has a stunning view across the valley to a range of 4,000-metre peaks. It also has the addition of a bathroom with an incongruous clawfoot bathtub looking out through French windows towards the mountains. It is a marker of proximity to the ski resort of Aspen's interior designers, but given that the spring has dried up, so there's no water for a bath, it's also a marker that nature doesn't care how much you pay for a fancy tub.

At almost 3,000 metres, set within aspen and Douglas fir forest, this is 105 acres of 'sanctuary' for Travis. Hummingbirds dart and hover at the bird feeders. A fox wanders past the deck, pounces on a mouse and disappears. Chipmunks and golden-mantel squirrels steal the bird food. Blue jays manage to look comical and threatening at the same time. In the past, during a difficult period, Travis lived here almost permanently on his own, but now he comes every week for a few days at a time, often with his partner, Veronica. He never stays longer than a week; if he did, he says he would probably never leave. 'This is the ultimate freedom because it doesn't matter what the hell is going on down there [in the valleys]. Arlo's [his neighbour] got guns, I've got pot in the basement, and food for a month.' He helpfully hands me bear spray: 30 feet and five seconds, aim for the eyes. The fire lit with too much wood, I put the can of bear spray by the bed and sleep with one ear open.

Next morning, we go visiting his neighbours, Arlo and Maeve. They live on the mesa permanently, some 500 metres away through the forest. Theirs is a more traditional two-storey cabin, open plan in the main room with a mezzanine for the bedroom warmed by rising heat from the central stove. It's still unfinished inside and rustic outside, with additions of a trailer and assorted sheds. After fifteen years,

Maeve still hasn't decided what to do about the kitchen. There is a large flat-screen television with two recliner leather rockers oriented towards it. There are also two dogs: Lego stretches on the back of Maeve's chair, almost around her neck, and the other lies on her lap. A holstered handgun hangs from the banister. When I mention it to Arlo, he retrieves his handmade semi-automatic with silencer to show me. He is an experienced hunter. The cabin is decorated with bear skins and other animal trophies, some his, some his daughter's. Maeve loves pistols and owns several but doesn't like to hunt. They are also an NRA household. 'I hope that we never get to the point where I cannot defend myself, or my family.'

Both are originally Southerners, Arlo from Georgia and Maeve from Florida, so there is always sweet iced tea in the fridge, no matter the temperature outside. Arlo doesn't 'get along' with big cities. 'Too many people.' When they left Florida, their rural neighbourhood was being swallowed up by suburbs. Now he has a feeling that it is getting too crowded on their mesa. Apart from Travis's cabin, hidden by Aspen forest, I can't see anyone else for miles.

They banter like a long-married couple, because they are. They met when Maeve was thirteen and Arlo eighteen and married two years later. Maeve laughs that that doesn't happen anymore. Maeve and I bond over stories of feeding the calves when we were growing up on a farm. She tells of her goat that ended in the freezer. I recount the story of Wilbur, the pet sheep who I'm pretty sure ended up the same way after an accident broke his leg. There are questions about my parents' farm. How big is the 'ranch'? What cattle? How many? How often we milked, once or twice a day? I talk about my chores.

From a first job at twelve years, Arlo went on to the military, a paratrooper, for 'twenty years and twenty-six days'. His grandfather and father were also airborne. He saw active service in Vietnam. His daughter, also in the military, had tours of duty in Iraq and Afghanistan. Arlo refers to military service as a 'responsibility', recognising 'it was not a popular opinion at the time'. On returning from fighting in Vietnam, he was harassed by strangers when wearing his uniform, but attitudes have changed: 'I showed you my hat. I wear that [military] hat with

the wings and everything on it more in protest now, because I can ...
it's one of my freedoms. But more people now come up and say "thank
you for your service".'

Having lived overseas with the military, there is a sense of gratitude
for the freedoms they have, summarised in the now familiar sketch:
'Unless it is a violation of someone else's freedom, we have freedom
to do just about anything.' He is a self-confessed optimist and the only
person I meet who says he trusts the government. Maeve, on the other
hand, reiterates the challenges facing democratic governance, including that rural areas 'don't count as much'.

Not wedded to a political party, like many others Arlo has switched
allegiance from Democrat to Republican, but 'it was the party that
changed', not him. During COVID-19 restrictions, Maeve proudly
wore a Trump mask, receiving a 'thumbs up' wherever she went.
Trump has a lot of approval in this part of the world, but when I asked
her why she supported him, her reply is not so straightforward: 'I
don't', not unequivocally at least.

Defying stereotypes ('uneducated hillbillies'), they both take voting
seriously as a civic responsibility and take part in all elections, from
local judges to the President. Arlo has voted in every election since
1964. His sense of duty is palpable. 'You have to do the research to be
informed. And if you don't know then you're really not doing what you
should do for your country.' They sometimes vote for opposite candidates and cancel each other out, but as a rule they will vote for who-
ever they believe addresses the issues important to them, for example
gun ownership, immigration and being in debt to China.

Shifting attitudes towards public service and patriotism are markers of intergenerational change in their family, indicative of a shift in
moral frameworks. Rural communities of affection, self-reliant, 'close
knit', 'doing their own thing' epitomise values of personal responsibility. But for Maeve, there's less 'morality' in the USA today, and less
discipline. Parents are too busy, houses are too big and kids hang out in
their bedrooms too much. Things she and Arlo value, like voting, the
'grandkids don't believe that'. Pointing to the impact of urbanisation,
Maeve draws a correlation between the hard work of farm life, where
kids have chores, and the likelihood of them getting into trouble. 'The

harder the work, the less likely the trouble' is a formula beloved of families and intergenerational nostalgia, although we found ample opportunity on our farm as kids to collect various scars and broken bones. More realistically, there is a nod to a stronger sense of community, to watching over families and to sharing the load. Looking after his grandchildren when his daughter was deployed to Iraq, Arlo soon confiscated their Game Boys and told them to go outside and play with the dog. They learned to catch crawdads in the creek.

For Arlo, freedom was at times coupled with the desire for hard boundaries, perhaps indicative of someone who has spent a lifetime in uniform. 'If it's a rule, it's a rule. Okay. Black and white. If it's a rule you do it, if it's not a rule you don't necessarily but it's no different to me.' The application of rules was illustrated in the inevitable conversation about the Southern border, an open wound that America First/MAGA poke a stick at daily on multiple channels in their media ecosystem. While there is empathy for those who want a better life, illegal migration is against the rules and generates a dystopian imagination of the future. The addition of strangers in large numbers brings discomfort to the surface for Maeve:

> It's like a balloon. And if you fill that balloon with water it's gonna pop. And if it pops, and you've got all these people, how are we going to feed them, take care of them? What are we going to do? With all these people the land is going to go. There's not going to be farmers and stuff [...]. So how are we going to survive foodwise? [...] It's the people coming over that will not stay and fight for their country.

The sum of care, land and national duty narrates a path to an anxious future: to not know if this land will be given to the next generation so that they will be remembered as part of one continuous story in which an individual life made a difference. Instead, they worry that their land will be taken by strangers or a tyrannical government. Add in the freedom-limiting precarity of ageing and inequality. As Maxmin and Woodward argue, rural America has few of the conditions that would enable a decent life, including access to a secure retirement:

> I've got back problems and knee problems. I can't do as much ... I used to do a lot [...] I could do anything in the world. Outside fence or haul 100-pound sack of feed. But when you start having pain and your knee wants

to give out. [...] It's like I have not figured out what we're going to do up here. I don't know how I'm going to clean the fan off.

Arlo suggests just taking the fan down.

Driving back to Denver, I choose again the longest route possible, taking as much time as I can in a landscape that will outlast our economic models. There are more diners to stop at, more pie to eat, as wild clouds scud across big skies and light fractures on black lakes. The precarity in rural America that I pass through highlights the importance of community and bonds of affection, especially in remote areas where individual freedoms may have less importance at times when compared to necessary cooperation. You need to know your neighbours will help even if they have different politics. Shared ditches need to be maintained to keep water flowing and equipment borrowed to keep roads clear. This is an imperfect affection, conditional to the extent that it serves a purpose, and complicating any arcadian depiction of rural life. But it is also an affection that defies polarisation and points towards how America's broken system may possibly be repaired. This form of love might just possibly trump hate sometimes.

11

'Figuring out' the future, writing new freedoms

Just a reminder. We won and they lost.[1]

Charlie Kirk, November 2024

I'm still okay my love (...) I had enough of his hatred. Some hate can't be negotiated out.[2]

Tyler Robinson, September 2025

That man, that young man ... I forgive him. (...) The answer to hate is not hate. The answer we know from the gospel is love, and always love. Love for our enemies and love for those who persecute us.[3]

Erika Kirk, September 2025

I hate my opponent and I don't want the best for them. (...) I can't stand my opponent.[4]

Donald Trump, September 2025

The Firehouse is in a busy part of New York that is gentrifying fast. Ed, Colin, Nick and Paul make me lunch in the kitchen and set the rules. No recording, no photos, no signing forms. The fire department has a high public approval rating, particularly post-9/11, but became embroiled in anti-mandate protests during the pandemic (they had to be vaccinated or lose their jobs) and claims of political partisanship in the 2024 presidential campaign.[5] They are 'a close society', 'not in public sight', very much part of the local community. A battalion of American hyphens, first-, second- and third-generation immigrants, many have family connections in the service: dad, older brother, uncles, grandfathers. There is a lot of 'banter', 'good-natured ribbing'. 'We all trust each other with our lives every day. There is no such thing as racism in this department.' One of the younger members is Hispanic, hugged by Colin and called a 'spic'. Everyone has to 'enjoy the comedy, not be offended by student jokes, pull their weight' – the organisational culture required to fit in. But outside, things are changing.

'Everything has become too expensive.' Despite the stressful nature of their work, many have side jobs to make ends meet, in construction and landscaping for example. There are several call outs during the morning. No one gets to relax. Ed notes it's not a healthy lifestyle. On night shift, they eat late then sleep with one ear open for the alarm.

Some have left the borough to live farther away, where it's cheaper. Paul's family moved when things 'got bad', with crime and immigration linked to things 'going bad'. Other explanations, such as the inequalities of capitalism or structural racism, do not cut through. They pay for their own lunch and clean the stations themselves. There is sarcasm from Nick, directed at debates on diversity: '[I]t's my privilege to clean toilets.'

There is the familiar list of dissent and pointed lack of trust in organisations that used to protect the working class. Government, 'elites' and unions are 'corrupt'. Trump is the exception. 'He already had money' and is not seen as enriching himself at taxpayers' expense. On the other hand, 'there's nothing wrong with working hard and making a ton of money. Elon Musk employs thousands and pays taxes. 'It's the American Dream right there.' Ed and I argue he's not paying enough taxes, but it's difficult to intervene when Colin and Nick are in full flight. '[Musk] isn't here to take care of the world, he's taking care of his family', the centre of obligations. 'No one else is going to take care of you.'

And yet they care – about each other, about what happens in the neighbourhood and in the country. Larger forces are blamed for the increasing dysfunction they see and feel – 'globalism', equated with 'socialism' at times, leading to 'communism'. There is the abstract 'they', the absent, unseen bringer of disorder and discomfort, taking away their freedoms. 'Who is they?' I ask. 'Liberals!' 'Ed!' Laughter. Ed is a Democrat, the others Republican leaning, Trump supporting. Colin believes Trump 'spoke to the people. You don't have to like the guy but you have to love what he did for the country. He punished China, closed borders, brought manufacturing back.' Ed intervenes: 'He raised taxes!' A debate follows.

Ed once voted for the libertarian businessman and independent presidential candidate Ross Perot but became more 'liberal' after 9/11, in opposition to the Iraq War. Nick voted for Clinton twice but Trump in

2020. Paul's parents voted Democrat. 'They were for the blue collar, pro-family, pro-working man. Unions were different back then, [pushing for] safe working conditions, job security, equal pay. Democrats took care of their community.' He gives the example of a former representative who would find jobs for people. 'Now it's AOC. This Democrat party is so ... extreme.' Ed remarks that AOC is 'his girl'.[6]

Common tropes are repeated. Globalists, of course, outside influences such as George Soros, China, Russia, the threat of a one world order, one world police force, rigged elections. J6 was either a legitimate protest ('it was our house') or 'treason'. There are myths on repeat. The lost cause narrative of the South gets an airing. Democrats want abortions during the ninth month of pregnancy. Big Government wants to increase taxes, nationalise health care, get rid of guns and legalise marijuana ('dumbing down society'). There is more criticism of Big Pharma and medical mandates. 'In a few years you will see it will be the biggest hoax. It's all about the money. We should seize all of China's assets.' One of the younger members of the battalion says 'kung flu' behind me. There are several references to Democrats being soft on crime. Colin is pro-gun and hunts. The others joke that he cries when he kills something. 'New York is liberal', full of 'transient people', whereas 'outside, people hunt, fish, there's a different view'.

On education, it's 'college kids brainwashed by their professors', so that 'they hate this country'. Nick makes a crack about 'gender studies'. I remind them I'm a professor who sometimes teaches gender studies and CRT, and Colin asks me why I'm teaching young people to hate their country. Again, I really don't have that much power, and students might have their own ideas. They are not convinced. Nick sends his kids to Catholic school.

Out of the jumble of feelings and truths and mis/dis-information is one overriding, visceral concern: immigration, particularly how 'third-world immigrants' will change the country. They don't want to go outside and speak another language. There is discussion of birth rates, large families and another culture 'taking over'. 'No one wants to become [American]. They just want to reap our freedoms.' Antebellum fears see the light of day: '[W]ith all the mixing you don't have a strong society.' Fear of numbers is layered over perceptions of unfairness. The

'Spanish' come and work for cheap, bringing down wages. The Chinese only hire Chinese, but at least they don't get into trouble. 'They stick with their kind.' 'The people who come here ruin it for everyone.'

Reminders of racism that may have affected their own families ('no blacks, no dogs, no Irish') do not invoke empathy. 'Eventually it turns to shit, because this race is going to get tired of that race.' Echoing the separatist approach that some libertarians and medical freedom activists support, Nick argues that 'you're not going to get everyone together. Everyone should just stay in their own different groups.' There's nothing wrong with having an identity, he argues, it keeps things in order. He wants the borders to be closed.

The three younger members of the battalion have withdrawn from the table and are having their own discussion behind us. I ask what they think, but they say they aren't interested in politics. The older members, however, are on a mission to find 'The Truth!' Fox News is popular, as is Tucker Carlson: '[He] speaks the truth.' Colin listens to Joe Rogan. He doesn't always agree with him, 'but he's pretty straight up'. My Rogan joke about Jefferson and the Constitution doesn't land well, or maybe it's just my delivery. It goes like this: Thomas Jefferson appears in twenty-first-century America. His first question is 'you guys didn't write any new shit?! Dude, I wrote the Constitution with a feather. I did it by fire! It was the only way I could see what I was writing! You lazy fucks!! You guys have phones in your pockets and spaceships!!' 'But the wisdom of the scrolls shall not be adjusted,' someone says. Jefferson replies, 'What the fuck does that even mean?! Who told you that bro?'[7]

For Colin, the Constitution is 'the most brilliant document written for its time. [The Founders] saw the future of what could happen. Everything would run smoothly if we just follow the Constitution.' If we just follow the rules ... made by free white men 250 years ago. Since January 2025, Donald Trump has himself shown scant regard for the Constitution or any other rules.

If things don't change, their vision of the future is 'dark', whether because of 'misinformation' (Ed) or 'greed' (Colin). But in their present frustration, there are surprising rays of hope. There is disagreement on every topic, the subject gets changed, we eat something, we move on. Despite their differences, there is absolute consensus that they must trust each other to keep each other safe. 'We have our different views but we have learned with this job that you have to find the middle ground. We still work together.' I ask if we can scale that idea up to the national level. 'If we are in charge [laughs], but that's not how it is.'

It only took a few hours at the Firehouse to confirm the feeling I'd had after that first AmFest rally: that America First/MAGA had a good chance of winning again in 2024. When Alexis de Tocqueville toured America, almost 190 years earlier, he described a country that had broken with the old authorities of European aristocracy and centralised religion.[8] This was a nation influenced by ideas of freedom that flowed with the movement of people to the 'New World'. Yet while admiring much of this America, de Tocqueville was prescient in his concern that this energy unleashed could in turn undermine freedom via a 'tyranny of the majority'.

In November 2024, the majority rejected a system that couldn't provide answers to the challenges they and the country faced. The conversations in this book happened before the election, but the themes that emerge tally with the autopsy of the Democrats' loss. The choices people made that day became part of managing the profound cultural and economic changes in America, embedded in calculations and trade-offs about what the future might look like.

Globalisation, immigration, social transformation, particularly attitudes to gender and sexuality, COVID-19, technology, geopolitical and demographic shifts. These changes have accumulated over decades, stretching and bending freedom out of shape so much that it no longer serves to define what it means to be good, or to protect things and people and ways of being in the world. Change has generated doubt that America is as free as it thought it was, or as exceptional. There is doubt that the future will be the same as the past, leading to fears of 'losing my country' or losing out in general. With no new compass, maps or rules for navigation, Democrats underestimated the strength of feelings like 'love of country' and 'hate the other side' that had become points of orientation instead.

Kamala Harris tried to use the power of freedom in her campaign, but too little, too late. While Trump and America First/MAGA made freedom feel real (prosperity, free speech, guns, patriotism), the Democrats made it seem lofty, idealistic or an abstract joy.[9] There was no redress for the tensions between individualism and affection for community, and no offer of a new social contract to replace the old one that was well and truly busted after the Global Financial Crisis (GFC).

The contested nature and contrasting imaginations of freedom played out in the politics and cultural infrastructure of everyday life, in families, schools, churches, rural and urban areas, while unfreedoms, immobilities and inequalities became starker in comparison. For those who felt marginalised, poorer, humiliated, ridiculed or forgotten, an America First/MAGA victory meant 'our voice still matters'. Their version of freedom could be restored. Change could be stopped, even rowed back. For a moment, in a voting booth, they had some control over the direction of change.

In fairness, I didn't predict that it would be Trump again in 2025. I thought Ron DeSantis or J.D. Vance would get in first to continue the America First/MAGA agenda. Trump outlasted many expectations and has been true to his word on taking office. His is an authoritarian freedom, imposing tariffs that stymie free trade, blocking freedom of choice for women and the trans community, cancelling free speech under threat of deportation and/or punitive legal measures, and rolling back rights like due process.

This authoritarianism became justified when positioned as 'saving freedom', saving the soul of the nation, saving the master narrative that threads America together. It shouldn't have come as a surprise. America First/MAGA commentators openly spoke of the need to restore 'the Republic' for America to flourish and re-find its virtue. Equating democracy with mob rule, in double speak, Charlie Kirk was clear: 'pure democracy leads to dictatorship'.[10]

Trump promised to reset the throughline of history and banish the unease of an anxious future created by strangers and the strange (e.g. immigrants and new pronouns). He made 135 executive orders, thirty-six memoranda and thirty-five proclamations in the first hundred days, designed to regain control, humiliate 'the other side' and erase shame in retribution. The inconsistencies and contradictions of restricting the freedoms of others in the name of freedom became inconsequential to the need to feel safe. Joe, one of the Texas libertarians, was right: people will trade off freedom for safety, including some of the most powerful people in terms of wealth and influence, like law firms, Tech Bros and university leaders. 'The world is laughing at us,' Trump insisted. Well, we're not laughing any more, as he called on leaders to 'kiss my ass'.[11] America has become reality TV, and we are all playing a part in the show. There is an excess of drama and emotion as sclerotic systems meet brittle egos unable to tolerate ambivalence and ever faster cycles of whiplash policy making.

But America First/MAGA's freedoms are reaching the limits of others' noses, and despite the boasts of MAGA, MAHA and MASA, the future appears poorer, sicker, less safe. A state of perma-crisis continues. It must continue; there is no reason for America First/MAGA and its associated organisations to exist if there is no struggle for the soul of America. There must be spectacle and an enemy, a 'they' trying to take away freedom. People must remain in a state of free fall so they reach out for something solid to hold on to, some concrete reality in the face of the unknown. There must be someone who can explain away the feelings of unease and precarity, who can reassert a benchmark of what it is to be American.

Without a sense of settlement or resolution, conversations in this book fell back on resignation: it's 'a mess, we're a mess'. 'We're tired, we're burned out.' 'Everything is going to hell.' Everything is elevated. Everything is at breaking point. We tumble exhausted into a vacuum of uncertainty about what comes next for the USA and the rest of the world. The nationalist populism of America First/MAGA isn't going anywhere, even if Trump steps aside in 2028. Precarity, and authoritarian responses to it, are part of our lives for the foreseeable future.

Back in New York towards the end of my travels, I meet with Hanima, who in Chapter 1 reminded me not to think of freedom in the abstract. She asks, after all the conversations I've had, 'Is there hope for America?' I can compile a list of factors driving cultural change that many feel threaten their freedoms, and consequently their future: immigration, the impact of globalisation and social alterations. I can point out how individuals attempt to manage the sense of instability by using the master narrative of freedom to give them a sense of orientation. However, reconciling the different approaches to managing change, to adapting to new ideas about what America represents, is more difficult. Supporters of Trump's approach hope it will usher in a new era of freedom. Less government, increased prosperity, order restored, safety felt. From my fairly liberal perspective, on the other hand, it's not looking good: oligarchy, plutocracy, corruption, the rolling back of the separation of powers, the rule of law and constitutional processes. Each of us thinks the other is a little delusional.

Cultural change can feel both rapid and glacial, as tectonic plates move at different speeds, grating against each other. It is a painful process. Structures that have held the USA together for so long are disassembling chaotically. It's gut wrenching to watch. There is speculation about a future civil war, but the USA is already fracturing, as states diverge on abortion, education, vaccines and religion. There are bellicose threats from Washington, DC, and there are a thousand little mutinies in response. Some see a balkanised future, with the federal government breaking up into blocks: west and east coast, middle and south. Others are prepping, stocking up on food and guns.

In this context, having the capacity to imagine alternative futures in which we are more free becomes very labour intensive. Yet there is always hope. In quiet and sometimes banal ways, the USA is not quite as divided as it appears on the surface. The conversations throughout this book indicate moments where people are 'figuring out' ways to bridge divides, to keep society civil, to find a collective future. De Tocqueville described the USA as an 'experiment', and that idea is repeated across the contemporary political and media landscape.[12] It can adapt. As the Firehouse showed, there is space for hope in the care the firefighters show each other and their neighbourhood. There is empathy and humility and love reclaimed from xenophobia. There is nostalgia for a time when 'we all got on'. People acknowledge they don't have to share the same values, and that's okay. People want to do good and contribute to something other than individual success.

People are creating alternative visions for collective futures, using a range of strategies deployed on a daily basis. These are often unremarked, unacknowledged, but keeping in place threads of resilience holding it all together, rebuilding trust, repairing the USA. Using freedom as a starting point, people encounter and navigate differences through dialogue, finding common ground and seeing the humanised individual rather than the demonised mob. Trust and connections are rebuilt and maintained in ordinary, everyday encounters. There are gatherers, those who bring people together to feel safe, and there are in-betweeners, those with bridging capital who cross divides. There is faith that allows us to think of a collective we have yet to meet, and faith that unknown others will stand by our side. We are all just trying to 'figure it out', to find a way of living together with our differences and creating new spaces that enable us to do that.

As a place to start, there was one point of agreement that emerged across the political spectrum when I asked how people imagined America's future: the current political system is failing and needs to change. So let's start with the Constitution. There are those who believe this is 'sacred'. As a guiding document, it has a 'brilliance' to it, 'the best historical document for freedom in the world'. A suggestion in one conversation that it could be rewritten was met with: 'Would you rewrite the Bible?' Well, probably, bits of it, yes. Yet while origi-nalists and textualists may argue over the nuances, shortcomings are recognised. It 'isn't perfect'. To continue to live by a document writ-ten in the eighteenth century 'just seems silly'. Even Joe Rogan agrees with that one. Adaptation is necessary: to climate change, a new geo-political world, shifting demographics, new cultural borders and chal-lenges the Founders never anticipated, like artificial intelligence. But making formal updates has been difficult. Legal fudges are possible using shadow spaces, for example, the Fourteenth Amendment's right to privacy. This has managed a multitude of ambiguities, including interracial marriage and abortion. Yet legislation like the Equal Rights Amendment (ERA) (guaranteeing equality under law regardless of sex), first introduced in 1923, remains unresolved due to a time limit for ratification imposed in 1972.[13]

There are arguments for starting again from scratch. A brand new Constitution could incorporate new forms of protection (the right to clean air and water, for example), as well as rectifying the glaring absence of people who weren't there the first time around. For Mark, a former Democrat congressional candidate, 'I think a freer future, hope-fully, would be one that has a chair at the table for the white Christian, but has fifteen other chairs for everybody else.' Given the vehement opposition from others to this idea, it seems an unlikely way forward any time soon. To get to the stage of rewriting a foundational document requires trusting relationships and a willingness to compromise. Yet this work is ongoing even in polarised times such as these.

People are starting small, creating spaces of hope and offering solutions, especially at the local scale. Proximity matters, as we see in conversations throughout this book. The details of other's lives can be understood as much more complex than political classifications. As Kathy, one of the Texas university students put it: 'It's harder to create a false narrative about your neighbour, right?' The chances of meaningful relationships are greater when we see each other more often. Someone encountered every day is no longer an abstract label but instead someone we could get to know and care about. We can also create a new narrative that can be shared, making it no longer a choice between left or right, Democrat or Republican, but instead, neighbour, friend, colleague.

Local interventions are also more likely to be built on foundations of affection. Coming together, 'one on one, people can have these changes of heart', as Pastor Jessie notes. Resilient personal relationships can be maintained even when fractures appear higher up the scale. During the white heat of a presidential campaign, for example, some conversations are not possible. But family, community, neighbourhood can enable a culture of rapprochement for people who are known and cared for, even if disagreed with. There is a 'conservative' or a 'liberal' in every family. There is disagreement in every group. Conversations get heated, especially on issues like abortion and immigration, but Democrats and 'Trump lovers' have lunch together and discuss plans for a party and play Bingo and pool. They recite the Pledge of Allegiance in unison. They sit together at the same table each week. There is friendship. Carol's best friend in rural Indiana has polar opposite political views. 'We can still be friends. There are things that we will never agree on, and we don't have to convince each other of those. We have enough common things that we do agree on, that we can base our friendship on.'

If people feel safe, and can trust others and institutions around them, it's also possible that they will be more willing to find common ground and even relinquish power. Decades of social experiments have shown this can work.[14] At its most basic, water, as residents of Colorado's western slopes know, creates a realisation that 'we are together in this'. Two mothers on different 'sides' want the same things for their children. 'Like you want to bring your kids up well and safely, you want your family to be fed and to have a home.' 'You love your kids. Sure you do. I love mine. Right? There's the cake in the room again, there's always common ground for everybody.' 'Bring out the cake' moments reminded us of points of connection.

Another point of common ground is that everyone cares in some way: we may prioritise those cares differently, but everybody understands what it is to love, to belong or, conversely, to feel unsafe and unmoored. Jeremy, a gun enthusiast in Austin, Texas, recognises that 'the root values of what people want out of life, the safety and security, I think is the same. It's the means to achieve or protect that we disagree on.' Mónica Guzman, author of *I never thought of it that way*, argues that we commit an error of judgement when we look at people across the aisle and mistake a different prioritising of values for an absence of them.[15] We may share many values with people, but the way we interpret and prioritise them, the moral trade-offs we are willing to make, is what creates the sense of difference.

With this realisation, connections can be forged, consensus and coalitions built, and certainty replaced with curiosity. Lorena, director of La Mujer Obrera in El Paso, will talk to whomever she needs to in order to bring in resources, employing different strategies depending on who they are. If it's a conservative politician, for example, she will focus on family. In Atlanta, Pamela works across the political divide to get her legislation on prison reform passed. Through shifting configurations, Reverend Danielle works with issue-based coalitions in Dallas, on urban renewal projects for example, as does New Yorker Cat, within the medical freedom movement. Cat argues that '[this] is the best way that we can work through things as opposed to [working with] candidates and parties'.

John Seago of Texas Right to Life works with coalitions of other 'pro-life' groups, but also coalitions including Democrats who will support some legislation he lobbies for, such as increasing funding for women's welfare. The ACLU opposes Texas Right to Life on abortion. 'They're always going to.' But John argues they both agree that it is an issue of justice. 'I have not had a discussion with someone who says, "Yes, I love taking innocent human life." No, that's not it.' There are other public policy issues where there is agreement, such as working to repeal poor medical ethics law. They may take different moral reasoning for why they oppose a law, but they both agree that it needs to change.

These are 'points of light' that show how progress can be made through coming to the table and being open to dialogue. There is power in conversations, as Reverend Danielle notes, with 'maybe everybody taking a deep breath and saying, "Okay, so maybe I'm open to having my assumptions challenged in this area, to pick a new and different way."' Others talk of wanting conversations 'without getting mad', to be 'a little bit more accepting of the other person's point of view', to understand that 'both have to give a little in order to get something'. 'We have to just not get personal about it.'

It's hard not to feel that it's personal when someone is telling you that you're wrong, but for Gary, one of the Dallas libertarians, a first step is entering into dialogue in good faith. 'I disagree with you about this, but I don't think that you're a piece of shit, right? I wish there was more of it that was going from a place of conviction, but also not from a place of malice.' This is recapturing what it looks like to do democracy, to disagree with someone, be okay with that and then go have a drink with them afterwards.

How we interact with people who disagree with us, how we demonise or humanise them, how we come to shared understandings, are all part of wider cultural speech norms. A feedback loop of social media echo chambers has created a relentless competition to 'join my team', pushing people to declare for one side or the other, Democrat or Republican, left or right. People and ideas are villainised, segregated, and expelled as a result.

Kevin Goldberg, a First Amendment specialist at Freedom Forum, holds to the principle that free speech is necessary to counteract bad speech. Shutting people down tends to make people angry. One of the first things he did when he took the job

> was to reach out to many of my more Republican friends and say, 'Who do you read? Who should I read?' [...] I invariably disagree with 90 per

cent of what those people write, but I read it, and every so often I see things that are just, you know, amazing, that I've never thought about.

Zach Greenberg, from the Foundation for Individual Rights and Expression, uses the legal system to protect free speech, but he is also aware of the need to come into a room with humility rather than humiliation:

> You learn more about yourself and the world around you and have the widest possible range of knowledge imparted upon you. [...] It takes courage. It takes humility right to admit that you may be wrong, to admit that maybe these beliefs you have are unfounded, like there could be change. It takes effort, it's a difficult thing to do. I'm not saying that everyone can go in there and do it. But would you think it's important for intellectual development, to becoming a functioning member of society to be able to have these discussions to seek out those you disagree with.

If the spaces for conversation are already too defined, new ones can be created. We don't have to meet in the middle in an enforced compromise; we can try somewhere completely different, a third space where there are no assumptions or expectations. Creativity excels at this role, as a form of repair and to imagine different futures – be it dreams of an international streetcar in El Paso or community projects among Hispanic women. Sidewalks, gardens, cafés, no man's land, can be co-opted with new meanings and new stories as people meet within them.

Jonel, on Akwesasne Mohawk land, reminds me of the power in gathering. 'If me and you right now came into agreement, that's power. If me and you and everybody [here] came into agreement, that's even more power.' Through time and cultural assimilation, things get lost, including people and communities. Gatherings then become a lifeline, a thread to remember that other ways of being in the world are still breathing, unforgotten, showing that 'we care for ourselves and for each other and for the world', in the past, present and future.

On a cold New York City night in December, as the AmFest rally is winding down in Phoenix, Elizabeth gathers people in the middle of gentrifying Brooklyn to celebrate the solstice with a firepit, shared food, a labyrinth of candles. Evoking ancient and cyclical wisdom, they sing freedom songs. Elders and children, doctors and sound-bath practitioners, farmers and social workers, lawyers and homeschooling mothers, artists and performers. They gather in good faith, unmediated by screens, connected in physical and spiritual ways, 'their hearts are bursting. They want to live a good life.' Elizabeth acknowledges that people who prefer 'fast cars, guns and BBQs' would probably 'not want to gather in the way we do. We allow for that in America. We should be free to gather in a way that is meaningful to us.'

The question then is how to balance a desire to gather with the like-minded, whether at a solstice celebration in Brooklyn or a MAGA youth rally in Phoenix, Arizona, each with their own repertoire of freedom songs, with the need to also encounter those different versions of freedom at some point. Despite the desires of some libertarians, I do not think it possible that we can just keep moving away from difference. A way forward together has to be found at some point.

It is hard work at times to encounter difference and deconstruct exceptionalism, but there are skills and dispositions that can help us 'figure out' how to get along, to bridge divides and make it a little less uncomfortable.[16]

To summarise all the advice from the conversations that make up this book, a good place to start is being curious. Suspend judgement: no one likes being looked down on or shamed, even gun enthusiasts, like Jeremy in Texas: 'I don't love being castigated as everything that the media, the anti-gun politicians, have people believe represents all of the gun owners.' Carol, in rural Indiana, like many others, wants to talk about our differences but not have people roll their eyes in disdain at her in the process. Her daughter, Monica, emphasises that foundational skill of non-violent, non-judgemental communication: to really listen.[17] 'Opening your ears and actually listening [...] digesting what they're saying [...] [rather than] just listening to respond with what you want them to hear.'

To 'actually listen' requires empathy and grace. It requires seeing how our pain is connected to the pain of others and even admitting we might be wrong sometimes. John Seago is okay with saying it.

'We have had terrible spokespersons, people throughout the history of our [pro-life] movement, who have used harmful rhetoric or religious rhetoric or just scientific inaccuracies. That doesn't hurt to admit our side is not perfect.' Pastor Jessie expresses an empathy for those who voted for Trump, understanding what the Democratic Party did not:

> [Trump's voters] have been working hard generationally to achieve some-thing and they don't see the fruits of their labour. [...] As a poor white person, instead of asking those systemic questions, they are looking out and saying, 'well, clearly it's because these other people are getting what was mine', which I guess is really human if you think about it. It's not very human to interrogate systems and ask where the systems are fail-ing. It is very human to say 'I blame you.' I blame you, 'group that I am not in touch with it, [that] I don't understand', for taking away what was mine.

To empathise presents us with an eternal moral question: can we bring ourselves to love others as we ourselves want to be loved? If we can do that, in Pastor Jessie's view, it might do a lot to help us repair the relationships in our lives that have been frayed or broken over political differences.

It all turns again on affection. There are those with bridging capital, embodied by the in-betweeners, people like Danni, in rural Indiana, and Travis, in Colorado, who can move between spaces of difference because they are trusted and loved. On the mesa, Seth and Travis trade banter.

Seth: Travis and I are best friends, he is one of my best friends, we're this far apart [gestures distance with hands].
Travis: I don't care if he's wrong. It's okay. [laughter]

Travis is a self-described 'liberal', Democrat/Independent, and Seth, his 'best friend', is Republican and a Trump supporter, with caveats. They exercise the right to avoid talking about politics in each other's company. There is a tussle at times for who has the final word, who blinks first, who ultimately claims the moral high ground, but there is a common project of friendship no matter how trenchant the opinions. Travis and Seth have worked together on local committees and know where each other stands. If Seth has 'liberal' clients coming to his ranch, the common ground is hunting: 'We've had those people with all those ideas that go against us, but hey man, we all have a good time at the end.'

For Seth, arguing with Travis is not like arguing with 'one of those anal liberals'. He is disentangled from the collective stereotype normally shouted in capitals and set apart with that phrase 'I don't mean you.' The difference is affection. 'We love Travis! He's our neighbour. Travis's our guy. Because he's a damn Democrat we don't hold that against him! [laughing] We love him!' Arlo and Maeve also speak of Travis, their neighbour, with affection, despite their political differences:

> We love Travis to death, but we don't have a problem with him being his affiliation and us what we are. [...] [Travis] comes over and visits and between the two of 'em ... can't get rid of Travis and can't get rid of [Arlo]. I mean they can just chat away.

Danni brings a similar level of bridging capital into her in-law's family. Her childhood home in suburban Ohio is not that far geographically from the farm in rural Indiana. But a suburban, Democrat family on the outskirts of a diverse city can feel a world away from the family she married into. Yet she is loved, as Carol acknowledges. 'She did not grow up the same as we did here [but] we love her like a daughter, like a sister, and it doesn't matter that maybe her politics are slightly different than what we are saying.' Danni aligns 'to an extent' with her own family's 'liberal' values, recognising where she lives now is 'more conservative', but living there has also changed her:

> There's perceptions of what rural areas are, and they're just not that. [...] I've watched Peter's father weep because he's lost a cow, like, it matters to him. I saw it two different ways. And I don't think either one is wrong or better than the other one. [...] Being able to live in two different places and seeing two different viewpoints has made me realise how much I didn't know one way and the other way.

For others in the family, like Monica, Danni's presence has shifted how they think about the world:

> Sometimes we need to hear something different because I think, again, listening to the news or whatever, and hearing the same thing over and over and over again, you start to really get this foundation of 'this is how I believe it should be'. And then you have someone like Danni who throws a curveball at you, it kind of brings you back to reality. [...] even

if it's hard, even if you're sitting in the moment, and you're thinking, alright, whatever. No, I don't think what you said was right. But then you start to think about it later and you're like why is that still itching me? Why is what she said still sitting there [...]. It's not exactly what I think but I should think of it a little bit more. That's what's important, not putting up this wall and not closing your ears off to what you don't want to hear. You don't always have to agree. And there can be stuff that you think well, that's not how I view it at all, and I probably will never change how I view that situation or that thing. That's okay too. But I can look at things differently.

There is also hope in the next generation that bridges two ways of being. Hanima sees 'a bunch of mixed babies out there who are going to grow up and maybe change the world just by being who they are, by knowing both sides, by living that duality'. It is perhaps an unfair burden to place all our hopes on Gen Z and Gen Alpha, particularly as election 2024 was marked by a significant number of young people leaning conservative. From Gen Z's perspective, there is both optimism and anxiety, as Anne outlines. 'I think a lot of my generation is very much like, a little bit fed up with it. Why are we like this? I think we'll figure it out eventually. [...] Eventually we'll be able to fix something.'

Beyond the next generation, hope starts to converge on the idea of a different life. For Hanima, this involves 'a freedom to be able to just put the grind to the side for a day'; for Lorena in El Paso, to not always be in survival mode and remembering that play is not just for children. Cat and Elizabeth are re-finding life in intentional communities outside mainstream economics.

As in Elizabeth's solstice gathering, the assumption that people 'are inherently good' is repeated surprisingly often, held on to tightly, with faith that the cycles of history will eventually swing back towards a time when it will feel better. There is recognition, summarised by Susan, a retired teacher in suburban Colorado, that

> at the core of everybody we just want to feel secure, we want to have our family supported, and to be able to support them, and I think eventually the pendulum is gonna swing and things are going to be easier to bring about changes. I don't know how it's happening but I have faith.

The long arc of history cycles through periods of cultural change: release and restraint, upheaval and stasis. Hanima places this current moment of anxiety into perspective. 'Fifty years ago, we [with her white husband] wouldn't have been able to get married; twenty-five years ago, my parents couldn't vote in South Africa. Like, we now have that freedom to be able to do these things.' Danni is also an optimist:

> Eventually we'll come to a point where people will realise that all these things are okay that people feel the way that they feel. [...] I think we're going to maybe get beat up a little bit and hurt, but then we're gonna be better from it. I'm hoping. I don't know if that will happen in my life-time. But I imagine it being a more empathetic, peaceful place.

We are all just 'figuring it out' and need 'the freedom to be able to figure it out'; finding the common ground from where to start build-ing rather than dig the hole deeper. Trying to figure out how to main-tain a system of democracy based on good principles, while grappling with where those principles are not fully applied. Figuring out how to deal with the constant tensions of navigating differences. Sometimes just figuring it out in good faith as we go along is the best we can do. Despite the trauma of unfreedom for Jonel, there remains the absolute faith that change for the better is possible:

> Creation shows up for you every day, the sun and the moon shows up for you every day. [...] [Y]ou can absolutely have more freedom to rethink, redesign, recreate the next part of our human existence. We are equipped with all of that intelligence. We do have the capacity to coexist with one another, [but] we have to be in the practice of putting things down in order to move forward. We have to form relationships, so that we can become family again. And so even me and you, having this moment, you know, you're going to feel like family to me, we're going to be in agree-ment, you're going to wander the earth, and I'm going to wander the earth, but there'll be an inner standing between the two of us that we're in agreement that I'm not going to hurt you, and you're not going to hurt me. And I can live with that.

This hope may seem to be taking a battering in the first year of Trump's second term. It is full-throated retribution for those who have slighted him. But underneath the storm there is faith in a network of resilient connections and conversations across difference that maintain the fab-ric of American society, at least for now.

Notes

PREFACE: WRITING FREEDOM

1 Donald J. Trump, 47th President of the USA, inaugural address, 20 January 2025.

2 In a speech to Parliament, 18 July 2022, before stepping down as Prime Minister, Boris Johnson referenced 'the Deep State' trying to prevent Brexit ('Brexit: Boris Johnson suggests Keir Starmer and "Deep State" plotting to take UK back into EU', *Independent*, 18 July 2022, www.independent.co.uk/news/uk/politics/brexit-boris-johnson-eu-deep-state-labour-b2125940.html [Accessed 21 August 2025]). Liz Truss, another former Conservative Prime Minister, has also apportioned blame for her 2022 downfall to 'the Deep State', speaking at a Conservative Political Action Conference gathering in the USA, 22 February 2024 ('Liz Truss' journey from Downing Street to "Deep State" conspiracist', Politico, 12 March 2024, www.politico.eu/article/liz-truss-unlikely-journey-from-downing-street-chief-to-deep-state-conspiracist/ [Accessed 21 August 2025]).

3 For example, in 2023, the US-based National Conservatism movement held its first conference in the UK attended by senior government ministers. TPUSA, who feature heavily in this book, now have a sister organisation, Turning Point UK (TPUK). Truss regularly attends conservative gatherings in the USA and repeats America First talking points. Elon Musk has reportedly considered donating to the populist UK Reform Party, and its leader Nigel Farage, who has also appeared at Conservative, MAGA, nationalist populist events and associated media outlets.

4 Eric Foner, *The story of American freedom* (Picador, 1998), p. xv.

5 'Steve Bannon holds nothing back', *Charlie Kirk Show*, AmFest, 21 December 2024, https://omny.fm/shows/the-charlie-kirk-show/steve-bannon-holds-nothing-back-exclusive-intervie [Accessed 26 December 2024].

ALL CHANGE

1 TPUSA is a conservative, America First/MAGA-aligned organisation, mobilising high school and university students.

2 Foner, *The story of American freedom*, p. xiii.

Notes

3   See 'Further reading' for detailed historical analysis of how freedom has evolved as a 'master narrative' in the USA.

4   Sarah Churchwell punctures the idea that the American Dream was founded on the pursuit of individual wealth. It was initially (around 1895) equated with democratic freedoms and social justice.

5   Condoleezza Rice, 'America's confidence in freedom', *Review of Faith & International Affairs* 4, no. 2 (2006): 37–40.

6   On a trip to the USA in the mid-2000s, I struck up a conversation with a young man in a frozen custard café, in Akron, Ohio. We were talking about travel, and he mentioned he had yet to go overseas. I said he was young and there was plenty of time. His response: 'I know. I'm an American, I can do whatever I want.' This may have been the starting point of *The trouble with freedom*.

7   'Bold fusion', Freedom Conservatism blog, 18 March 2024, www.freedom conservatism.org/p/bold-fusion [Accessed 4 August 2025].

8   See Sophia Rosenfeld, *The age of choice: A history of freedom in modern life* (Princeton University Press, 2025).

9   Stephen Tomkins, *The journey to the Mayflower: God's outlaws and the invention of freedom* (London, 2020).

10 While there is a certain romanticism associated with mobility in these works, going 'off-grid' to be free of consumer society, there are other drivers including relationship breakdown, health crises, economic precarity, unemployment and substance abuse (see Jessica Bruder, *Nomadland: Surviving America in the 21st century* [Swift Press, 2017]).

11 Jean Baudrillard, *America* (Verso, 2010), p. 5.

12 Ibid., p. 82.

13 Ibid., p. 129.

14 '10 Facts on global inequality in 2024', World Inequality Database, n.d., https://wid.world/news-article/10-facts-on-global-inequality-in-2024/ [Accessed 27 December 2024].

15 Timothy Snyder, *The road to unfreedom: Russia, Europe, America* (Vintage, 2018), p. 268.

16 For writers who focus in-depth on the history of enslavement and racism in the United States, see 'Further reading'.

17 'Wealth gaps across racial and ethnic groups', Pew Research Center, 4 December 2023, www.pewresearch.org/2023/12/04/wealth-gaps-across-racial-and-ethnic-groups/ [Accessed 4 August 2025].

18 Tyler Stovall, *White freedom: The racial history of an idea* (Princeton University Press, 2021).

19 See, e.g., Nikole Hannah-Jones, *The 1619 Project* (New York Times, 2019).

20 'This nation, for all its hopes and all its boasts, will not be fully free until all its citizens are free', John F. Kennedy, 1963 speech proposing the 1964 Civil Rights Act.

21 Pro-Trump advertising included messaging such as: 'Under Kamala Harris, over 13,000 illegals convicted of murder are living in American communities, while an additional 15,000 convicted of sexual assault and rape are also living amongst you tonight. How will your family survive another four years if you

Notes

may not be able to survive the night?' Created by the PAC Right for America;
'Living amongst you', Right for America, n.d., host2.adimpact.com/admo/
viewer/74dc381f-acoc-4356-a6co-1fec8dcd5b62 [Accessed 4 November 2024].

22 See, e.g., 'Buffalo supermarket shooting', *New York Times*, 14 May 2022,
www.nytimes.com/live/2022/05/14/nyregion/buffalo-shooting#in-buffalo-
and-some-other-mass-shootings-a-shared-belief-that-white-people-could-be-
wiped-away [Accessed 4 August 2025].

23 Isabel Brown livestream, Gettr, 3 February 2022, 7pm, www.youtube.com/
@theisabelbrown [Accessed 4 August 2025].

24 Snyder, *Road to unfreedom*.

25 See interview between conservative columnist Ross Douthat and venture
capitalist and billionaire Tech Bro Marc Andreessen: 'How Democrats drove
Silicon Valley into Trump's arms', *New York Times*, 17 January 2025, www.
nytimes.com/2025/01/17/opinion/marc-andreessen-trump-silicon-valley.
html [Accessed 24 January 2025]. According to Andreessen, 'You'd get berated
at an all-hands meeting as a C.E.O., where you'd have these extremely angry
employees show up and they were just completely furious about how there's
way too many white men on the management team. "Why are we a for-profit
corporation? Don't you know all the downstream horrible effects that this
technology is having? We need to spend unlimited money in order to make
sure that we're not emitting any carbon."'

26 See, e.g., independent journalist, Julio Rosas, in conversation with Charlie
Kirk. , 'Live from Tampa at the Student Action Summit', *The Charlie Kirk
Show*, 11 July 2025, https://thecharliekirkshow.com/podcasts/the-charlie-
kirk-show/live-from-tampa-at-the-student-action-summit [Accessed 18 July
2025].

27 See social psychologist Jonathan Haidt's analysis, 'Life after Babel: Adapting
to a world we no longer share', 2025, https://lifeafterbabel.com [Accessed 4
August 2025].

28 Amartya Sen, *Rationality and freedom* (Oxford University Press, 2022).

29 Sebastian Junger, *Freedom* (HarperCollins, 2022), p. 17.

30 Oren Cass, American Compass, 'Life, liberty, and the over adjusted to 38.5
parlayed with the money-line', Understanding America Substack, 7 December
2024, www.commonplace.org/p/life-liberty-and-the-over-adjusted [Accessed
7 December 2024].

31 Patrick Deneen, *Why liberalism failed* (Yale University Press, 2018).

32 Long-form podcasting, with shows sometimes lasting three hours, has become
a mainstay of the conservative/America First media ecosystem, often interconnected with hosts appearing on each other's podcasts. Well-known hosts
include: Steve Bannon, Glen Beck, Dan Bongino, Sebastian Gorka, Benny
Johnson, Charlie Kirk, Christopher Rufo, Ben Shapiro, Allie Beth Stuckey,
Matt Walsh. A 'liberal' media ecosystem has its equivalents including Ezra
Klein, Keith Olbermann, Pod Save America and Michael Popok (Legal AF).

33 'Breaking: Trump announces presidential transition team leaders', Right Side
Broadcasting Network (RSBN), online, 16 August 2024, www.rsbnetwork.
com/featured/breaking-trump-announces-presidential-transition-team-leaders
[Accessed 25 August 2024].

Notes

34   See, e.g., Adam Serwer, *The cruelty is the point: The past, present, and future of Trump's America* (One World, 2021).

35   Ibid., p. 54.

36   Veena Das, *Life and words: Violence and the descent into the ordinary* (University of California Press, 2007).

37   Elaine Scarry, *The body in pain: The making and unmaking of the world* (Oxford University Press, 1985).

38   Sara Ahmed, *The cultural politics of emotion*, 2nd ed. (Edinburgh University Press, 2014).

39   Christina Pazzanese, 'Democrats and Republicans do live in different worlds', *The Harvard Gazette*, 16 March 2021, https://news.harvard.edu/gazette/story/2021/03/democrats-and-republicans-live-in-partisan-bubbles-study-finds/ [Accessed 30 July 2024].

40   See also Maggie Nelson, *On freedom: Four songs of care and constraint* (Jonathan Cape, 2021).

41   See advertisement: 'Kamala Harris launches her campaign for president', YouTube, 25 July 2024, www.youtube.com/watch?v=sHky_Xopyrw [Accessed 27 December 2024].

DEFENDING FREEDOM, SAVING AMERICA

1   Posted on Donald Trump's fundraising website the day after an assassination attempt. 'Alert from Trump', n.d., https://secure.winred.com/trump-national-committee-jfc/lp-website-trump-response-v4-00 [Accessed 15 July 2024].

2   Each has a slightly different flavour to their economic, social and foreign policies; priorities can differ and come into conflict. Manifestos and mission statements are available online.

3   National Conservatism is a project of the Edmund Burke Foundation: 'National Conservatism: A statement of principles', Edmund Burke Foundation, n.d., https://nationalconservatism.org/national-conservatism-a-statement-of-principles/ [Accessed 4 August 2025].

4   Organisations aligned with America First/MAGA that were monitored for this book include: Advancing American Freedom; Alliance Defending Freedom; America First Policy Institute; America First Works; American Cornerstone Institute; Center for Renewing America; Citizens Defending Freedom; Conservative Political Action Conference; Heritage Foundation; Look Ahead America; Patriot Academy; TPUSA. There is a media ecosystem, primarily podcasting and digital channels but also Fox TV, that supports America First/MAGA messaging, as well as a raft of associated state and local organisations 'defending freedom'. Sources also included speeches and social media content of leading conservative commentators, as well as e-newsletters and websites of America First/MAGA organisations, 2021–2025.

5   This chapter includes material from the inaugural AmFest 2021, interwoven with material from other America First/MAGA rallies and conservative commentary to highlight the repetition of this play book throughout the conservative ecosystem.

6   On 10th September 2025, Charlie Kirk was shot and killed while speaking at Utah Valley University. A twenty-two-year old man, Tyler Robinson, has been charged with his murder. At the time of publication, Robinson's motives are

Notes

still unclear but may be related to Kirk's denigration of the trans-community (see Chapter 5). Kirk's murder led to increased calls from Donald Trump and members of his administration to crack down on 'the left'. His widow, Erika Kirk, has been named as the new CEO of TPUSA.

7 'Staff', TPUSA, n.d., www.tpusa.com/staff [Accessed 24 August 2025].

8 TPUSA now has a sister organisation, TPUK, but with a much lower profile, focused mostly on protests against Drag Queen Story Hours in London.

9 'Freedom must win!', TPUSA, n.d., www.tpusa.com/freedom [Accessed 4 August 2025]. In the immediate aftermath of Kirk's murder, spokespeople for TPUSA suggested they had received over 60,000 requests to establish new chapters.

10 American Cornerstone Institute, e-newsletter, 14 May 2024.

11 'Thought crime: The Trump verdict special', *Charlie Kirk Show*, 31 May 2024, https://thecharliekirkshow.com/podcasts/the-charlie-kirk-show/thoughtcrime-the-trump-verdict-special [Accessed 1 June 2024].

12 Jack Posobiec is a former naval intelligence officer and now podcaster at 'Human Events'.

13 M. Stanton-Evans, 'A Conservative case for freedom', *Intercollegiate Review* (Autumn 2015). Stanton-Evans was not an advocate of authoritarian freedom but preferred a 'fusion' of libertarianism with Christian ideas of virtue.

14 Donald Trump speech, Faith and Freedom Coalition, 17 June 2022, Tennessee.

15 See, e.g., Serwer, *Cruelty is the point*; and Sarah Churchwell, *Behold, America: A history of America First and the American dream* (Bloomsbury Publishing, 2018).

16 American Cornerstone Institute, e-newsletter, 14 May 2024.

17 'Taylor Swift: Deep State op?', *Charlie Kirk Show*, 12 January 2024, https://thecharliekirkshow.com/podcasts/the-charlie-kirk-show/taylor-swift-deep-state-op [Accessed 28 July 2024].

18 For different approaches to understanding 'culture wars', see Robert Samuels, *Culture wars, universities and the political unconscious* (Palgrave MacMillan, 2024); Andrew Hartman, *A war for the soul of America: A history of the culture wars*, 2nd ed. (University of Chicago Press, 2019).

19 See Chapter 5 for a more in-depth analysis.

20 For example, Tucker Carlson's *The end of men* documentary, Fox News, April 2022, www.foxnews.com/video/6313315096112 [Accessed 27 December 2024].

21 Source: 'Madison Cawthorn calls for mothers to raise "monster" men in terrifying speech against "demasculation"', *Independent*, 19 October 2021, www.independent.co.uk/news/world/americas/us-politics/north-carolina-madison-cawthorn-masculinity-b1940849.html [Accessed 4 August 2025].

22 Source: 'Eyebrow-raising Madison Cawthorn video at center of new ethics complaint', Fox News, 29 April 2022, www.foxnews.com/politics/madison-cawthorn-video-aide-new-ethics-complaint [Accessed 25 April 2025].

23 The National Association of Police Organizations endorsed Trump for President in July 2024.

24 Various National Conservatism outlets have addressed this, for example the Heritage Foundation: see Thomas Spoer, 'The rise of wokeness in the military', Heritage Foundation, 30 September 2022, www.heritage.org/defense/commentary/the-rise-wokeness-the-military [Accessed 4 August 2025].

Notes

25 See Paige Williams' overview of the case, 'Kyle Rittenhouse: American vigilante', *The New Yorker*, 28 June 2021, www.newyorker.com/magazine/2021/07/05/kyle-rittenhouse-american-vigilante [Accessed 4 August 2025].

26 There are now a multitude of conservative online channels and 'citizen journalists', including Project Veritas, Human Events and the O'Keefe Media Group.

27 'Donald Trump's foreign policy masterclass', *Charlie Kirk Show*, 27 January 2025, https://thecharliekirkshow.com/podcasts/the-charlie-kirk-show/donald-trumps-foreign-policy-masterclass [Accessed 6 April 2025].

28 Authored by Hiram Evans, 'The Klan's fight for Americanism', cited in Churchwell, *Behold, America*.

29 Dinesh d'Souza, fundraising email, 26 July 2024.

30 Naomi Klein, *Doppelganger: A trip into the mirror world* (Allen Lane, 2023).

31 See Hannah Arendt's 1951 analysis of authoritarian rule, *The origins of totalitarianism* (Schocken Books, 1951). This book had a resurgence of popularity after Trump's first election victory in 2016.

32 Posted on Truth Social, 14 July 2024, following an assassination attempt, 13 July 2024.

33 Referred to as an 'insurrection' or 'coup' by liberal-leaning commentators, and 'legitimate political discourse' by the Republican National Committee (4 February 2022), J6 denotes the riots that took place on 6 January 2021, in which Trump followers attempted to overturn the 2020 election results.

34 Trump Speech, Faith and Freedom Coalition, 17 June 2022, Tennessee.

35 'They tried to assassinate Trump', *Charlie Kirk Show*, 14 July 2024. https://thecharliekirkshow.com/podcasts/the-charlie-kirk-show/they-tried-to-assassinate-trump [Accessed 25 April 2025].

36 TPUSA, e-newsletter, 4 July 2024.

37 Jane Mayer, *Dark money: The hidden history of the billionaires behind the rise of the radical right* (Anchor Books, 2017).

38 See also Kenneth Vogel, Shane Goldmacher and Ryan Mac, 'Dissatisfied with their party, wealthy Republican donors form secret coalitions', *New York Times*, 6 April 2022, www.nytimes.com/2022/04/06/us/politics/republican-donors-rockbridge-network-trump.html [Accessed 4 August 2025]; Jane Mayer, 'The big money behind the big lie', *The New Yorker*, 2 August 2021; and 'Turning Point USA', Source Watch, www.sourcewatch.org/index.php/Turning_Point_USA [Accessed 22 February 2025].

39 The Democratic Party felt it had the better 'ground game' in elections. For example, Stacey Abrams, Democrat politician, lawyer and author, was widely regarded as turning Georgia blue in 2020 through her community organising.

40 'How Turning Point action delivered the White House', *Charlie Kirk Show*, 21 November 2024, www.charliekirk.com/podcasts/how-turning-point-action-delivered-the-white-house [Accessed 24 November 2024].

41 'RNC reactions day 2', *Charlie Kirk Show*, 17 July 2024, https://thecharliekirkshow.com/podcasts/the-charlie-kirk-show/rnc-reactions-day-2 [Accessed 18 July 2024].

42 Focusing on farming, the environment and Biden legislation (the EATS Act), MfA began discussing the quality of food, the health of children and fears of Chinese control over US farming. 'American farmers at risk with EATS Act', YouTube, 17 May 2024, www.youtube.com/watch?v=eElEc1qfRmc [Accessed 27 December 2024].

43 'Oren Cass on the conservative case for labor unions', American Compass, 17 December 2020, https://americancompass.org/oren-cass-on-the-conservative-case-for-labor-unions/ [Accessed 27 December 2024].

44 J.D. Vance, *Hillbilly elegy: A memoir of a family and culture in crisis* (William Collins, 2017).

45 'Chris Widener', n.d., https://redreferralnetwork.com [Accessed 28 July 2024].

46 'The Taylor Swift question and 2024', *Charlie Kirk Show*, 1 February 2024, https://thecharliekirkshow.com/podcasts/the-charlie-kirk-show/the-taylor-swift-question-and-2024 [Accessed 5 March 2024].

47 George Lakoff, *Moral politics: How liberals and conservatives think* (University of Chicago Press, 2016).

48 'As partisan hostility grows, signs of frustration with the two-party system', Pew Research Center, 9 August 2022, www.pewresearch.org/politics/2022/08/09/as-partisan-hostility-grows-signs-of-frustration-with-the-two-party-system/ [Accessed 27 December 2024].

49 Rachel Treisman, 'JD Vance went viral for "cat lady" comments: The centuries-old trope has a long tail', NPR, 29 July 2024, www.npr.org/2024/07/29/nx-s1-5055616/jd-vance-childless-cat-lady-history [Accessed 27 December 2024].

RE-IMAGINING FREE MOVEMENT: EL PASO/CIUDAD JUÁREZ

1 See Josh Meredith, 'El Paso industrial market: The birth of the "borderplex"', Rebusiness Online, 20 April 2022, https://rebusinessonline.com/el-paso-industrial-market-the-birth-of-the-borderplex [Accessed 28 December 2024]. See also 'Borderplex statistics show major economic activity', *Albuquerque Journal*, 15 January 2022, www.abqjournal.com/2461525/borderplex-statistics-show-major-economic-activity.html [Accessed 24 August 2025]; 'The city of El Paso: Discover the borderplex region', Elpasotexas.gov, www.elpasotexas.gov/economic-development/economic-snapshot/industry-and-jobs/ [Accessed 4 August 2025]; Erik Lee and Christopher Wilson, eds, *The U.S.–Mexico border economy in Transition* (Woodrow Wilson Center, 2015), www.wilsoncenter.org/sites/default/files/media/documents/publication/Border_Economy_Transition_Wilson_Lee.pdf [Accessed 4 August 2025].

2 See 'Manufacturing resources pages', Southern Border Partners, 18 April 2016, https://southernborderpartners.com/manufacturing-resources-pages/2016/4/18/nafta-and-the-maquiladora-program [Accessed 31 July 2024].

3 See 'Regional snapshot', Borderplex Alliance, n.d., www.borderplexalliance.org/regional-snapshot [Accessed 28 December 2024]. See also 'The city of El Paso: Discover the borderplex region', Elpasotexas.gov, www.elpasotexas.gov/economic-development [Accessed 4 August 2025].

4 See 'How Americans view the situation at the U.S.–Mexico border, its causes and consequences', Pew Research Center, 15 February 2024, www.pewresearch.org/politics/2024/02/15/how-americans-view-the-situation-at-the-u-s-mexico-border-its-causes-and-consequences/ [Accessed 4 August 2025].

5 Dave Davies, 'How NYC is coping with 175,000 migrants from the Southern border', NPR, 15 February 2024, www.npr.org/2024/02/15/1231712535/how-nyc-is-coping-with-175-000-migrants-from-the-southern-border [Accessed 31 July 2024].

6   Charlie Kirk, 'Liberty ledger' (e-newsletter), 24 June 2024.
7   See, e.g., the Homeland Security website using the MASA phrase during the second Trump presidency: https://www.dhs.gov/making-america-safe-again [Accessed 18 August 2025].
8   See Ieva Jusionyte, *Exit wounds: How America's guns fuel violence across the border* (University of California Press, 2024).
9   Estimates from the 1990s suggest 60 per cent of labour in the maquiladoras are women, but accurate statistics are difficult to find. Exploitation and discrimination are documented by several labour NGOs working in the area. See, e.g., 'Maquiladoras', Women on the Border, n.d., https://womenontheborder.org/women-and-globalization/maquiladoras/ [Accessed 28 December 2024]; also 'Together we can defend ourselves: For the opening of a supporting and counseling center for workers in Ciudad Juárez', ProDesc, https://prodesc.org.mx/en/gomujeres-campaign-for-women-workers-from-the-maquiladoras-of-ciudad-juarez/ [Accessed 4 August 2025].
10 Maquiladoras have been operating in the border region since the 1960s; however, the creation of the free trade zone saw numbers increase rapidly. 'Maquiladoras', Women on the Border, n.d., https://womenontheborder.org/women-and-globalization/maquiladoras/ [Accessed 28 December 2024] [Accessed 31 July 2024].
11 For their critique, see Wendy Brown, *In the ruins of neo-liberalism* (Colombia University Press, 2019); and J.-K. Gibson-Graham, *A postcapitalist politics* (University of Minnesota Press, 2006).
12 See sociologist and activist Stellan Vinthagen's recent work in this area.
13 See Phil Helsel, 'Man sentenced to 5 years in "We Build the Wall" fraud case', NBC News, 26 July 2023, www.nbcnews.com/news/us-news/man-sentenced-5-years-build-wall-fraud-case-rcna96345 [Accessed 31 July 2024].
14 Migrants crossing illegally into the USA are temporarily taken into custody to await a decision on whether they can remain. Migrants who are not granted asylum are typically deported. See Ted Hesson and Mica Rosenberg, 'Biden imposes sweeping asylum ban at US–Mexico border', Reuters, 5 June 2024, www.reuters.com/world/us/biden-expected-block-migrants-asylum-us-mexico-border-sources-say-2024-06-04/ [Accessed 28 December 2024].
15 See John Gramlich, 'Migrant encounters at U.S.–Mexico border have fallen sharply in 2024', Pew Research Center, 1 October 2024, www.pewresearch.org/short-reads/2024/10/01/migrant-encounters-at-u-s-mexico-border-have-fallen-sharply-in-2024/ [Accessed 28 December 2024].
16 Those coming from the 'Northern Triangle', El Salvador, Guatemala and Honduras, used to be the majority, but in December 2023, more than 54 per cent came from other countries, in particular Venezuela, and increasingly China. Gramlich, 'Migrant encounters at U.S.–Mexico border have fallen sharply in 2024'. See also Will Freeman, Steven Holmes and Sabine Baumgartner, 'Why six countries account for most migrants at the U.S.–Mexico border', Council on Foreign Relations, 9 July 2024, www.cfr.org/article/why-six-countries-account-most-migrants-us-mexico-border [Accessed 5 August 2025]; on Chinese migration: Cate Cadell, Nick Miroff and Li Qiang, 'Walking the line', *Washington Post*, 29 July 2024, www.washingtonpost.com/immigration/interactive/2024/china-migrants-us-border-san-diego-new-york/ [Accessed 5

Notes

August 2025]; on African migration: 'African migration to the U.S. soars as Europe cracks down', *New York Times*, 5 January 2024, www.nytimes.com/2024/01/05/us/africa-migrants-us-border.html [Accessed 5 August 2025].

17 See 'The city of El Paso'; Lee and Wilson, *The U.S.–Mexico border economy*.

18 In 1853, the US government agreed to pay Mexico $10 million for a tract of land of almost 30,000 square miles, now part of Arizona and New Mexico. This became known as the Gadsden Purchase after James Gadsden, the US negotiator.

19 See 'Migrant crisis', Elpasotexas.gov, n.d., www.elpasotexas.gov/migrant-crisis/ [Accessed 5 August 2025].

'POWER AND CONTROL, BABY': STORIES OF (UN)FREEDOM AND (IN)JUSTICE

1 There is a similar law in the UK, known as 'joint enterprise'. See '5 Things You Need to Know about Joint Enterprise', Liberty, 7 April 2022, www.libertyhumanrights.org.uk/issue/5-things-you-need-to-know-about-joint-enterprise/ [Accessed 24 August 2025].

2 See the Prison Policy Initiative for an overview of the data, as of April 2024: '56 facts about mass incarceration', Prison Policy Initiative, n.d., https://static.prisonpolicy.org/factsheets/56facts_2024.pdf [Accessed 24 August 2025]; and Wendy Sawyer and Peter Wagner, 'Mass incarceration: The whole pie 2024', Prison Policy Initiative, 14 March 2024, www.prisonpolicy.org/reports/pie2024.html [Accessed 24 August 2025]; also the Vera Institute of Justice: Jacob Kang-Brown and Jess Zhang, 'People in jail and prison in 2024', Vera Institute of Justice, October 2024, https://vera-institute.files.svdcdn.com/production/downloads/publications/People-in-Jail-and-Prison-in-2024-Full-Reportpdf.pdf [Accessed 24 August 2025]; and research at Tufts University, 'What is the prison industrial complex?', Tufts University Prison Divestment, https://sites.tufts.edu/prison divestment/the-pic-and-mass-incarceration/ [Accessed 30 December 2022].

3 See 'Prison population over time', Sentencing Project, n.d., www.sentencing project.org/research/ [Accessed 5 August 2025]. After the 1973 Rockefeller Drug Law was introduced, New York state's prison population grew from 12,500 to 71,500 in 1999, see Kenneth W. Mentor, 'Rockefeller Drug Laws', Critical Criminology, 15 April 2010, https://critcrim.org/rockefeller-drug-laws.htm [Accessed 2 January 2023]; Juhohn Lee, 'America has spent over a trillion dollars fighting the war on drugs: 50 years later, drug use in the U.S. is climbing again', CNBC, 17 June 2021, www.cnbc.com/2021/06/17/the-us-has-spent-over-a-trillion-dollars-fighting-war-on-drugs.html [Accessed 6 January 2022]; 'Mass incarceration', ACLU, n.d., www.aclu.org/issues/smart-justice/mass-incarceration [Accessed 30 December 2022].

4 Women in state prisons are more likely than men to have been incarcerated for a drug or property offence. The proportion of imprisoned women convicted of a drug offence increased from 12 per cent in 1986 to 25 per cent in 2021. Source: Kristen M. Budd, 'Incarcerated women and girls', Sentencing Project, 25 July 2024, www.sentencingproject.org/fact-sheet/incarcerated-women-and-girls/ [Accessed 5 August 2025]. See also Aleks Kajstura, 'Women's mass incarceration: The whole pie 2019', Prison Policy Initiative, 29 October 2019, www.prisonpolicy.org/reports/pie2019women.html [Accessed 30 December 2022].

Notes

5   See 'Immigration detention in the United States', Immigration Justice Campaign, 8 July 2024, https://immigrationjustice.us/immigration-detention-in-the-united-states/ [Accessed 24 August 2025]; see also Tufts University Prison Divestment project: http://sites.tufts.edu/prisondivestment/the-pic-and-mass-incarceration/ [Accessed 8 January 2023].

6   'Mass incarceration', ACLU.

7   See 'Trials are rare in the federal criminal justice system, and acquittals are even rarer', Pew Research Centre, 14 June 2023, www.pewresearch.org/short-reads/2023/06/14/fewer-than-1-of-defendants-in-federal-criminal-cases-were-acquitted-in-2022/sr_23-06-12_federalconvictions-png/ [Accessed 5 August 2025]; 'U.S. district courts: Criminal defendants disposed of, by type of disposition and offense, during the 12-month period ending September 30, 2022', US Courts, n.d., www.uscourts.gov/sites/default/files/data_tables/jb_d4_0930.2022.pdf [Accessed 24 August 2025]; and Jeffrey Q. Smith and Grant R. MacQueen, 'Going, going, but not quite gone: Trials continue to decline in federal and state courts; Does it matter?', *Judicature* 101, no. 4 (2017), https://judicature.duke.edu/articles/going-going-but-not-quite-gone-trials-continue-to-decline-in-federal-and-state-courts-does-it-matter/ [Accessed 5 August 2025].

8   Serwer, *Cruelty is the point.*

9   See 'Education levels of federally sentenced individuals', United States Sentencing Commission, December 2023, www.ussc.gov/research/research-reports/education-levels-federally-sentenced-individuals [Accessed 5 August 2025]; see also Caroline Wolf Harlow, 'Education and correctional populations', Bureau of Justice Statistics, January 2003, https://bjs.ojp.gov/content/pub/pdf/ecp.pdf [Accessed 5 August 2025].

10   The Vera Institute for Justice have reported on the poor quality of food in US prisons. 'Cheap jail and prison food is making people sick: It doesn't have to', Vera Institute for Justice, 27 February 2024, www.vera.org/news/cheap-jail-and-prison-food-is-making-people-sick-it-doesnt-have-to [Accessed 28 December 2024].

11   'Criminal justice reform', Equal Justice Initiative, n.d., https://eji.org/criminal-justice-reform [Accessed 5 August 2025].

12   What French philosopher Michel Foucault described as 'bio-power' in *Society must be defended: Lectures at the Collège de France, 1975–76* (Picador, 2003 [1997]), p. 247.

13   Sawyer and Wagner, 'Mass incarceration'. The ACLU argues that criminal justice is the second-fastest growing spending area for states, behind Medicaid, and 90 per cent of that spending goes to prisons, 'Fiscal cost of mass incarceration', ACLU, n.d., www.aclu.org/issues/smart-justice/mass-incarceration/fiscal-cost-mass-incarceration [Accessed 5 August 2025]. See also the 'Criminal justice reform', Equal Justice Initiative.

14   See 'Why is the opioid epidemic overwhelmingly white?', NPR, 4 November 2017, www.npr.org/2017/11/04/562137082/why-is-the-opioid-epidemic-overwhelmingly-white [Accessed 10 January 2023].

Notes

15 'Proud Boys leader sentenced to 22 years in prison for seditious conspiracy and other charges related to U.S. Capitol breach', US Department of Justice, 5 September 2023, www.justice.gov/opa/pr/proud-boys-leader-sentenced-22-years-prison-seditious-conspiracy-and-other-charges-related [Accessed 5 August 2025].

16 From a BBC television news report, 10pm, 6 January 2021.

17 'Inside the Capitol riot: An exclusive video investigation', *New York Times*, 30 June 2021, www.nytimes.com/2021/06/30/us/jan-6-capitol-attack-takeaways.html [Accessed 20 December 2024].

18 See CNN coverage of Donald Trump's town hall. 'Trump tells skeptical Republican voter Jan. 6 was a "day of love"', CNN, 16 October 2024, https://edition.cnn.com/2024/10/16/politics/video/donald-trump-univision-town-hall-jan-6-digvid [Accessed 28 December 2024].

19 Ted Rivers, J6 Patriot News, YouTube, 11 January 2022, www.youtube.com/watch?v=lVOvWWiqzmg [Accessed 10 January 2023].

20 For an overview of this case, see Casey Hicks, 'Timeline of Hillary Clinton's email scandal', CNN, 7 November 2016, https://edition.cnn.com/2016/10/28/politics/hillary-clinton-email-timeline/index.html [Accessed 28 December 2024].

21 Ted Rivers, J6 Patriot News, 11 January 2022.

22 CAPP, https://www.youtube.com/@citizensagainstpoliticalpe1908 [Accessed 24 August 2025]; 'Letter to the American people from J6 political prisoners', CAPP, YouTube, 11 January 2022, www.youtube.com/watch?v=lVOvWWiqzmg [Accessed 5 August 2025].

23 From the US Department of Justice: almost 1,600 have been charged in nearly all fifty states and the District of Columbia. 'Trump gave broad clemency to all Jan. 6 rioters: See their cases in 3 charts', CNN, 26 January 2025, https://edition.cnn.com/2025/01/26/politics/january-6-rioters-charges-convictions-dg [Accessed 24 August 2025].

24 Valerie Pavilonis, 'Fact check: Thousands of Black Lives Matter protesters were arrested in 2020', USA Today, 22 February 2022, https://eu.usatoday.com/story/news/factcheck/2022/02/22/fact-check-thousands-black-lives-matter-protesters-arrested-2020/6816074001/ [Accessed 11 January 2023].

25 Parole involves release from incarceration before the end of a sentence. Supervised release is an additional term of supervision, or 'restricted freedom', that must be completed after a person completes their term of federal custody. 'Supervised release (parole)', Congressional Research Service, 28 September 2021, https://sgp.fas.org/crs/misc/RS21364.pdf [Accessed 28 December 2024].

26 Supported by Kamala Harris, among others. 'The Dignity for Incarcerated Women Act', Now.org, n.d., https://now.org/wp-content/uploads/2017/09/Dignity-for-Incarcerated-Women-Act.pdf [Accessed 28 December 2024].

27 See David M. Reutter, 'Georgia enacts massive probation reform bill', Prison Legal News, 1 October 2021, www.prisonlegalnews.org/news/2021/oct/1/georgia-enacts-massive-probation-reform-bill/ [Accessed 28 December 2024].

Notes

LET'S HEAR IT FOR THE GIRL

1 'RNC reactions day 2', *Charlie Kirk Show*, 17 July 2024, with Charlie Kirk, Jack Posobiec, Tyler Bowyer, Blake Neff, following J.D. Vance's acceptance speech as Trump's running mate.

2 I use the term 'woman' throughout this chapter as expansively as possible. All are welcome: trans, cis, non-binary.

3 Judith Butler, 'Why is the idea of "gender" provoking backlash the world over?', *The Guardian*, 23 October 2021, www.theguardian.com/us-news/com mentisfree/2021/oct/23/judith-butler-gender-ideology-backlash [Accessed 5 August 2025].

4 Timothy Snyder uses Viktor Orbán, president of Hungary, as an example. *Road to unfreedom*, p. 52.

5 Agnieszka Graff and Elzbieta Korolczuk, *Anti-gender politics in the populist moment* (Routledge, 2021).

6 See, e.g., Hungary's tax exemptions for mothers of four or more children. The Trump administration announced it was looking into ways of supporting a higher birth rate in the USA in April 2025.

7 'Kamala Harris, nervous wreck', *The Charlie Kirk Show*, 30 August 2024, www.charliekirk.com/podcasts/kamala-harris-nervous-wreck [Accessed 29 December 2024].

8 Helen Andrews, *Boomers: The men and women who promised freedom and delivered disaster* (Sentinel, 2021), p. xiii.

9 'The revolution heads to Washington', *The Charlie Kirk Show*, 22 November 2024, https://omny.fm/shows/the-charlie-kirk-show/the-revolution-heads-to-washington [Accessed 23 November 2024].

10 Thomas Gallatin, 'Missing the real red flag', Patriot Post, 27 May 2022, https://patriotpost.us/articles/88668 [Accessed 27 August 2024]. In the space of two weeks, between May and June 2022, there was a spate of mass shootings by young men. An eighteen-year-old murdered ten people at a supermarket in Buffalo, New York state (16 May). An eighteen-year-old massacred nine-teen children (eight- to ten-year-olds) and two teachers at Robb Elementary school, Uvalde, Texas (24 May). A week later, a man killed four people and himself at a medical facility in Tulsa, Oklahoma (1 June). The next day, a man shot and killed two women then himself outside a church in Ames, Iowa (2 June). A nineteen-year-old tried to assassinate Donald Trump in July 2024. A twenty-two-year old was charged with the murder of Charlie Kirk in 2025.

11 'In brief: Not all masculinity is toxic', Patriot Post, 6 June 2022, https://patriotpost.us/articles/88856-in-brief-not-all-masculinity-is-toxic-2022-06-06 [Accessed 29 December 2024]; see also Mark Alexander, 'The common denominator of violence: Fathers who abandon children', Patriot Post, 15 June 2022, https://patriotpost.us/alexander/89121 [Accessed 21 August 2024].

12 Douglas Murray, 'Not all masculinity is toxic', *The Spectator*, 1 June 2022, https://thespectator.com/topic/not-all-masculinity-toxic/ [Accessed 29 December 2024].

13 *The Kevin Roberts Show* (Heritage Foundation), with Virginian politician Nick Freitas, YouTube, 28 August 2024, www.youtube.com/watch?v=3ikcoyhR5YU [Accessed 1 December 2024].

Notes

14   See Melissa Deckman, *The politics of Gen Z: How the youngest voters will shape our democracy* (Columbia University Press, 2024). See also 'Donald Trump courts the manoverse', *New York Times*, 30 August 2024, www.nytimes.com/2024/08/30/us/politics/trump-politics-nelk-boys.html [Accessed 5 August 2025]; John Otis, 'The gender gap among Gen Z voters explained', *New York Times*, 27 August 2024, www.nytimes.com/2024/08/27/insider/the-gender-gap-among-gen-z-voters-explained.html [Accessed 5 August 2025]; Claire Cain Miller, 'Many Gen Z men feel left behind: Some see Trump as an answer', *New York Times*, 24 August 2024, www.nytimes.com/2024/08/24/upshot/trump-polls-young-men.html [Accessed 5 August 2025]; Carter Sherman, 'Young women are the most progressive group in American history: Young men are checked out', *The Guardian*, 7 August 2024, www.theguardian.com/us-news/ng-interactive/2024/aug/07/gen-z-voters-political-ideology-gender-gap [Accessed 5 August 2025]; Sean Illing and David French discuss 'the GOP's masculinity panic' on the Vox podcast: Sean Illing, 'The GOP's masculinity panic', Vox, 5 January 2022, www.vox.com/vox-conversations-podcast/22834353/vox-conversations-david-french-republican-party-trump-masculinity [Accessed 29 December 2024].

15   Interview on Right Response Ministries, reposted on X by Right Wing Watch, 15 August 2024, https://x.com/CalltoActivism/status/1824169764916486403, [Accessed 17 August 2024].

16   Calvin Robinson, *Fox and Father*, 2 August 2024, clipped for X by Truth Checkers, https://x.com/i/status/1819270725154337122 [Accessed 17 August 2024]. His response to race riots in Britain, August 2024. Robinson announced his move to the USA in 2024.

17   To ratchet up emotions, Trump at times appeared at rallies with family members of the young women murdered. There is a long tradition of men calling for violence in the name of protecting women. See, e.g., George W. Bush's reference to 'rape rooms' in his justification for removing Saddam Hussein in the Gulf War. 'President Bush addresses Australian Parliament', The White House, 22 October 2003, https://georgewbush-whitehouse.archives.gov/news/releases/2003/10/20031022-12.html [Accessed 5 August 2025]. In the UK, attacks on asylum hotels in the summer of 2025 were accompanied by slogans such as 'safety of women and children before foreigners', https://www.bbc.co.uk/news/articles/c4gerg74y710 [Accessed 30 September 2025].

18   Donald Trump, 2024 election campaign rally, Indiana, Pennsylvania, 23 September 2024. 'Former President Trump campaigns in Indiana, Pennsylvania', C-Span, 23 September 2024, www.c-span.org/video/?538501-1/president-trump-campaigns-indiana-pennsylvania [Accessed 23 October 2024].

19   'Our movement vs the machine', *The Charlie Kirk Show*, 21 June 2024, https://thecharliekirkshow.com/podcasts/the-charlie-kirk-show/our-movement-vs-the-machine [Accessed 27 August 2024].

20   See 'More women are becoming gun owners', Harvard School of Public Health, 14 July 2021, https://hsph.harvard.edu/news/more-women-are-becoming-gun-owners/ [Accessed 5 August 2025].

21   For a summary of these incidents, see 'US election: Full transcript of Donald Trump's obscene videotape', BBC, 9 October 2016, www.bbc.co.uk/news/election-us-2016-37595321 [Accessed 5 August 2025]; Madeline Halpert, 'Key

moments from E. Jean Carroll's civil rape trial against Donald Trump', BBC, 9 May 2023, www.bbc.co.uk/news/world-us-canada-65502792 [Accessed 5 August 2025]; 'Trump reposts crude sexual remark about Harris on Truth Social', *New York Times*, 28 August 2024, www.nytimes.com/2024/08/28/us/politics/trump-truth-social-posts.html [Accessed 5 August 2025].

22 Anandita Datta, 'The genderscapes of hate: On violence against women in India', *Dialogues in Human Geography* 6, no. 2 (2016): 179–181, https://journals.sagepub.com/doi/10.1177/2043820616655016 [Accessed 5 August 2025].

23 Oren Cass, 'When the bough breaks', Understanding America (Substack), 16 November 2024, www.commonplace.org/p/when-the-bough-breaks [Accessed 23 November 2024].

24 Promotional email for Ben Carson's new book, *The perilous fight: Overcoming our culture's war on the American family* (Zondervan, 2024), American Cornerstone Institute, 14 May 2024.

25 Ben Carson, American Cornerstone Institute, e-newsletter, 31 May 2024.

26 'The right's big lie about a sexual assault in Virginia', *New York Times*, 28 October 2021, www.nytimes.com/2021/10/28/opinion/loudoun-county-trans.html [Accessed 5 August 2025].

27 See, e.g., Oren Cass (American Compass) and Kevin Roberts (Heritage Foundation) emphasising the importance of family and removing barriers to having more children. Ronald Reagan Foundation & Institute, YouTube, 26 January 2022, https://youtu.be/mGTGYBH_g7Y [Accessed 28 August 2024].

28 The National Conservatism statement of principles: https://national conservatism.org/national-conservatism-a-statement-of-principles [Accessed 5 November 2024].

29 'Freedom Conservatism: Statement of principles', www.freedomconservatism.org/p/freedom-conservatism-a-statement [Accessed 7 December 2024]; the Libertarian Party official platform states: 'Consenting adults should be free to choose their own sexual practices and personal relationships.' 'Our platform', Libertarian Party, www.lp.org/platform/ [Accessed 7 December 2024].

30 See, e.g., Helen Lewis, 'Taylor Swift's three-word burn of J.D. Vance', *The Atlantic*, 11 September 2024, www.theatlantic.com/politics/archive/2024/09/taylor-swift-kamala-harris-cats/679781/ [Accessed 29 December 2024].

31 *Tucker Carlson Tonight*, Fox News, 29 July 2021, www.foxnews.com/video/6265796735001 [Accessed 18 August 2024].

32 For example, TPUSA and the Daily Wire produced the documentary *Identity crisis* (2025), critiquing 'gender ideology' and trans-activism, www.dailywire.com/videos/identity-crisis [Accessed 13 February 2025]. The film was inspired by the 2023 Matt Walsh documentary *What is a woman?*, https://rumble.com/v2rpv4w-what-is-a-woman-matt-walsh-full-documentary.html [Accessed 13 February 2025].

33 Alabama, Florida, Georgia, Idaho, Indiana, Kentucky, Louisiana, North Carolina, North Dakota, Ohio, Oklahoma, Tennessee and Texas had litigation proceedings challenging these bans at the time of writing. Some states, such as Louisiana, already implemented a prohibition on gender-affirming care for minors. Sources: 'Map: Attacks on gender affirming care by state', Human Rights Campaign, www.hrc.org/resources/attacks-on-gender-affirming-care-by-state-map [Accessed 25 August 2025] and 'Trans youth healthcare ban

Notes

FAQ', Louisiana Trans Advocates, 8 January 2024, www.latransadvocates.org/healthcare-ban-faq [Accessed 24 August 2025].

34 Minnesota, for example, is a 'Trans Refuge' state due to a 2023 law that prevents out-of-state laws from interfering in the practice of gender-affirming health care there. 'New law establishes Minnesota as a "Trans Refuge" state', Minnesota House of Representatives, n.d., www.house.mn.gov/NewLaws/story/2023/5541 [Accessed 8 August 2025].

35 Butler, 'Why is the idea of "gender" provoking backlash the world over?'.

36 In summary, Title IX protects staff and students from sex discrimination in education settings.

37 Charlie Kirk, 'Liberty ledger', e-newsletter, 24 April 2024.

38 'America's civilizational death spiral', *The Charlie Kirk Show*, 3 April 2024, https://omny.fm/shows/the-charlie-kirk-show/americas-civilizational-death-spiral [Accessed 25 August 2024].

39 Attendees at the 2024 TPUSA Young Women's Leadership Summit could listen to the wisdom of speakers such as Holistic Hilda: see website at www.holistichilda.com/ [Accessed 8 August 2025].

40 Kevin Roberts, 'It's time Republicans really put family first', The Daily Signal (Heritage Foundation), 5 August 2024, www.dailysignal.com/2024/08/05/why-its-time-for-family-first-conservatism/ [Accessed 7 December 2024].

41 Sanjana Karanth and Jennifer Bendery, 'New DOT memo directs funds to communities with higher "marriage and birth rates"', Huffington Post, 31 January 2025, www.huffingtonpost.co.uk/entry/dot-memo-funds-communities-marriage-birth-rates_n_679bf8d8e4b0e1faebeef9c8 [Accessed 15 March 2025].

42 Moms for Liberty was designated an 'extremist' organisation in 2023 by the SPLC for their denigration of LGBTQi+ communities.

43 Source: 'Moms for America®: Love of liberty begins at home', MfA, 9 August 2021, https://momsforamerica.us/moms-for-america-love-of-liberty-begins-at-home/ [Accessed 30 March 2025].

44 Interview with founder and president Kimberly Fletcher, 9 May 2024, in 'Meet Kimberly Fletcher', Voyage Ohio, 9 May 2024, https://voyageohio.com/interview/meet-kimberly-fletcher/ [Accessed 29 December 2024].

45 The text book: W. Cleon Skousen, *The 5000-year leap: A miracle that changed the world* (National Center for Constitutional Studies, 1981). Its basic premise is that the USA is an economic miracle, having leap-frogged 5,000 years of development because of the principles of freedom established at its founding.

46 Following the decision, the country divided. Abortion law returned to individual states, several of which began to introduce restrictions and outright bans. Others became designated 'sanctuary states' for women who could travel for health care. Trump has taken credit for rowing back Roe vs Wade by his conservative appointments to SCOTUS.

47 For example, public comments by J.D. Vance made in 2022, supporting a national ban in order to stop women travelling interstate for abortions, resurfaced in 2024: 'JD Vance's resurfaced abortion comment sparks anger: "Dystopia scary"', Newsweek, 26 July 2024, www.newsweek.com/jd-vance-abortion-audio-travel-banned-1930761 [Accessed 24 August 2025].

48 In February 2024, the Alabama supreme court ruled that frozen embryos could be considered 'children' and halted IVF treatment in the state. Andrea Rice, 'Harris vs. Trump on reproductive access in 2024 presidential election', Healthline, 30 October 2024, www.healthline.com/health-news/trump-vs-harris-abortion-ivf-reproductive-rights-2024-presidential-election#ivfl [Accessed 8 August 2025].

49 Jason Arunn Murugesu, 'People opposed to abortion in the US would still help a friend get one', *New Scientist*, 18 February 2022, www.newscientist.com/article/2308925-people-opposed-to-abortion-in-the-us-would-still-help-a-friend-get-one/ [Accessed 29 August 2024].

50 Maggie Haberman and Shane Goldmacher, 'On Truth Social, Donald Trump tries to refashion himself as supportive of abortion rights', *New York Times*, online ed., 23 August 2024, www.nytimes.com/2024/08/23/us/politics/trump-abortion-truth-social.html [Accessed 7 December 2024].

51 The National Abortion Federation shows rising incidents of violence against abortion providers. 'Provider security', National Abortion Federation, n.d., https://prochoice.org/our-work/provider-security/ [Accessed 5 August 2025].

52 See Donald Trump 2024 campaign video, 8 April 2024, https://truthsocial.com/@realDonaldTrump/posts/112235238031827342 [Accessed 30 March 2025].

53 We Testify: https://wetestify.org/ [Accessed 8 August 2025].

54 See 'History of abortion laws', Texas State Library, n.d., https://guides.sll.texas.gov/abortion-laws/history-of-abortion-laws#s-lg-box-29043273 [Accessed 8 August 2025].

55 According to the Texas Department of Health, 85 per cent of all abortions among Texas residents occurred at eight or less weeks post-fertilisation and 92 per cent at ten weeks or less post-fertilisation (2021). Source: '2021 induced terminations of pregnancy for Texas residents', Texas Health and Human Services, n.d., www.hhs.texas.gov/sites/default/files/documents/2021-itop-narrative-tx-residents.pdf [Accessed 8 August 2025].

56 Charlie Kirk promoted donations to 'Pre-Born', an organisation that provides ultrasounds to women, 'saving moms from a lifetime of pain and regret'. '$280 can save 10 babies'; see 'Our movement vs. the machine', *The Charlie Kirk Show*.

57 Source: Michael Li and Julia Boland, 'Anatomy of the Texas gerrymander', Brennan Center for Justice, 7 December 2021, www.brennancenter.org/our-work/analysis-opinion/anatomy-texas-gerrymander [Accessed 8 August 2025].

58 According to the Guttmacher Institute, the Texas state spent $140 million on its 'alternatives to abortion' programme in 2024–2025, Kimya Forouzan and Rosann Mariappuram, 'Midyear 2024 state policy trends: Many US states attack reproductive health care, as other states fight back', Guttmacher Institute, June 2024, www.guttmacher.org/2024/06/midyear-2024-state-policy-trends-many-us-states-attack-reproductive-health-care-other [Accessed 21 April 2025].

59 Planned Parenthood, attorneys and other abortion rights advocates filed law-suits, including several against Texas Right to Life and John Seago, challeng-ing the constitutionality of the Heartbeat Act. However, the Texas supreme court looks likely to reject their claim (November 2024). Source: Toluwani

Osibamowo, 'Challenge to Texas "Heartbeat Law" could be thrown out after Texas supreme court ruling', Texas Public Radio, 22 November 2024, www.tpr.org/bioscience-medicine/2024-11-22/challenge-to-texas-heartbeat-law-could-be-thrown-out-after-texas-supreme-court-ruling# [Accessed 8 August 2025].

60 See, e.g., the work of Maureen Condic: https://neuroscience.med.utah.edu/faculty/condic.php [Accessed 8 August 2025].

61 Details of the case and the contested reporting around it can be found here: David Folkenflik and Sarah McCammon, 'A rape, an abortion, and a one-source story: A child's ordeal becomes national news', NPR, 13 July 2022, www.npr.org/2022/07/13/1111285143/abortion-10-year-old-raped-ohio [Accessed 29 December 2024].

62 Parental leave is regulated by labour laws that only require twelve weeks of unpaid leave for mothers, and only if they work for a company with fifty or more employees. Estimates range from 5 per cent (for low-income families) to 12 per cent on average of Americans receiving paid parental leave. 'Paid maternity leave by state 2025', World Population Review, n.d., https://worldpopulationreview.com/state-rankings/paid-maternity-leave-by-state [Accessed 8 August 2025].

63 Women's March is a loose affiliation of women's organisations that formed after Trump was elected in 2016.

64 Source: 'Violence against abortion providers continues to rise following Roe reversal, new report finds', National Abortion Federation, 11 May 2023, https://prochoice.org/violence-against-abortion-providers-continues-to-rise-following-roe-reversal-new-report-finds/ [Accessed 8 August 2025].

65 Women's March, e-newsletter, 22 December 2023.

TEACHING FREEDOM: THE (MIS-)EDUCATION OF AMERICA

1 One of the origin stories for how DEI initiatives became a flashpoint was reported in the *New York Times*, October 2021 ('Energizing conservative voters, one school board election at a time'): Milwaukee school boards were recalled because some introduced an hour-long video on racism after parents requested information on how to talk to their children about the murder of George Floyd. Other parents later objected. 22 October 2021, A1, A12. (Also available online: https://www.nytimes.com/2021/10/21/us/republicans-schools-critical-race-theory.html [Accessed 24 August 2025].)

2 David Davenport, 'Civics education: Let it bloom', Hoover Institution, 20 August 2021, www.hoover.org/research/civics-education-let-it-bloom [Accessed 19 October 2024].

3 Ronald Reagan Foundation & Institute, e-newsletter, 23 July 2024.

4 West Virginia State Board of Education v. Barnette, 1943, cited by Jill Lepore in 'The parent trap', *The New Yorker*, 21 March 2022, p. 21. See also Jill Lepore, *These truths: A history of the United States* (W.W. Norton, 2019).

5 For example, 'Critical race theory', MfA, n.d., https://momsforamerica.us/mom-watch/critical-race-theory/ [Accessed 8 August 2025].

Notes

6   Lepore, 'The parent trap'.

7   Heritage Foundation, e-newsletter, 12 April 2024.

8   Recorded at AmFest 2021, see also 'Groomer schools 1: The long cultural Marxist history of sex education', New Discourses, 19 November 2021, https://newdiscourses.com/2021/11/groomer-schools-1-long-cultural-marxist-history-sex-education/ [Accessed 12 February 2025].

9   'DEI, CRT, and the plan to take down AMERICA!', MfA, with Dr Carol Swain, podcast available on demand, https://momsforamerica.us/webinars-on-demand/ [Accessed 8 August 2025].

10 Heritage Foundation, 'Saved by the (Heritage) bell', e-newsletter, 12 April 2024.

11 'Leading the fight against the left-wing ideological regime', activist, author and Manhattan Institute senior research fellow, Christopher Rufo, has campaigned for greater transparency for parents and an end to teaching CRT. He has, along with other conservative organisations such as the Heritage Foundation, proposed a 'pro-parent education agenda' to encourage parents to have greater input into their children's education. As an advisor to Florida Governor Ron DeSantis, he has been instrumental in developing education policy in that state. See Christopher F. Rufo, 'Welcome to my Substack', Substack, n.d., https://christopherrufo.com/about [Accessed 8 August 2025].

12 Ben Carson, 'Preparing for this summer', American Cornerstone Institute, e-newsletter, 23 May 2024.

13 See 'Coalition calls on states to increase transparency, end critical race theory in schools', Heritage Foundation, 2 December 2021, www.heritage.org/article/coalition-calls-states-increase-transparency-end-critical-race-theory-schools [Accessed 8 August 2025]; Christopher F. Rufo, 'The anti-CRT parent guidebook', Substack, 23 November 2021, https://christopherrufo.com/p/crt-parent-guidebook [Accessed 8 August 2025].

14 See Lepore, 'The parent trap'.

15 'Alabama voters pass Amendment 4 to address Constitution's legacy of racial injustice', Equal Justice Initiative, 4 November 2020, https://eji.org/news/amendment-4-addresses-alabama-constitutions-legacy-of-racial-injustice/ [Accessed 8 August 2025].

16 See, e.g., MfA, 'The true corrective', e-newsletter, 21 February 2024; https://momsforamerica.us/homeschool-mom-2-mom/ [Accessed 8 August 2025].

17 Mike Pence, former vice president, 'Advancing American freedom', fundraising email, 7 September 2022.

18 Heritage Foundation, 'Saved by the (Heritage) bell', e-newsletter, 12 April 2024.

19 Pizzagate was a conspiracy theory that began circulating on social media during the 2016 presidential election campaign. The conspiracy falsely claimed that Democratic Party leaders were involved in a paedophile ring linked to a pizzeria in Washington, DC.

20 Isabel Brown livestream, Gettr, 3 February 2022, 7pm, www.youtube.com/@theisabelbrown [Accessed 8 August 2025].

21 Heritage Foundation, 'The kids are not alright', fundraising email, 18 July 2024.

22 His 2022 book was titled *The college scam: How America's universities are bankrupting and brainwashing away the future of America's youth* (Winning Team Publishing, 2022).

23 Source: 'Professor watchlist', www.professorwatchlist.org/ [Accessed 8 August 2025].

24 MfA, e-newsletter, 23 July 2024; see also MfA podcast on public school indoctrination, 9 July 2024, with Alex Newman, YouTube, https://www.youtube.com/watch?v=GyJwSHUhy3g [Accessed 24 August 2025].

25 MfA podcast, 'Taking back our schools and children's education', YouTube, 1 March 2022, www.youtube.com/watch?v=yLchclGsfuM [Accessed 8 August 2025].

26 MfA, e-newsletter, promoting the podcast 'Freedom, faith and folklore: Unraveling the TRUTH about our nation's foundation' (their caps). 1 November 2024.

27 MfA, podcast, 'By now we have all heard about CRT: Critical race theory', 25 May 2022, Rumble, https://rumble.com/v162r2e-by-now-we-have-all-heard-about-crt-critical-race-theory.html [Accessed 8 August 2025]; see also MomForce resources on education options: 'Empower moms: Education options', n.d., https://momsforamerica.us/empower-moms/resources-education-options/ [Accessed 8 August 2025].

28 'Cat litter for pupils rumour denied by school in letter', BBC News online, 10 November 2023, www.bbc.co.uk/news/uk-wales-67377626 [Accessed 15 December 2024].

29 Ben Carson, 'Commonsense pledge', American Cornerstone Institute, e-newsletter, 5 June 2024.

30 Ben Carson, 'How can we stop this', American Cornerstone Institute, e-newsletter, 25 May 2024.

31 Hillsdale is an independent Christian college focusing on 'learning, character, faith, and freedom', with K-12 as well as higher education programmes, providing an 'American classical education'. 'Reviving the American tradition of K-12 education', Hillsdale College, n.d., https://k12.hillsdale.edu [Accessed 8 August 2025]. See promotional videos 'An American classical education: An inside view of the work Hillsdale College is doing', YouTube, 26 July 2022, https://youtu.be/PSHOx_36dAo [Accessed 8 August 2025]; 'Teaching for virtue: K12; An American classical education', YouTube, 12 November 2021, https://youtu.be/S14dw_pLi2g [Accessed 8 August 2025].

32 Kevin Roberts, Heritage Foundation, e-newsletter, 4 July 2024.

33 Compare, for example, Rebecca Futo Kennedy's work on 'the uses of Greco-Roman antiquity in racism and supremacisms', 'Academy of Athens seminar (10/2): Uses of antiquity in racism & supremacisms', YouTube, 24 February 2022 (www.youtube.com/watch?v=jZSCsXAytWI [accessed 8 August 2025]), with Jeffrey Rosen's *The pursuit of happiness: How classical writers on virtue inspired the lives of the founders and defined America* (Simon & Schuster, 2024) (https://constitutioncenter.org/go/the-pursuit-of-happiness [Accessed 8 August 2025]). See also the Hoover Institute's paper 'Duelling populisms', by Victor Davis Hanson, who likens today's populism to conflicts between rural and urban Rome.

Notes

34 Ronald Reagan Foundation & Institute, e-newsletter, 23 July 2024; see also Charlie Kirk, 'Liberty ledger', e-newsletter, 7 August 2024, expressing 'shock' 'at how uneducated students are about their own country's founding'.

35 American Cornerstone Institute, e-newsletter, 29 February 2024.

36 'American values, one story at a time', Heroes of Liberty, n.d., https://heroesofliberty.com/#shopify-section-template--15213910753442__1635286773decf0c44 [Accessed 8 August 2025].

37 Source: 'DeSantis doubles down on claim that some Blacks benefited from slavery', *Washington Post*, 22 July 2023, www.washingtonpost.com/politics/2023/07/22/desantis-slavery-curriculum/ [Accessed 8 August 2025].

38 The SPLC surveyed teachers and found that when they didn't teach the history of enslavement it was primarily because they were afraid of what emotions it would evoke in their students. They also lacked confidence about how much they knew about the period. SPLC then created resources to support teachers. From interview with Lecia Brooks, SPLC. See Kate Shuster, 'Teaching hard history', SPLC, 31 January 2018, www.splcenter.org/20180131/teaching-hard-history [Accessed 8 August 2025].

39 'The 1619 Project', *New York Times*, 14 August 2019, www.nytimes.com/interactive/2019/08/14/magazine/1619-america-slavery.html [Accessed 8 August 2025].

40 'Training & equipping', n.d., Turning Point Academy, www.turningpointacademy.com/training [Accessed 8 August 2025]; 'Turning Point education', Turning Point Academy, www.tpusa.com/academy [Accessed 8 August 2025]; see also Charlie Kirk, podcast: 'The myth of "neutral" education: My speech to the TP Academy Educators Summit', *The Charlie Kirk Show*, 29 July 2024, https://thecharliekirkshow.com/podcasts/the-charlie-kirk-show/education-summit-the-myth-of-neutral-education-my [Accessed 8 August 2025].

41 'American Cornerstone Institute's Little Patriots Program introduces free curriculum for celebrating American liberty', American Cornerstone, 18 September 2024, https://americancornerstone.org/wp-content/uploads/2024/09/Press-Release-for-CFW.pdf [Accessed 8 August 2025].

42 Heritage Foundation, 'Saved by the (Heritage) bell', e-newsletter, 12 April 2024.

43 Heritage Foundation, 'Will American ideals survive the next generation?', e-newsletter, 8 December 2023.

44 Patriot Academy, e-newsletter, 13 May 2024, https://coach.patriotacademy.com/learn-more/ [Accessed 8 August 2025].

45 'From revolution to republic: Cottage meetings for teens': '[T]his interdisciplinary course weaves together American history, classic literature, and the power of personal story to help teens explore the timeless themes of freedom and liberty.' MfA e-newsletter, 14 February 2025.

46 America First Works, 'Bootcamp for patriots', e-newsletter, 12 April 2024, https://amac.us/bootcamp/?mc_cid=c5e3adbf7f&mc_eid=7aedcc4aff [Accessed 8 August 2025].

47 EdChoice is founded on the classical liberalism principles of economists Milton and Rose Friedman, 'Who we are', EdChoice, n.d., www.edchoice.org/who-we-are/ [Accessed 8 August 2025].

Notes

48 See 'Coalition for TJ, plaintiff – appellee, v. Fairfax County School Board, defendant – appellant', United States Court of Appeals for the Fourth Circuit, no. 22-1280, p. 8, www.ca4.uscourts.gov/opinions/221280.P.pdf [Accessed 8 August 2025].

49 See the ruling here: https://pacificlegal.org/wp-content/uploads/2023/05/2023-05-23-circuit-opinion-coalitition-for-tj-v-fairfax-county-school-board.pdf; Further explanation: Colleen Kelleher, 'Thomas Jefferson High School admissions policy stays in place; Supreme Court won't hear case', *Northern Virginia Magazine*, 20 February 2024, https://northernvirginiamag.com/culture/news/2024/02/20/thomas-jefferson-high-school-admissions-policy-stays-in-place-supreme-court-wont-hear-case/ [Accessed 8 August 2025].

50 For example: Jeremy B. White, 'Parental fury propels San Francisco school board ouster', Politico, 14 February 2022, www.politico.com/news/2022/02/14/san-francisco-school-board-ouster-00008422 [Accessed 8 August 2025].

51 See Keith Nickolaus, 'The Supreme Court on affirmative action: The decision, its context, and future impact', Crimson Education, 25 July 2023, www.crimsoneducation.org/ca/blog/affirmative-action-and-college-admissions/ [Accessed 8 August 2025]; also, Nina Totenberg, 'Supreme Court guts affirmative action, effectively ending race-conscious admissions', NPR, 29 June 2023, www.npr.org/2023/06/29/1181138066/affirmative-action-supreme-court-decision [Accessed 8 August 2025].

52 There have been multiple examples of cancellations in universities in the USA and UK, with virulent debates among academics about the limits of academic freedom and free speech. Examples of high-profile cases at the University of Michigan and Prof. Kathleen Stock in the UK: 'A blackface "Othello" shocks, and a professor steps back from class', *New York Times*, 15 October 2021, www.nytimes.com/2021/10/15/arts/music/othello-blackface-bright-sheng.html [Accessed 8 August 2025]; 'Kathleen Stock: University of Sussex free speech row professor quits', BBC News, 29 October 2021, www.bbc.com/news/uk-england-sussex-59084446 [Accessed 8 August 2025].

53 This is to fund 'tuition, curriculum, textbooks, testing fees, and other educational goods and services'. Source: Keri D. Ingraham, 'Louisiana to become 12th state to adopt Universal School Choice', Discovery Institute, 6 June 2024, www.discovery.org/education/2024/06/06/louisiana-to-become-12th-state-to-adopt-universal-school-choice [Accessed 8 August 2025].

54 See 'Court blocks Louisiana law requiring public schools to display Ten Commandments in every classroom', ACLU, 12 November 2024, www.aclu.org/press-releases/court-blocks-louisiana-law-requiring-public-schools-to-display-ten-commandments-in-every-classroom [Accessed 8 August 2025].

55 See Steve Gorman, 'Louisiana becomes first US state to classify abortion pills as controlled substances', Reuters, 25 May 2024, www.reuters.com/world/us/louisiana-governor-signs-bill-classifying-abortion-pills-controlled-substances-2024-05-24/ [Accessed 8 August 2025].

56 See 'Private school enrollment', National Center for Education Statistics, May 2024, https://nces.ed.gov/programs/coe/indicator/cgc/private-school-enrollment [Accessed 8 August 2025]; see also Ruth Graham, 'Christian schools boom in a revolt against curriculum and pandemic rules', *New York Times*,

19 October 2021, www.nytimes.com/2021/10/19/us/christian-schools-growth.html [Accessed 8 August 2025].

57 The evangelical Association of Christian Schools International experienced a 12 per cent increase in its K-12 enrolment from 2019/2020 to 2020/2021. In 2023, the *Washington Post* published findings indicating a 51 per cent increase in the transition from traditional educational settings to homeschooling over the previous six academic years. Source: Peter Jamison et al., 'Home schooling's rise from fringe to fastest-growing form of education', *Washington Post*, 31 October 2023, www.washingtonpost.com/education/interactive/2023/homeschooling-growth-data-by-district/ [Accessed 8 August 2025].

58 I was unable to find any reference to this sex education programme. There was a Bill (House Bill 22–1136) introduced in Colorado in 2022 that would have required schools to show a five-minute video of the development of a foetus over time, but it was not passed. Source: 'Ultrasound video demonstration in sex education', Colorado General Assembly, HB22-1136, https://leg.colorado.gov/bills/hb22-1136 [Accessed 8 August 2025].

59 Lepore is citing Sigal R. Ben-Porath and Michael C. Johanek's, *Making up our mind: What school choice is really about* (University of Chicago Press, 2019), p 3. For the full article, see 'Why the school wars still rage', *The New Yorker*, 21 March 2022, www.newyorker.com/magazine/2022/03/21/why-the-school-wars-still-rage [Accessed 8 August 2025].

60 'Messaging guide and digital toolkit: Freedom to learn', We Make the Future Action, n.d., www.wemakethefutureaction.us/resources-documents/freedom-to-learn-messaging-guide [Accessed 8 August 2025].

THE MANY INCARNATIONS OF JESUS CHRIST'S LOVE

1 See, e.g., as part of The American Conservative's Constitutional Fellows programme, participants learn the moral and cultural underpinnings of the Constitution, including its 'ancient and Christian origins'. 'TAC Announces Constitutional Fellows Program', The American Conservative, 25 November 2019, www.theamericanconservative.com/the-american-conservative-announces-constitutional-fellows-program/ [Accessed 22 February 2025].

2 See, e.g., the National Conservative statement of principles: 'Where a Christian majority exists, public life should be rooted in Christianity and its moral vision, which should be honored by the state and other institutions both public and private.' 'National Conservatism: A statement of principles', National Conservatism, n.d., https://nationalconservatism.org/national-conservatism-a-statement-of-principles/ [Accessed 13 March 2025].

3 'Evangelicals for Harris: The world's worst oxymoron', *The Charlie Kirk Show*, 17 August 2024, https://members.charliekirk.com/evangelicals-for-harris-the-worlds-worst-oxymoron-ad-free/ [Accessed 24 August 2025]. Kirk interviews the director of TPFaith, Lucas Miles, who refers to 'the Marxism of Liberation Theology' and states that 'Evangelicals for Harris' 'makes about as much sense as Jews for Hitler', https://thecharliekirkshow.com/podcasts/the-charlie-kirk-show/evangelicals-for-harris-the-worlds-worst-oxymoron [Accessed 22 August 2024].

Notes

4   Mike Pence, 'Advancing American freedom', e-newsletter, 19 November 2022.
5   Ben Carson, American Cornerstone Institute, e-newsletter promoting his new book, *Perilous fight*, 14 May 2024.
6   Karen Jordan, 'A Christian vision of freedom and democracy: Neutrality as an obstacle to freedom', *Tennessee Journal of Law and Policy* 9, no. 3 (2014), article 4.
7   Jordan Peterson, quoted in an Alliance for Responsible Citizenship e-newsletter, 19 January 2024.
8   The authors of *The founders Bible: The origin of the dream of freedom* (Shiloh Road Publishers, 2012) selected 15,000 quotes from the Founding Fathers and found that a third originated or were influenced by the Bible.
9   Jean Baudrillard, *America* (Verso, 2010), p. 105.
10 See e.g. Laleh Khalili, *Extractive capitalism: How commodities and cronyism drive the global economy* (Verso, 2025).
11 See, e.g., Susanna Park et al., 'Digital methods for the spiritual and mental health of Generation Z: Scoping review', *Interactive Journal of Medical Research* 6, no. 13 (2024), https://pmc.ncbi.nlm.nih.gov/articles/PMC10879969/#ref7 [Accessed 24 August 2025].
12 The Free Thinkers mission statement.
13 Pew Research Center, sources: 'About three-in-ten U.S. adults are now religiously unaffiliated', Pew Research Center, 14 December 2021, www.pewresearch.org/religion/2021/12/14/about-three-in-ten-u-s-adults-are-now-religiously-unaffiliated/ [Accessed 8 August 2025]; 'Compared with in 2016, fewer Republicans and Democrats now say being Christian and being born in the U.S. are important to being "truly American"', Pew Research Center, 24 May 2021, www.pewresearch.org/short-reads/2021/05/25/in-both-parties-fewer-now-say-being-christian-or-being-born-in-u-s-is-important-to-being-truly-american/ft_2021-05-25_nationalidentity_01-png/ [Accessed 8 August 2025].
14 See Gregory A. Smith et al., 'Decline of Christianity in the U.S. has slowed, may have leveled off', Pew Research Center, 26 February 2025, www.pewresearch.org/religion/2025/02/26/decline-of-christianity-in-the-us-has-slowed-may-have-leveled-off/ [Accessed 13 March 2025].
15 See, e.g., 'Meet the Christians pushing back on Christian nationalism', NPR, 24 October 2024, www.npr.org/2024/10/24/1211597179/1a-10-24-2024 [Accessed 29 December 2024]; see also John Blake, 'The relentless focus on white Christian nationalism is spreading a racist myth', CNN, 3 February 2024, https://edition.cnn.com/2024/02/03/us/white-christian-nationalism-racist-myth-cec/index.html [Accessed 8 August 2025].
16 Ryan Burger, 'Why evangelical is becoming another word for Republican', *New York Times*, 26 October 2021, www.nytimes.com/2021/10/26/opinion/evangelical-republican.html [Accessed 29 December 2024].
17 For in-depth analysis of these trends, see Ryan Burger, 'Are we all evangelicals now? How the term has grown to blur theology and ideology', Religion Unplugged, 11 March 2021, https://religionunplugged.com/news/2021/3/11/are-we-all-evangelicals-now-how-the-term-has-grown-to-blur-theology-and-ideology [Accessed 17 March 2025].

Notes

18 In June 2023, SCOTUS ruled that on the basis of free speech, states could not enforce anti-discrimination laws against Christian businesses refusing services to gay people. In May 2022, SCOTUS ruled that Boston city council cannot exclude religious groups from displaying flags at its city hall installation. Kennedy vs Bremerton School District (27 June 2022) found praying in public schools was protected by the First Amendment. Carson vs Makin (21 June 2021) overturned Maine's exclusion of religious schools from a state tuition programme.

19 SPLC named Christian nationalism in its 2023 annual report, 'The year in hate and extremism', SPLC, www.splcenter.org/resources/year-hate-extremism-2023 [Accessed 8 August 2025]; see also FFRF response to study showing majority of Americans reject Christian nationalism: 'FFRF welcomes study showing Americans strongly reject Christian', FFRF, 9 February 2023, https://ffrf.org/news/releases/ffrf-welcomes-study-showing-americans-strongly-reject-christian-nationalism/ [Accessed 24 August 2025].

HOW TO BECOME A LIBERTARIAN: 'DON'T HIT OTHER PEOPLE, DON'T TAKE THEIR STUFF AND KEEP YOUR PROMISES'

1 See the Free State Project for more details of libertarianism in New Hampshire: 'The Free State Project mission statement: "Liberty in your lifetime!"', n.d., www.fsp.org/mission [Accessed 8 August 2025].

2 Matthew Hongoltz-Hetling, *A libertarian walks into a bear: The utopian plot to liberate an American town (and some bears)* (Public Affairs, 2020).

3 For an overview of what happened, see Cheng-Chun Lee, Mikel Maron and Ali Mostafavi, 'Community-scale big data reveals disparate impacts of the Texas winter storm of 2021 and its managed power outage', *Nature: Humanities and Social Sciences* 9 (2022), www.nature.com/articles/s41599-022-01353-8; www.ncei.noaa.gov/news/great-texas-freeze-february-2021 [Accessed 8 August 2025]; Joshua W. Busby et al., 'Cascading risks: Understanding the 2021 winter blackout in Texas', *Energy Research & Social Science* 77 (2021), www.sciencedirect.com/science/article/pii/S2214629621001997 [Accessed 8 August 2025].

4 Mostly European and North American, mostly bespectacled men in tweed suits and bow ties, with the occasional woman, including: Richard Epstein, Milton Friedman, F.A. Hayek, John Locke, Robert Nozick, Ayn Rand, Murray Rothbard, Adam Smith, Morrison and Linda Tannehill. Contemporaries such as David Boaz and Milton Friedman's son, David, continue the tradition.

5 David Friedman, *The machinery of freedom: Guide to a radical capitalism*, 3rd ed. (Open Court Publishing, 2014 [1973]), p. xv.

6 David Boaz, *The libertarian mind: A manifesto for freedom* (Simon & Schuster 2015 [1997]), p. 23.

7 Morris and Linda Tannehill, *The market for liberty* (Ludwig von Mises Institute, 2007 [1970]), p. 9.

8 See 'Atlas Society', n.d., www.atlassociety.org/ [Accessed 8 August 2025].

9 Boaz, *The libertarian mind*, p. 78.

10 Tannehill and Tannehill, *The market for liberty*, p. 42.

11 Boaz, *The libertarian mind*, p.179.

Notes

12   Source: 'Freedom Conservatism: A statement of principles', 13 July 2023, www.freedomconservatism.org/p/freedom-conservatism-a-statement [Accessed 8 August 2025].

13   A contested metaphor, often misquoted. See Brandon Dupont and Yvonne Durham, 'Adam Smith and the not so invisible hand: A revision for the undergraduate classroom', *International Review of Economics Education* 36 (2021), www.sciencedirect.com/science/article/abs/pii/S1477388020300323 [Accessed 8 August 2025]. The original quote can be found here: Adam Smith, *An inquiry into the wealth of nations* (MetaLibri, 2007), www.ibiblio.org/ml/libri/s/SmithA_WealthNations_p.pdf [Accessed 8 August 2025].

14   According to Boaz, freedom emerged out of a contest between church and state in medieval Europe that allowed individualism to develop; an argument that would be contested.

15   See historian Sarah Churchwell's work on the origins of the American Dream: *Behold, America* .

16   See, e.g., David Graeber, *The ultimate hidden truth of the world* (Allen Lane, 2024); David Harvey, *The ways of the world* (Oxford University Press, 2016).

17   See, e.g., Daniel Kahneman, Olivier Sibony and Cass Sunstein, *Noise: A flaw in human judgement* (Little, Brown, 2021).

18   For example: in 2020, Libertarian Party candidate Jo Jorgensen received more votes than Biden's winning margins in several key states. If his voters had supported Trump instead, Trump would have been re-elected due to the electoral college, although he would have lost the popular vote. Source: Matthew R. Kerbel and John Kenneth White, *American political parties: Why they formed, how they function, and where they're headed* (University Press of Kansas, 2023), Chapter 9, 'Third parties in the twenty-first century', Project Muse, https://muse.jhu.edu/pub/266/oa_monograph/chapter/3171480 [Accessed 8 August 2025].

19   Sebastian Junger, *Freedom* (4th Estate, 2022), p. 116.

20   Tannehill and Tannehill, *The market for liberty*, p. 10. The example given is of a mother who goes without a new dress in order to buy a new coat for her daughter whom she loves; the child's comfort outweighing the value of the dress. But, if she deprives both herself and the child, and gives the money to a charity instead so that people won't think she's 'selfish', that is a sacrifice.

21   Friedman, *The machinery of freedom*, pp. 14–17.

22   Alexis de Tocqueville, *Democracy in America* (Penguin Classics, 2003 [1835, 1840]). .

23   In Adam Smith's *The wealth of nations*, he uses the manufacture of pins to illustrate the division of labour that goes into the production of goods. This division of labour extends from extracting the raw materials needed to make a pin, to its manufacture and distribution. According to Smith, as people begin to specialise in particular jobs in this production chain, it makes societies more efficient, able to produce more and therefore wealthier.

24   Boaz, *The libertarian mind*, p. 120.

25   The actual quote is: 'Hard times create strong men. Strong men create good times. Good times create weak men. And, weak men create hard times',

appearing in G. Michael Hopf's post-apocalyptic 2016 novel, *Those who remain* (n.p., 2016).

26 Boaz, *The libertarian mind*.

27 Section 8 of the USA government's Housing Act of 1937 provides rental assistance vouchers to low-income households to access private rental accommodation. See 'Section 8', USAGOV, 17 June 2025, https://www.usa.gov/housing-voucher-section-8 [Accessed 25 August 2025].

28 Source: Art Carden, 'The aristocracy of pull', Atlas Society, 28 September 2020, www.atlassociety.org/post/the-aristocracy-of-pull [Accessed 8 August 2025]; see also Hoover Institution analysis: David R. Henderson, 'The aristocracy of pull', Hoover Institution, 8 September 2022, www.hoover.org/research/aristocracy-pull [Accessed 8 August 2025]. Others may argue it's structural inequality by another name.

29 'About the untreated syphilis study at Tuskegee', Centers for Disease Control and Prevention, www.cdc.gov/Tuskegee [Accessed 8 August 2025].

30 See Richard Beck's 2024 review of 'Waco: I will give thee Madonna', *London Review of Books* 4, no. 6 (21 March 2024), www.lrb.co.uk/the-paper/v46/n06/richard-beck/i-will-give-thee-madonna [Accessed 29 December 2024].

31 See the following case study: Jeanine Santucci, 'Old legal quirk lets police take your money with little reason, critics say', USA Today, 18 August 2024, https://eu.usatoday.com/story/news/nation/2024/08/18/civil-asset-forfeiture-explained/74802279007/ [Accessed 8 August 2025].

32 From the World Inequality Database: 'The United States is the most unequal country in the OECD, with 21% of national income going to the richest 1%.' '10 facts on global inequality in 2024', World Inequality Database, 19 November 2024, https://wid.world/news-article/10-facts-on-global-inequality-in-2024/ [Accessed 31 December 2024].

33 According to the Pew Research Center, the government's total public debt was $31.46 trillion in 2023. Source: Drew Desilver, '5 facts about the U.S. national debt', Pew Research Center, 14 February 2023, www.pewresearch.org/short-reads/2023/02/14/facts-about-the-us-national-debt/ [Accessed 8 August 2025].

34 Student debt has now reached $1.75 trillion, including federal and private loans. Biden announced a programme of forgiving student debt (2023–2024), but it was blocked by SCOTUS in 2023. Alicia Hahn, 'Student loan debt statistics: Average student loan debt', *Forbes*, 18 April 2024, www.forbes.com/advisor/student-loans/average-student-loan-debt-statistics/ [Accessed 31 December 2024].

35 See 'Trade wars and Trump's tariffs harm everybody', Libertarian Party, n.d., https://lp.org/trade-wars-trumps-tariffs-harm-everybody/ [Accessed 29 April 2025].

36 According to census data, Florida added 819,000 domestic migrants to its population between 2020 and 2023. Texas added 656,000. See 'National population totals and components of change: 2020–2024', United States Census Bureau, n.d., www.census.gov/data/tables/time-series/demo/popest/2020s-national-total.html [Accessed 8 August 2025]. Source: Jeffrey H. Anderson, 'Moving to red America', City Journal, 30 January 2024, www.city-journal.org/article/moving-to-red-america [Accessed 8 August 2025].

37 Boaz, *The libertarian mind*, p. 138.

38 On membership, see 'Libertarian Party registration surges 92% in 10 years', Libertarian Party, n.d., www.lp.org/libertarian-party-registration-surges-92-10-years/ [Accessed 8 August 2025]; on results in the 2024 presidential elections, see 'What happened to the minor party presidential candidacies?', *New York Magazine*, 17 November 2024, https://nymag.com/intelligencer/article/november-surprise-minor-party-candidacies-nearly-vanished.html [Accessed 8 August 2025]; see also Drew Desilver, 'Third-party and independent candidates for president often fall short of early polling numbers', Pew Research Center, 27 June 2024, www.pewresearch.org/short-reads/2024/06/27/third-party-and-independent-candidates-for-president-often-fall-short-of-early-polling-numbers/ [Accessed 8 August 2025].

THE ENCHANTMENTS OF MEDICAL FREEDOM AND FUTURE DYSTOPIAS

1 See *New York Times* election coverage, www.nytimes.com/live/2024/11/05/us/trump-harris-election [Accessed 5 November 2024].

2 *Tucker Carlson Show*, Fox News, 19 April 2022, 8.25pm.

3 Up to 2022, New York City required evidence of vaccination to access indoor spaces such as theatres and restaurants.

4 By Hi Rez and Jimmy Levy: https://genius.com/Hi-rez-and-jimmy-levy-this-is-a-war-lyrics [Accessed 29 December 2024].

5 This transnational conspiracy extended to a belief that policies linked to 'fifteen-minute cities' and managing pollution (ultra-low emission zones in the UK) were also attempts to 'control' and geo-fence. See, e.g., '15 minute cities: How they got caught in conspiracy theories', BBC News, 3 October 2023, www.bbc.co.uk/news/uk-politics-66990302 [Accessed 29 December 2024].

6 See, e.g., Graeber, *The ultimate hidden truth of the world*; David Harvey, *The ways of the world* (Oxford University Press, 2016).

7 Heritage Foundation, e-newsletter, January 2024.

8 This became an election issue in 2024. See 'Fact sheet: President Biden takes new steps to lower prescription drug and health care costs, expand access to health care, and protect consumers', White House, 6 March 2024, https://bidenwhitehouse.archives.gov/briefing-room/statements-releases/2024/03/06/fact-sheet-president-biden-takes-new-steps-to-lower-prescription-drug-and-health-care-costs-expand-access-to-health-care-and-protect-consumers/ [Accessed 24 August 2025].

9 For differing arguments, see Jean Tirol, 'Why Google and Facebook can't be broken up like a utility', Columbia Business School, 13 August 2018, https://business.columbia.edu/cgi-media-tech/chazen-global-insights/why-google-and-facebook-cant-be-broken-utility [Accessed 8 August 2025]; Oren Cass, 'Curtailing Big Tech requires much more than breaking it up', *Financial Times*, 30 May 2021, www.ft.com/content/4d3df1d9-971f-4e1d-ad45-b73881dcd965 [Accessed 8 August 2025]; and Daren Acemoglu and Simon Johnson, 'Big Tech is bad: Big A.I. will be worse', *New York Times*, 9 June 2023, www.nytimes.com/2023/06/09/opinion/ai-big-tech-microsoft-google-duopoly.html [Accessed 8 August 2025].

Notes

10 Santa, People's Convoy organiser and founder of the now defunct 1776 Restoration movement, interviewed on First Responders Media (YouTube channel, now defunct), 25 May 2022.

11 Patrick Deneen, 'Why liberalism failed', Yale University Press, 20 February 2019, https://yalebooks.yale.edu/2019/02/20/why-liberalism-failed/ [Accessed 8 August 2025].

12 Alexandra Roginski and Cristina Rocha argue that 'this mode of establishing and defending truth (...) becomes more visible and meaningful in moments of great change, uncertainty and epistemological contestation'; 'The body as evidence of truth: Biomedicine and enduring narratives of religious and spiritual healing', *Journal for the Academic Study of Religion* 35, no. 2 (2022): 168–191, at p. 171; see also Cristina Rocha, *John of God: The globalisation of Brazilian faith healing* (Oxford University Press, 2017).

13 For statistics on bankruptcies, see 'Medical bankruptcies by country 2025', World Population Review, n.d., https://worldpopulationreview.com/country-rankings/medical-bankruptcies-by-country [Accessed 8 August 2025].

14 See William Davies, 'Antimarket', *London Review of Books* 4, no. 7 (4 April 2024): 23.

15 Legislation was passed in December 2021 to allow 800,000 legal non-citizens to vote in local elections. Source: 'New York City will allow 800,000 noncitizens to vote in local elections', NPR, 15 December 2021, www.npr.org/2021/12/15/1064385999/new-york-city-will-allow-legal-non-citizens-to-vote-in-local-elections [Accessed 8 August 2025].

16 Alliance for Responsible Citizenship e-newsletter, 'Dr Jordon B. Peterson on identity and meaning', 19 January 2024.

'IT ALL TURNS ON AFFECTION': FAMILY, FREEDOM AND THE LAND

1 Consisting of 'reddi-whip', cherries and pineapple, it's not totally offensive in small doses.

2 Wendell Berry, *It all turns on affection: The Jefferson lecture and other essays* (Counterpoint, 2012).

3 For an in-depth profile of Wendell Berry's life and legacy, see Dorothy Wickenden, 'Wendell Berry's advice for a cataclysmic age', *The New Yorker*, 21 February 2022, www.newyorker.com/magazine/2022/02/28/wendell-berrys-advice-for-a-cataclysmic-age [Accessed 8 August 2025].

4 For their overview of how Democrat policies and politics abandoned rural America, see Chloe Maxmin and Canyon Woodward, *Dirt road revival: How to rebuild rural politics and why our future depends on it* (Beacon Press, 2022).

5 Barry Goodwin and Vincent Smith, 'Is the US losing farms at an alarming rate?', American Enterprise Institute, 15 July 2024, www.aei.org/research-products/report/is-the-us-losing-farms-at-an-alarming-rate/ [Accessed 8 August 2025]. See the report here: www.aei.org/wp-content/uploads/2024/07/RPT_Is-the-US-Losing-Farms-at-an-Alarming-Rate.pdf [Accessed 29 December 2024].

Notes

6 'Many rural Americans are still "left behind"', Institute for Research on Poverty, University of Wisconsin, Madison, January 2020, www.irp.wisc.edu/resource/many-rural-americans-are-still-left-behind/ [Accessed 8 August 2025]; see also Tanya Lewis, 'People in rural areas die at higher rates than those in urban areas', Scientific American, 14 December 2022, www.scientificamerican.com/article/people-in-rural-areas-die-at-higher-rates-than-those-in-urban-areas/ [Accessed 29 December 2024].

7 Wickenden, 'Wendell Berry's advice'.

8 For an overview of Freedom to Farm from the perspective of the conservative Heritage Foundation, see John Frydenlund, 'The erosion of Freedom to Farm', Heritage Foundation, 8 March 2002, www.heritage.org/agriculture/report/the-erosion-freedom-farm [Accessed 29 December 2024].

9 Maxmin and Woodward, *Dirt road revival*.

10 See Tom Carter-Brookes, 'Protesting farmers are having to fight off the radical right, conspiracy theorists and climate sceptics', The Conversation, 13 December 2024, https://theconversation.com/protesting-farmers-are-having-to-fight-off-the-radical-right-conspiracy-theorists-and-climate-sceptics-245725 [Accessed 29 December 2024]. See also Robert Finger et al., 'Farmer protests in Europe 2023–24', *EuroChoices* 23, no. 3 (2024): 59–63.

11 In 2022, the Biden administration was criticised for shortages in baby formula after the largest producer recalled items and halted production. The shortage highlighted the dangers of having few companies controlling production of essential goods.

12 See 'Explainer: How four big companies control the U.S. beef industry', Reuters, 17 June 2021, www.reuters.com/business/how-four-big-companies-control-us-beef-industry-2021-06-17/ [Accessed 8 August 2025].

'FIGURING OUT' THE FUTURE, WRITING NEW FREEDOMS

1 'The elites would rather blow up the world than give up power', *The Charlie Kirk Show*, podcast, 19 November 2024, www.charliekirk.com/podcasts/the-elites-would-rather-blow-up-the-world-than-giv [Accessed 24 November 2024].

2 Text sent from Tyler Robinson, after he allegedly shot and killed Charlie Kirk. See https://www.bbc.co.uk/news/articles/c99g1eoz2ero [Accessed 28 September 2025].

3 Erika Kirk, speaking at her husband, Charlie Kirk's funeral, 21 September 2025, https://thecharliekirkshow.com/podcasts/the-charlie-kirk-show/he-blinked-and-saw-his-savior-in-paradise-mrs-erika-kirk [Accessed 28 September 2025].

4 Donald Trump, speaking at Charlie Kirk's funeral, 21 September 2025, https://thecharliekirkshow.com/podcasts/the-charlie-kirk-show/a-martyr-for-american-freedom-president-trump-honors-charlie-kirk [Accessed 28 September 2025].

5 'FDNY turns up heat on firefighters who cheered Trump, booed Letitia James with scolding internal letter', *NY Post*, 10 March 2024, https://nypost.com/2024/03/10/us-news/fdny-turns-up-heat-on-firefighters-who-cheered-trump-booed-letitia-james-with-scolding-internal-letter/ [Accessed 17 December 2024].

Notes

6   AOC refers to Democrat New York Congresswomen Alexandria Ocasio-Cortez.

7   Joe Rogan, *Strange times* (Netflix, 2018).

8   Alexis De Tocqueville, *Democracy in America* (Penguin Classics, 2003 [1835]).

9   Annaliens de Dijn discusses this point in *Freedom: An unruly history* (Harvard University Press, 2020) (see 'Further reading'). The concept of freedom expanded in the eighteenth–nineteenth centuries from the political into the economic realm, with the 'left' then relinquishing the idea and leaving space for more conservative views to co-opt it.

10 'Ask Charlie Kirk Show 127', *Charlie Kirk Show*, 7 November 2022, https://thecharliekirkshow.com/podcasts/the-charlie-kirk-show/ask-charlie-kirk-show-127-trump-or-desantis-why-ca [Accessed 24 August 2025].

11 Source: 'Trump brags other countries are "kissing my a**" to negotiate tariffs', CNN, n.d., https://edition.cnn.com/2025/04/09/politics/video/donald-trump-nrcc-president-dinner-tariff-negotiations-digvid [Accessed 8 August 2025].

12 For example, Barak Obama: 'The Fourth of July is about celebrating the big, bold, inclusive experiment that is our American democracy. And it has always been an experiment. Our democracy has never been guaranteed, which means we can't take it for granted. We need to keep fighting for it, keep improving it, and keep making sure it reflects the better angels of our nature instead of the worst', 4 July 2024, https://x.com/barackobama/status/1808863940878696768,.

13 The ERA still hadn't been formally recognised as part of the Constitution at the time of writing. Despite attempts to suspend the time limit in 2021 and 2023, it remains unresolved.

14 Going back to the 1950s, studies of intergroup conflict and cooperation have found that setting shared goals can reduce conflict.

15 See *Divided we fall* podcast for an overview: https://dividedwefall.org/a-conversation-with-monica-guzman-on-bridging-partisan-divides/ [Accessed 8 August 2025].

16 There is a wealth of data across social science, psychology, human resources management and communications disciplines that has identified key cultural competencies, knowledge, attitudes and behaviours that enable us to work across differences. Many are noted in this chapter, including curiosity, empathy, managing ambiguity, suspending judgement.

17 Non-violent communication techniques were developed by the American psychologist Marshall Rosenberg, beginning in the 1960s. They are now widely used in mediation and counselling settings.

Further reading

A history of the USA

Andersen, Kurt. *Fantasy land: How America went haywire; A 500-year history.* Penguin Random House, 2017.

Churchwell, Sarah. *Behold, America: A history of America First and the American dream.* Bloomsbury Publishing, 2018.

Cowie, Jefferson. *Freedom's dominion: A saga of white resistance to federal power.* Basic Books, 2022.

Engel, Jeffrey A. *The four freedoms: Franklin D. Roosevelt and the evolution of an American idea.* Oxford University Press, 2016.

Foner, Eric. *The story of American freedom.* W.W. Norton & Co., 1998.

Hahn, Steven. *Illiberal America: A history.* W.W. Norton & Co., 2024

Hannah-Jones, Nikole. *The 1619 Project.* New York Times, 2019.

Hartman, Andrew. *A war for the soul of America: A history of the culture wars.* 2nd ed. University of Chicago Press, 2019.

Hartman, Saidiya. *Wayward lives, beautiful experiments.* W.W. Norton & Co., 2019.

Jones, Reece. *White borders: The history of race and immigration in the United States from Chinese exclusion to the border wall.* Beacon Press, 2021.

Kruse, Kevin M. and Julian E. Zelizer, eds. *Myth America: Historians take on the biggest legends and lies about our past.* Basic Books, 2022.

Lepore, Jill. *These truths: A history of the United States.* W.W. Norton & Co., 2019.

Rana, Aziz. *The two faces of American freedom.* Harvard University Press, 2014 [2010].

Richardson, Heather Cox. *To make men free: A history of the Republican Party.* Basic Books, 2014.

Ryan, Alan. *On Tocqueville: Democracy and America.* Liveright Publishing, 2014.

Slotkin, Richard. *A great disorder: National myth and the battle for America.* Belknap Press of Harvard University Press, 2024.

Stovall, Tyler. *White Freedom: The racial history of an idea.* Princeton University Press, 2021.

Tomkins, Stephen. *The journey to the Mayflower: God's outlaws and the invention of freedom.* Hodder & Stoughton, 2020.

Further reading

Contemporary society and politics in the USA

Anker, Elizabeth. *Ugly freedoms*. Duke University Press, 2022.

Bruder, Jessica. *Nomadland: Surviving America in the 21st century*. Swift Press, 2017.

Dallek, Matthew. *Birchers: How the John Birch Society radicalized the American Right*. Basic Books, 2023.

Ehrenreich, Barbara. *This land is their land: Reports from a divided nation*. Holt Books, 2008.

Ehrenreich, Barbara. *Nickel and dimed: On (not) getting by in America*. Picador, 2011.

Hochschild, Arlie Russell. *Strangers in their own land: Anger and mourning on the American right*. New Press, 2016 [2018].

Hunter, James Davison. *Democracy and solidarity: On the cultural roots of America's political crisis*. Yale University Press, 2024.

Klein, Ezra. *Why we're polarized*. Simon & Schuster, 2020.

Klein, Naomi. *Doppelganger: A trip into the mirror world*. Allen Lane, 2023.

Lakoff, George. *Whose freedom? The battle over America's most important idea*. Picador, 2007.

Lakoff, George. *Moral politics: How liberals and conservatives think*. 3rd ed. University of Chicago Press, 2016.

Levitsky, Steven and Daniel Ziblatt. *Tyranny of the minority: How to reverse an authoritarian turn and forge a democracy for all*. Viking, 2023.

Marche, Stephen. *The next civil war: Dispatches from the American future*. Simon & Schuster, 2022.

Martin, Jonathon and Alexander Burns. *This will not pass: Trump, Biden, and the battle for America's future*. Simon & Schuster, 2022.

Maxmin, Chloe and Canyon Woodward. *Dirt road revival: How to rebuild rural politics and why our future depends on it*. Beacon Press, 2022.

Packer, George. *The unwinding: Thirty years of American decline*. Vintage, 2013.

Payne, Keith. *Good, reasonable people: The psychology behind America's dangerous divide*. Penguin Random House, 2024.

Pierson, Paul and Eric Schickler. *Partisan nation: The dangerous new logic of American politics in a nationalized era*. University of Chicago Press, 2024.

Press, Eyal. *Dirty work: Essential jobs and the hidden toll of inequality in America*. Farrar, Straus & Giroux, 2021.

Samuels, Robert. *Culture wars, universities and the political unconscious*. Palgrave MacMillan, 2024.

Serwer, Adam. *The cruelty is the point: The past, present, and future of Trump's America*. One World, 2021.

Wilkerson, Isabel. *Caste: The origins of our discontents*. Random House, 2020.

Wolff, Michael. *All or nothing: How Trump recaptured America*. Bridge Street Press, 2024.

Wuthnow, Robert. *The left behind: Decline and rage in rural America*. Princeton University Press, 2018.

Further reading

On freedom

Balagopalan, Sarada, Cati Coe and Keith M. Green, eds. *Diverse unfreedoms: The afterlives and transformations of post-transatlantic bondages*. Routledge, 2019.

Dijn, Annelien De. *Freedom: An unruly history*. Harvard University Press, 2020.

Fromm, Erich. *The fear of freedom*. Routledge Classics, 2001 [1952].

Mill, John Stuart. *On liberty*. Penguin Classics, 1982 [1859].

Nelson, Maggie. *On freedom: Four songs of care and constraint*. Jonathan Cape, 2021.

Snyder, Timothy. *The road to unfreedom: Russia, Europe, America*. Vintage, 2018.

Snyder, Timothy. *On freedom*. Vintage, 2024.

Ypi, Lea. *Free: Coming of age at the end of history*. W.W. Norton & Co., 2022.

Žižek, Slavoj. *Freedom: A disease without cure*. Bloomsbury Academic, 2023.

Acknowledgements

This work exists thanks to the kindness of strangers who trusted me with their contacts and stories. I hope I have been able to do them justice. To all who gave up their time to have a conversation: thank you. Not everyone appears 'in person', but you are all there in some way: providing context, adding to the story.

To all the friends who tested ideas, especially Annaliki Antoniou, Cathy Byrne, Pat Coy, Sophie Hawkins, Connie Stambush and Helen Yanacopulos.

To Greg Donovan and Amy Aronson at Fordham University.

Saher for fact checking and Tim for copy editing. Any errors remaining are my responsibility.

To Tom Cull for taking a punt, and Tom Dark and Alun Richards for helping me beat words into shape.

For Dad, who didn't get to see the final version. You will be missed.

And to Daniel, who came along at just the right time, much love.

Index

Index

EU authorised representative for GPSR:
Easy Access System Europe, Mustamäe tee 50,
10621 Tallinn, Estonia
gpsr.requests@easproject.com

www.ingramcontent.com/pod-product-compliance
Lightning Source LLC
Chambersburg PA
CBHW011537260326
41914CB00036B/1976/J